£2.99

8

Southern A...

CW00418788

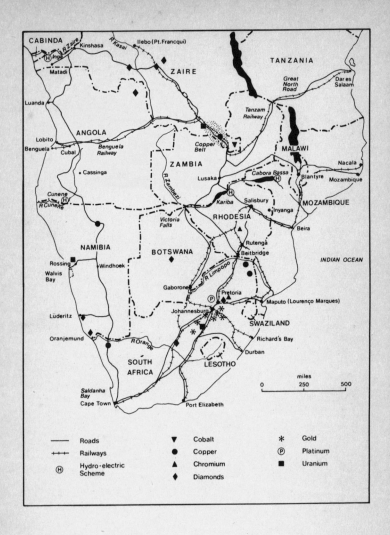

Alex Callinicos and John Rogers

Southern Africa after Soweto

Pluto Press

First published 1977 by Pluto Press Limited
Unit 10 Spencer Court, 7 Chalcot Road, London NW1 8LH

Copyright © Pluto Press 1977
ISBN 0 904383 42 3

Cover designed by David King
Map on page ii by Joyce Batey

Typeset by Red Lion Setters, Holborn, London
Printed in Great Britain by
Lowe & Brydone Printers Limited, Thetford, Norfolk

Contents

Maps

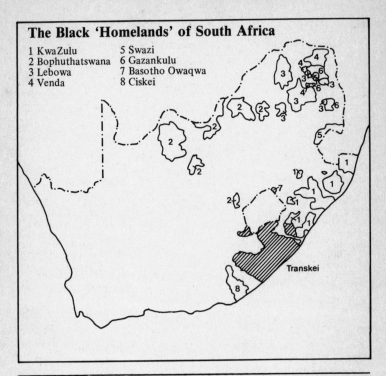

The Black 'Homelands' of South Africa

1 KwaZulu
2 Bophuthatswana
3 Lebowa
4 Venda
5 Swazi
6 Gazankulu
7 Basotho Owaqwa
8 Ciskei

Transkei

Southern Africa at the End of 1975

See map page ii

	POPULATION million	INCOME per head	TRADE $ million imports	TRADE $ million exports	RESERVES $ million
Angola	5.8	500	624*	1229*	?
Botswana	0.7	340	included with South Africa		
Mozambique	9.2	300	385	212	?
Rhodesia	6.3 (white 0.3)	500	541*	652*	n.a.
South Africa	25.5 (white 4.3)	1150	9080	8400+	1216
Namibia (South West Africa)	0.9	800	included with South Africa		
Tanzania	15.3	150	714	349	65
Zaire	24.9	125	904	827	51
Zambia	4.9	400	1075	763	129

* end of 1973   + including gold 3480

Black Township Uprisings, 1976

Two months of 'calm and order' after Soweto

This map shows the areas of unrest between June 16 and August 18.

1. June 16: Soweto.
2. June 18: Alexandra township, north-east of Johannesburg.
3. June 18: University of Zululand at Ngoye, near Empangeni.
4. June 18: Tokosa and Daveytown, near Benoni.
5. June 18: Natalspruit and Kathlehong, Germiston.
6. June 18: Vosloorus at Boksburg.
7. June 18: Tembisa, near Kempton Park.
8. June 18: Kagiso at Krugersdorp, West Rand.
9. June 18: University of the North, Turfloop, near Pietersburg.
10. June 20: Seshego township, Pietersburg.
11. June 21: Duduza township, Nigel.
12. June 21: Townships surrounding Pretoria: Mamelodi, Mabopane, Atteridgeville, Hammanskraal.
13. June 22: Lowveld; Lekozi township near Nelspruit.
14. June 22: CaRankuwa in Bophuthatswana homeland.
15. June 23: Jouberton township, near Klerdsdorp, Western Transvaal.
16. July 18: University of Fort Hare.
17. July 20: Witbank, Middelburg and Carletonville.
18. July 22: Boipatong township, Vanderbijlpark (Vereeniging).
19. July 25: Zulu Training School, Vryheid.
20. July 26: Ndwedwe, Natal.
21. August 2: UWC boycott at Bellville South.
22. August 4: Soweto violence flares again.
23. August 7: New Brighton, Port Elizabeth (boxing match).
24. August 8: Montshiwa township, near Mafeking.
25. August 9: Mdantsane township, near East London.
26. August 11: Cape Town's three townships; Langa, Nyanga, Guguletu.
27. August 18: New Brighton, Port Elizabeth.
28. August 28: Athlone Training College, Guguletu.

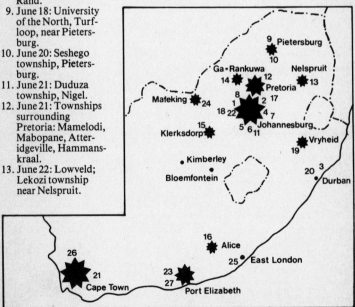

Preface

This book is a collective work in more senses than one. The analysis it offers was developed during discussions over the last four years within the Socialist Worker Africa Group. Chris Harman encouraged us to write it. Mike Kidron edited it, suggesting a number of improvements in its structure as well as in many points of detail. Baruch Hirson read a draft of Chapter 2, and his criticisms led us to make many changes in it. We learned a great deal from the discussions we have had with members of the South African and Zimbabwean resistance. Of course, only we are responsible for any errors of fact or of judgement the book may contain.

February 1977

Note on Terminology

The name you choose to use for a country or a people in Southern Africa often involves a political decision. This note is aimed at helping the reader through the resulting terminological jungle.

In this book, we use the term African to cover the original populations of Southern Africa. The official name for them in South Africa is Bantu, after the family of languages they speak. The older white names for Africans - Kaffirs or Natives - are now only used as terms of racist abuse (although South African gold shares are still called 'Kaffirs' on the London stock exchange). The word Coloured refers to the people of mixed race in South Africa, the descendants of the white settlers, and their Indonesian slaves, as well as the Khoi Khoi or Hottentots, displaced by the Dutch at the Cape. Asian or Indian refers to the descendants of the Indians imported during the last century to work as indentured labourers in the sugar plantations of Natal.

Africans, Coloureds and Asians make up the black population (sometimes called non-White or non-European in South Africa). Because Africans make up the mass of the black population we often use the terms African and black interchangeably.

The original white settlers in South Africa were of Dutch origin; today they call themselves Afrikaner. The old name, Boer, has dropped into disuse. The other main group of settlers in South Africa and Zimbabwe are English-speaking, of British descent. The settlers sometimes call themselves Europeans.

Since 1961, when it left the British Commonwealth, South Africa has been called the Republic of South Africa (before that time it was known as the Union of South Africa). Following independence, the other British colonies in the area, with the exception of Swaziland, changed their names: Northern Rhodesia has become Zambia, Nyasaland Malawi, Bechuanaland Botswana, Basutoland Lesotho.

Since the Smith regime illegally seized independence in 1965 Southern Rhodesia has come to be known as Rhodesia. The name given to the country by black people is Zimbabwe. Similarly South-West Africa is now called Namibia everywhere outside South Africa.

Tanganyika became Tanzania after fusion with Zanzibar in 1964. The Belgian Congo became Congo Kinshasa and then Zaire after independence.

Currencies

On 15 February 1977:

£1 sterling = 1.4826 rand (South Africa)
             1.0470 dollars (Rhodesia)
             1.37 kwacha (Zambia)

Introduction

On 3 February 1960 the then British Prime Minister, Harold Macmillan, addressed the all-white South African Parliament in Cape Town. He was on the last leg of a tour of Africa. His speech undoubtedly reflected the predominant view among the rulers of the West: 'The most striking of the impressions I have formed since I left London a month ago is of the strength of this African national consciousness... The wind of change is blowing through the continent... Our national policies must take account of it.'[1]

Three years before, Ghana had become the first British colony in Africa to gain independence on the basis of black majority rule. The pace of decolonisation in Africa was rapidly gathering speed, spreading to the other great colonial empires in Africa. In Algeria the French government under de Gaulle was prepared to use force in its efforts to break the hold of the white settlers on the colony and hand over power to the FLN independence movement. The Belgian Congo was to gain independence in 1960.

Within South Africa itself the situation appeared more and more threatening for the white minority. For more than a decade the Nationalist government had faced mass opposition from black people. One African nationalist party, the Pan-Africanist Congress, had decided on 'decisive and positive action' against the pass laws as the first step towards freedom and independence by 1963. A series of mass demonstrations against the pass laws were planned. It seemed merely a matter of time before a tide of black nationalism swept away the white minority regime in South Africa.

Ten years later, in 1970, the picture was very different. A few weeks after Macmillan's visit, police had fired on a peaceful black demonstration at Sharpeville in the Transvaal. 67 people were killed and 186 wounded. The massacre was a prelude to a wave of repression unprecedented even in South Africa's bloody history. The main nationalist organisations, the African National Congress (ANC) and the Pan-Africanist Congress (PAC), were banned and their leaders gaoled, driven underground or into exile. The urban and rural guerilla campaigns launched by ANC and PAC were crushed and a massive military and police regime was erected to hold down the black population and any isolated white opponents of apartheid that there might be.

The triumphant Nationalist regime went on to preside over the biggest boom in South Africa's history, fuelled by a massive influx of foreign capital. Between 1960 and 1970 the South African economy grew by 76 per cent - a growth rate comparable only to that of Japan.[2] This economic expansion was used to finance the construction of the most powerful military machine in Africa. The defence budget grew from R44 million in 1960-1 to R272 million in 1968-69.[3] The apartheid state appeared impregnable within and without.

The propagandists of apartheid drew a contrast between the prosperity and stability of South Africa and the economic backwardness and political weakness of black Africa. And the facts seemed to bear them out. Decolonisation - political independence - did not alter black Africa's economic dependence upon the West. Often the contradiction between the anti-imperialist rhetoric of many African nationalists' programmes and their inability to implement these programmes when in power accentuated this dependence. The states of black Africa remained semi-colonies of Western capital, politically independent but economically subordinate. This semi-colonial status set the stage for the political instability of black Africa, as the ruling classes of the new states fought among themselves over the meagre spoils left them by the departing colonial power. The result was a succession of military coups and civil wars in the black African states.

Yet one issue united the rulers of black Africa. They were pledged to overthrow the minority regimes in Southern Africa. The Organisation of African Unity failed dismally to realise the Pan-Africanist dream of a united Africa. But it did organise a programme of military and financial aid to the liberation movements fighting minority rule in South Africa, Rhodesia and the Portuguese colonies of Angola, Mozambique and Guinea-Bissau.

South Africa retaliated in kind. Subversion and sabotage were organised in the black states bordering on white-ruled Southern Africa - most notably in Zambia. White politicians threatened black states that harboured nationalist guerillas with Israeli-style 'hot pursuit' raids.

But to an outsider it appeared that white power in Southern Africa was secure. The black guerillas in the Portuguese colonies were a threat, but they could be contained with the backing of South Africa and NATO, which was readily forthcoming. A National Security Council memorandum prepared under Henry Kissinger's supervision for the incoming Nixon administration in 1969 spelled out what appeared from the standpoint of the US to be the most realistic perspective in Southern Africa:

> The whites are here to stay and the only way that construct-ive change can come about is through them. There is no hope for the blacks to gain the political rights they seek through violence, which will only lead to chaos and increased opportunities for the communists.[4]

Events since 1974 have shattered this picture. Let us briefly sum up these developments. The aim of this book is to explain them, and to map out future prospects on the basis of that explanation.

The catalyst for these changes was the Portuguese coup of 25 April 1974. The burden of the colonial wars broke the back of the weakest capitalist state in Western Europe and bred in its barracks a circle of officers - the Armed Forces Movement - which overturned the Caetano dictatorship. In Portugal the coup unleashed the biggest revolutionary upsurge of a West European working-class since Barcelona in 1936. In Southern Africa it drastically undermined the position of the white minority regimes. In particular it weakened the white settlers in Rhodesia, who were already fighting a bitter war with black guerillas in the north-east of the country and who were now faced with the prospect of a radical nationalist regime taking over Mozambique along their eastern border.

The Portuguese coup led to the second major development: what appeared to be the sudden and dramatic reversal in foreign policy by the Vorster regime in South Africa. In October 1974 Vorster made a speech in the South African Senate calling for co-operation with the new black nationalist regimes in the former Portuguese colonies.

The response from black Africa was equally dramatic. Kenneth Kaunda of Zambia described Vorster's speech as 'the voice of reason for which Africa and the rest of the world has been waiting'.[5]

After a decade of near-war between the two states, the South African and Zambian regimes launched a policy of detente aimed at resolving the main differences between them. The focus of their efforts was the search for a settlement between the Smith regime in Rhodesia and the black nationalists attempting to overthrow it. The Lusaka agreement of December 1974 gave Zambian and South African backing to negotiations between Smith and the nationalists. In pursuit of a settlement Kaunda gaoled more than a thousand Zimbabwean guerillas opposed to detente.

This operation reached its climax in August 1975. The Smith regime and the nationalist leaders met at the Victoria Falls to discuss a settlement. Also present were Kaunda and Vorster to give their backing for detente. The *Times of Zambia* commented on their meeting:

A year ago a psychiatrist would have been recommended for you if you even thought about it, let alone talked about it.

But it happened - rather it's happening - and the thousands of people who witnessed the historic occasion are as sober and sane as a High Court judge.[6]

To grasp what a drastic reversal of policies was involved in the Vorster-Kaunda alliance we have only to remember the two men's backgrounds.

In the 1950s and 1960s as the leader of the movement for Zambian independence, Kaunda was gaoled a number of times by the British colonial authorities. After independence in 1964, in close collaboration with Julius Nyerere of Tanzania, Kaunda went on to attempt to construct a version of African socialism specially suited, it was claimed, to Zambia's needs. He and Nyerere were in the forefront of the African left, the most committed supporters of the armed struggle in Southern Africa.

John Vorster's record is quite different. During the second world war he was interned for opposing South Africa's involvement in the war. He was a general in the *Ossewa Brandwag*, a pro-Hitler fascist movement organised along military lines, which argued that the interests of Afrikaner nationalism lay in alliance with the Nazis against the British. It was at this time that Vorster made the notorious statement:

We stand for Christian Nationalism which is an ally of National Socialism. You can call this anti-democratic principle dictatorship if you wish. In Italy it is called Fascism, in Germany German National Socialism, and in South Africa Christian Nationalism.[7]

In the early 1960s it was Vorster as Minister of Justice and Police who took charge of ruthlessly crushing all opposition to the regime.

Yet events thrust these two men, white fascist and black humanist - and the classes they represent - into open collaboration.

The Angolan war broke up the Vorster-Kaunda alliance. The war, another product of the collapse of Portuguese colonialism, pitted the tried and tested national liberation movement, MPLA, against an unholy alliance of two other

Angolan nationalist groups, FNLA and Unita, the US, Zambia, Zaire, South Africa, and - 'People's' China. When South African armour and troops invaded the country in October 1975 they did so at the invitation of Zambia and Zaire. This was confirmed by Jonas Savimbi, leader of Unita:

> In mid-October 1975 Savimbi 'asked President Mobutu [of Zaire - AC and JR], President Kaunda of Zambia and President Houphouet Boigny of the Ivory Coast to ask for secret assistance from South Africa.
>
> 'This was done ... and shortly afterwards a South African armoured column moved rapidly up the west coast to Port Amboine about 100 miles south of Luanda.'[8]

The defeat of this alliance at the hands of MPLA, backed by Russia and Cuba, was a turning point in Southern Africa. It wrecked the Vorster-Kaunda alliance, already shaken by its failure to bring about a settlement in Rhodesia. More important still, as we pointed out at the time:

> South Africa has lost the war. The last time black people inflicted such a heavy defeat on the white rulers of South Africa was in 1879 at Isandlwhana when the British colonial army invading Zululand was destroyed by the *impis* of Cetiwayo. This is the message that is now spreading through the shantytowns, the all-male workers' hostels, the farm and mine compounds into which the black working-class of South Africa are herded by their white masters: black people can defeat the apartheid regime.[9]

The effect was dramatic. The black rebellion within South Africa itself began in Soweto in June 1976 and spread throughout the townships in the following months. Triggered off by the issue of compulsory Afrikaans teaching in Soweto schools, and fuelled by the courage and militancy of black youth, who braved the guns, tear-gas, helicopters, armoured cars, dogs and truncheons of one of the most effective and ruthless security forces in the world, the explosion undoubtedly owed much of its force to MPLA's victory over the regime's troops in Angola.

The embattled Vorster regime thus faces massive black opposition at home. On its borders in Zimbabwe and Namibia there are burgeoning guerilla wars. White power in Southern Africa is more threatened than it has ever been.

This crisis has led to direct US intervention in the region. Previously America's rulers were content to leave the care of Western capitalist interests in Southern Africa in the hands of the old colonial power, Britain. The Angolan war changed all that. The US Administration launched its biggest 'covert' (i.e. CIA-run) military intervention in Africa since the Congo crisis of the early 1960s. The American government is directly intervening in the region in order to complete the detente operation initiated by Vorster and Kaunda. Henry Kissinger, after ignoring Africa for most of his time in office, launched another 'peace' mission to add to his other trophies, dubiously won in Vietnam and the Middle East. His attempts seemed to be met with success, when in September 1976 he produced a seemingly miraculous settlement in Rhodesia.

These developments, packed together in the space of less than three years, have changed the face of politics in Southern Africa. The argument of this book is that they result from Western domination of the region. This domination operates through the existence in South Africa of a powerful capitalist state whose political, economic and military influence spreads far beyond its borders, deep into black Africa. And that the resolution of the crisis of Southern Africa, a crisis that reaches as far as Lusaka and Kinshasa, lies in the hands of the massive black working class concentrated in the townships and mine-compounds of South Africa.

1. Apartheid and Capitalism

South Africa today has most of the features of a developed capitalist economy. It outpaces the rest of Africa, producing 22 per cent of the continent's gross domestic product, and 40 per cent of her manufacturing output, while accounting for 53 per cent of her energy consumption.[1] Yet this economy rests upon an apparently 'archaic' system which denies the mass of the working class any rights in the areas where they live and work.

The result of this paradoxical situation can be seen in most writing on South Africa. Almost without fail, writers hostile to apartheid assume that there is a conflict between the capitalistic organisation of the South African economy and the apartheid system.

This assumption takes different forms depending on the writer's politics. Liberal critics argue that there is a conflict between the rational capitalist economy and the irrational political order. This situation, they claim, arises from the control of the state by Afrikaner nationalists, steeped in the racialist, pre-capitalist traditions of the rural *volk* (people); given time, however, and the continued expansion of the 'modern' sector of the economy, the pressures of economic rationality will force Afrikanerdom into the twentieth century. The argument serves as an implicit justification for the role of Western capital in South Africa as a force for economic rationality and change. Within South Africa the argument is identified with the 'liberal' Progressive Reform Party and its backer, the Oppenheimer Anglo-American mining empire.[2]

Among radical opponents of apartheid, the argument goes rather differently. Apartheid is the product, it is claimed, of the co-existence of two types of economic relationship. The first is that characteristic of an advanced capitalist economy; the second is an 'archaic' one, that between a metropolitan power and a colonised people.

This analysis underlies the programme of the South African Communist Party:

> *South Africa is not a colony but an independent state. Yet masses of our people enjoy neither independence nor freedom. The conceding of independence to South Africa by Britain in 1910 was not a victory over the forces of colonialism and imperialism. It was designed in the interests of imperialism. Power was transferred not into the hands of the masses of people of South Africa, but into the hands of the white minority alone. The evils of colonialism, in so far as the non-white majority was concerned, were perpetuated and reinforced. A new type of colonialism was developed, in which the oppressing White nation occupied the same territory as the oppressed peoples themselves and lived side by side with them.*[3]

This theory of 'colonialism of a special type' or 'internal colonialism', according to which 'Non-White South Africa' is 'the colony of White South Africa', which is itself 'an advanced capitalist country in its final stage of imperialism',[4] also has certain political implications. If the main struggle is against the colonising national embodied in the settler state, victory requires the unity of all oppressed groups and classes. This in its turn imposes a limit on the programme of the liberation movement: its target must be national independence and the destruction of white supremacy. Any more radical social demands would scare off groups like the African commercial class, whose development into a full-blown capitalist class is blocked by the apartheid system, and who would therefore support a struggle for national liberation, but not one for socialism. For the South African Communist Party the fight against apartheid represents merely a necessary stage in the struggle for socialism:

> *The destruction of colonialism and the winning of national
> freedom is the essential condition and key for the future
> advance to the supreme aim of the Communist Party: the
> establishment of a socialist South Africa, laying the
> foundations of a classless, Communist society.*[5]

What the liberal and the Communist Party analyses share is
a view of capitalism as a pure abstraction. Certain ideal
economic and political relationships are identified with
capitalism. These relationships are derived from the liberal-
democratic regimes of the advanced Western capitalist
countries. Any deviation from this ideal norm - the denial of
political or trade-union rights to workers, the use of racialism as
a means of controlling the labour-force, open and brutal
repression of opposition parties - is treated as evidence that the
country in question is not a 'developed' capitalist country.[6]

But what makes a country capitalist is not how things
appear on the surface, but the underlying relations of
production - the separation of the workers from the means of
production, their subordination to competing capitalists
organising production to extract and accumulate surplus value
at their expense. These relations take different forms depending
on the particular phase through which the world economy is
going and the place of that country within this world economy.
The Britain of 1815 and of 1976 were very different societies, but
in both the dominant relations of production were capitalist.

As a capitalist country South Africa has some special
features. First, the overwhelming majority of the working class
is denied any political rights because it is black and is subjected
to a series of controls aimed at preventing it from becoming a
stable, settled urban class with the sort of trade-union and
political organisations that workers in Western Europe and
North America take for granted. Second, gold-mining plays a
central role in the South African economy. Third, the state not
only manages the economy, but also owns large sections of
South African industry. Fourth, capitalist control of the state in
South Africa is organised under the hegemony of the Afrikaner

bourgeoisie and this hegemony is exercised through the Nationalist Party, which has been in power since 1948.

Not all these features are unique. Capitalist dictatorships are two a penny; there are plenty of entrenched ruling parties, and the directly economic role of the state is one of the main characteristics of late capitalist society. But the combination is unique, and, more important, the system's political basis is unique in resting on the disenfranchisement of the African population and their subjection to the migrant labour system.

Migrant Labour and the Gold-Mines

The facts of apartheid are well known. Black people possess no political rights. The main African nationalist organisations are banned. African trade unions are not recognised by the government and any dispute involving African workers is referred to a government-appointed regional labour committee or to the all-white Central Bantu Labour Board. Under the Bantu Labour (Settlement of Disputes) Act of 1953 all strikes by African workers are illegal.

Not only are African workers denied any opportunity to organise in defence of their interests; their movements are subjected to the system of rigid controls known as the pass laws. All Africans must carry a reference book, containing their photograph, their race identity card, their registered number, details of their tribal connections, their ethnic classification, the official authorisation to be in the relevant urban area, their current tax receipt, the labour bureau permit to be employed or to seek work, the name, address and monthly signature of their employer, and various other details. Any African who does not produce an up to date reference book on demand is liable to immediate arrest.

The country is divided into a number of urban areas under the pass laws. Africans do not have the right to move from area to area. Unless an African has lived there continuously from birth or for 15 years with government permission, or has worked continuously for one employer for at least 10 years, he or she cannot stay in a given urban area for more than 72 hours. If such a person loses a job, he or she must register at the local labour bureau. The government district labour officer can deport Africans or make them take up a job in a different urban area. If an African refuses a job offered by the labour officer three times or is guilty of 'misconduct' (anything from getting drunk to going on strike), then he or she is an 'idle person' and must be deported. Africans deported from urban areas - the unemployed, the militant, the old, the ill - are dumped in barren 'resettlement areas' in the African reserves or 'Homelands' in the countryside.

The aim of the pass laws is, according to government spokesmen, to turn all African workers in the 'white areas' (over 87 per cent of South Africa, including all the urban, industrial and mining areas) into migrant workers. Since 1968 every African, whether or not he lives in one of the tribal reserves, must register as a workseeker at a tribal labour bureau. Any workseeker, unless he qualifies under the 10-15-year residence rule, cannot work in a white area for longer than a year. He then returns to the tribal labour pool; if his old employer wants him back, he must file a special request.

The pass laws and the migrant labour system give the government and employers tremendous power over African workers. Atomised and denied political and trade-union rights, their every movement is subjected to detailed government control. Obviously, this system means that it is very difficult for African workers to combine against the employers and the state. Management's bargaining position over wages, conditions etc is strengthened immeasurably.

The other side of the coin is that, while black workers are impoverished and disenfranchised, the minority of white workers enjoy an entrenched, privileged position. A statutory colour bar reserving skilled jobs in the mining industry for white workers was introduced in 1911. Under section 77 of the Industrial Conciliation Act of 1956 the Minister of Labour is empowered to introduce the colour bar - or 'job reservation' - into any industry (Africans had already been banned from doing skilled construction jobs in 'white' areas in 1951). An informal but powerful colour bar closes apprenticeships in skilled trades to Africans.

The result is that, on the one hand, black workers in South Africa suffer the most appalling poverty, and, on the other, white workers enjoy the advantages of membership of the settler community, including job security (there is hardly any white unemployment) and black servants. It has been calculated that between 1911 and 1966 African wages in the gold mines remained static or even fell in real terms. Meanwhile, the black/white earnings gap grew from 11.7 to 1 in 1911 to 17.6 to 1 in 1966.[7]

But why has South African capitalism come to depend on cheap, disenfranchised black labour? Only a primitive marxist would argue that capitalism *always* involves a fall in working-class living standards. In Western Europe and North America real wages rose in the decades following the second world war. The fact that they have fallen as a result of the crisis of the mid 1970s is a sign of the difficulties the system is in. Why do starvation wages, pass laws and the denial of liberty appear to be a necessary feature of South African capitalism?

The answer must be sought in gold mining. Even today, when mining in South Africa has been outpaced by manufacturing, the gold mines are still immensely important to the country's economy. In 1975 their revenue totalled R2,670 million and the mines employed 37,000 white workers and 359,000 black workers.[8]

Historically, the gold mines were even more important. The discovery of gold in the Transvaal in 1886 was the turning point in the development of capitalism in South Africa. Previously, the overwhelming majority of the population, both black and white, were pastoral farmers providing for their own needs. The gold mines changed all that.

The foundations for the development of the new industry had been laid when diamonds were discovered in Kimberley in 1867. The small diggers who flocked there were rapidly absorbed by the big mining companies. The latter then proceeded to fight it out among themselves for mastery. The victor was Cecil John Rhodes' company, De Beers, which absorbed its major rival, Barney Barnato, in 1888. By the end of the century De Beers controlled 90 per cent of the world's diamond production.[9]

Rhodes and De Beers also came up with what proved to be the classic system of labour control and theft prevention in Southern African mines:

> They hit on the idea of confining African miners in closed compounds for four or six months of their contract period … The compound was an enclosure surrounded by a high corrugated iron fence and covered by wire-netting. The men lived, twenty to a room, in huts or iron cabins built against the fence. They went to work along a tunnel, bought food and clothing from the company's stores, and received free medical treatment but no wages during sickness, all within the compound. Men due for discharge were confined in detention rooms for several days, during which they wore only blankets and fingerless leather gloves padlocked to their wrists, swallowed purgatives, and were examined for stones concealed in cuts, wounds, swellings and orifices.[10]

In 1886 the Witwatersrand in the Transvaal was declared to be a gold-bearing area. It proved to have the richest deposits of gold in the world. Because the average gold content of the Witwatersrand ore is very low, mining the gold involved from the start massive applications of labour and technology. The large investments involved were financed by a huge influx of foreign capital in alliance with established mining capitalists like Rhodes. Between 1887 and 1932 £148 million was invested in the Rand. £120 million was foreign capital, most of it British.[11]

Speculative booms and slumps hastened the amalgamation of the industry. By 1897 the basic structure of the gold-mining industry was established, with about fifty mining companies owned by six mining finance houses or groups.[12] The groups were banded together in the Chamber of Mines. Rhodes's group, Consolidated Goldfields, was probably the most powerful of the finance houses. The Johannesburg Stock Exchange was established to deal in gold shares. The amalgamation of South African banking was also accelerated; by 1920 there were two big banks - the Standard Bank and the National Bank (taken over by Barclays a few years later) - closely linked to British capital.

The invasion and transformation of the South African economy by Western capital reflected developments in the world economy. Britain at the end of the nineteenth century was no longer the sole industrial capitalist state. It had been joined by others - the United States, Germany, Japan, France - whose intense competition led them to expand the productive forces beyond the limits imposed by the national state. Competition and technological development brought about a greatly accelerated concentration and centralisation of capital. Individual national economies became dominated by great trusts. Capital flowed out of the advanced capitalist countries in search of more profitable investments. The result was a huge transfer of capital from Europe and North America to Asia, Africa and Latin America where raw materials and cheap labour power were in plentiful supply. The different imperialist powers thrust each other aside in the desperate hunt for colonies. The percentage of Africa owned by European colonial powers grew from 10.8 in 1876 to 90.4 per cent in 1900.[13]

In South Africa the attraction was gold which then, as now, tied the country closely to the world economy and the international monetary system and which could be mined at deep level from the low-grade ores of the Rand only with the application of vast numbers of very low-paid workers. These were the Africans, subject to the migrant labour system, the pass laws and the tyranny of the mine compounds, and made available to the mines through the expropriation of the African tribes. There was another component of the new industrial working class: a group of skilled white workers imported from Britain and other parts of the white Empire. They brought with them their traditions, including craft unionism and, among the more militant, syndicalism. From the start, however, since they enjoyed the privileges of the white settler minority, they were alienated from the African workers.[14]

The Formation of the African Working Class

The exploitation of African labour in the gold-mines of the Rand presupposed that Africans had no choice but to sell their labour-power to the white capitalists. This situation in its turn presupposed the final expropriation of the African tribes living in South Africa, which had been the source for centuries of struggle between the white invaders and the African peoples.

The colonial occupation of the country began in 1652, when the Dutch East India Company established a settlement on the Cape of Good Hope. The Company's main interest was in the Far East, where its fleets were carving out a vast colonial empire; the colony on the Cape was intended to provide fresh provisions for Dutch ships on their way to and from the Indies. However, the Dutch farmers, or Afrikaners as they came to call themselves, settled by the Company gradually spread beyond the reach of the colonial administration with its restrictions and taxes. They became *trekboers* - pastoral subsistence farmers pushing deeper into the subcontinent in search of better land in the areas of high rainfall.

They encountered - and enslaved or wiped out - the remnants of aboriginal races - the Khoi Khoi (Hottentots) and San (Bushmen). Slaves were also imported from Holland's Far Eastern possessions. The settler economy was built upon a quasi-feudal basis. The white farmers provided for most of their own needs on their huge farms (6,000 acres was considered normal for a farm) exploiting a labour force of slaves and indentured African and Coloured workers.

A more serious obstacle blocking settler expansion was provided by the Bantu-speaking collectivist African peoples who had already spread over most of the Southern African continent by the time the Dutch arrived at the Cape.[15] The first of these were the Xhosa on the eastern border of the Cape, against whom the Afrikaners launched a series of bitter wars of conquest, the 'Kaffir wars'.

A South African historian explains the dynamic underlying the settler expansion beyond the frontiers of the Cape Colony:

> The search for water and grass was the first principle in the life of Boer and Bantu, for it was in their herds that both counted their wealth. When Boers and natives finally met in the last third of the eighteenth century, the natives had already penetrated beyond the area of comparatively high average rainfall. The frontier, commonly known as the Eastern Frontier, because of its position from Cape Town, lay in an area of uncertain rainfall and subject to drought … The area of low rainfall lay behind the Boers, while the area of more bountiful rains lay behind the natives. This circumstance alone was enough to force the Boers to take the offensive. To secure sufficient grazing for their herds and especially in order to penetrate beyond the native frontier to the better-watered lands, the Boers were bound to press heavily upon the natives.[16]

The settlers also found themselves clashing with an unsympathetic colonial administration. Following the Napoleonic wars, which ended in 1815, the Cape passed into British hands. The new administration considered the slave system on which the white farmers relied for much of their labour irrelevant to Britain's rulers, whose interest in the Cape was largely strategic, since it dominated the route from Europe to their possessions in India; moreover, it contradicted the economic foundation of the industrial capitalism that was overwhelming British society at the same time. The industrial revolution rested on the exploitation of free (i.e. propertyless) labourers, not on colonial slavery. Slavery was abolished in 1834.

The emancipation of the slaves precipitated the mass settler migration to Natal, the Orange Free State and the Transvaal, known as the Great Trek. There were other, underlying factors. The British colonial administration was asserting its authority on the Eastern frontier. Its policy was to halt the Afrikaner migration and force the settler farmer to adopt more efficient agricultural methods and produce for the market. But it was the colonial power's interference with the settlers' control over the black labour force that rankled most deeply. Apart from emancipating the slaves, the government had, by Ordinance 50 of 1828, freed Coloured workers from many controls, including the pass laws that restricted their movements. Piet Retief, one of the leaders of the trek, stated in a declaration of grievances:

> We are resolved, wherever we go, that we will uphold the just principles of liberty; but, whilst we will take care that no-one shall be held in a state of slavery, it is our determination to maintain such regulations as may suppress crime, and preserve proper relations between master and servant.[17]

In their trek northwards the settlers were able to take advantage of what in African history is known as the *difaqane* - the forced migration - which had thrown many of the African tribes in their path into turmoil. This was caused by the emergence of the highly centralised military Nguni kingdoms of the Zulu and the Ndebele (Matabele):

> These fighting tribes were an effect not a cause. It is clear that throughout a large part of South Africa there had developed an intense competition between the tribes for grazing and sowing land and, in the vast arid regions, for the 'eyes' of land where springs provided an adequate supply of water... Tribes like the Zulus under Chaka, and their offspring the Matabele under Moselekatze [Mzilikazi] found refuge in military organisations born in times of depression and unrest. They used their discipline to tyrannise and plunder their neighbours. Amongst the causes of this singular crisis that smashed tribes, scattered others, and dashed the fragments into new combinations, the halting of the Bantu vanguard on the Eastern frontier probably had much influence.[18]

The Afrikaner Voortrekkers established themselves on the land of these peoples by armed conquest. Equipped with rifles, and expert shots, they fought and won a series of bloody battles with the tribes they encountered. The Ndebele under Mzilikazi were driven across the Limpopo to establish their kingdom in parts of Zimbabwe. In the battle of Blood River on 16 December 1837, 500 settlers slaughtered 3,000 Zulus for the cost of three wounded.

Eventually the trekkers established two settler states, the South African Republic in the Transvaal and the Orange Free State. Their military strength lay in the commandos, a general mobilisation of all adult male whites. Politically and economically the settlers were roughly equal, each with a huge farm, while the black people whose land it was were denied all rights. The constitution of the South African Republic stated: 'The people desire to permit no equality between coloured people and the white inhabitants either in Church or State.'[19]

The white conquest of South Africa was completed by the British colonial power. The wars against the Xhosa on the Cape's eastern frontier were fought to the finish. Natal was annexed because of the strategic importance of the port of Durban. The process was accelerated after diamonds were discovered in Griqualand West between the Cape Colony and the Orange Free State (the area was rapidly annexed by Britain) and gold in the Transvaal in 1884. More African land was annexed by the Cape Colony between 1872 and 1894 than during the entire preceding century. It came not without struggle. In early 1879, 900 white and 800 black troops of the invading army of Lord Chelmsford were slaughtered by the Zulu in Natal under Cetiwayo. It took an imperial expeditionary force and the artillery bombardment of the royal *kraal* at Ulungi to force them into submission.

The effect on the African tribes of the loss of land was catastrophic. Land and the cattle it supported were the basis of African society. Before the white conquest,

Between population and land there was a reasonable

balance. As the tribes exhausted the soil or grass they could move on to fresh soil and find new pastures. The freedom to exploit new resources of land ... was the balance-wheel of tribal economic life.[20]

This freedom was now taken away. Throughout the colonies and settler republics, white farmers and land speculators carved out great blocks of land for themselves. Some absentee landlords owned tracts of 200,000 or 300,000 acres.[21] The Africans found themselves crowded into portions of land too small to maintain them and their beasts. Traditional agricultural methods, appropriate to a mode of production where land resources were virtually unlimited, led to soil erosion and falling productivity when restricted to particular areas. Taxes imposed by the white state and the inroads made by the market through the intermediary of traders intensified the pressure on African peasants. Increasingly they went to work for white farmers in order to earn money for taxes, to cover their debts to the traders for guns, tools, blankets and to meet their subsistence needs. The migrant labour system was beginning to emerge.

A variety of measures inspired by the mineowners were used to complete the expropriation of the African peasantry. Hut and poll taxes were imposed on Africans to force them to take up wage labour. As Prime Minister of the Cape, Rhodes introduced the Glen Grey Act of 1894, which replaced the communal land tenure of the Xhosa in the Transkei with individual landholding. By placing a minimum limit on the size of plots and imposing a labour tax, Rhodes hoped to force the Africans to work in the mines. He explained that he hoped 'by the gentle stimulant of the labour tax to remove them from a life of sloth and laziness; you will thus teach them the dignity of labour'.[22]

Other measures were taken to control the movement of labour to and from the mining compounds. Masters and servants laws made black workers criminally liable for breach of contract with the employers. Pass laws made it compulsory for blacks to carry identification papers. Rhodes explained in 1887: 'Either you have to receive them on an equal footing as citizens or you call them a subject race. I have made up my mind that there must be class legislation, that there must be pass laws.'[23]

The spread of market relations into the countryside speeded up the process. The mining companies, which formed the Witwatersrand Native Labour Association in 1896, employed recruiting agents in different areas and paid local traders 25 shillings for every African they found for the mines. Peasant indebtedness was used to force Africans to sell their labour power. Already by 1902 a Transkei magistrate could claim that three out of every four able-bodied men were migrating for work. The President of the Chamber of Mines explained in 1912 that it was only through 'paying out large sums to recruiters, who in turn endeavour to induce the natives to come to work by offers of loans and the wherewithal to pay their taxes and their debts to the local traders who have given them credit, that we have been able to keep up the supply of labour to what it is today'.[24] In 1912 the mining companies went further and set up the Native Recruiting Corporation, whose function it was to enlist all the African workers for the mines. The object of this move was to end the competition for workers between different mines which was pushing up wages and lowering profits. African miners faced a single employer.

By then the mineowners were recruiting labour beyond the borders. After cutting wages by 30 per cent in 1896, and having then to face a large-scale withdrawal of labour, which rather confounded their claim that Africans worked in the mines only to supplement their incomes from agriculture, and therefore would work more if wages fell,[25] active steps were taken to find labour outside South Africa. In 1904 60,000 indentured Chinese workers were imported to meet the labour shortage in the mines. Later black workers were recruited nearer to hand, although outside South Africa itself. By 1910 half the mines' African labour force consisted of 'East Coast natives' from Mozambique.[26]

Once recruited, the mineworkers were worked on by the

machinery of the pass laws, the master and servant laws and the compound system. They were forced to sign long-term contracts (minimum of 6-9 months for Africans from 'British South Africa' and 12 months for 'Portuguese' Africans). Breach of contract was a criminal offence and, under the pass laws, extended to all African mineworkers by the Native Labour Regulation Act of 1911, any African who did not have a job within a week of entering an urban area could be fined, imprisoned or deported. Skilled jobs were reserved under the Mines and Works Act of 1911 to white workers.

In 1913 the Native Land Act limited African rights to own land to about 13 per cent of the country. Within these areas - the Reserves (now the 'Homelands') - only Africans could own land.

The object of this measure was to prevent the complete proletarianisation of the African peasantry by halting the disintegration of their economy. Already white carpetbaggers like those in the American south after the civil war had gobbled up much of the land the settler conquerors of the nineteenth century had neglected to seize.[27] If they were not stopped, an African working class with no ties to the land and nothing to sell but their labour-power would result. Not only would this development be politically threatening, but the migrant workers would require higher wages to feed and house their dependents, whom the land could no longer keep. It was therefore imperative to preserve the fiction that African workers were peasants who only visited the towns in search of jobs and who had no right to settle in towns with their families. It was also useful that the Act inhibited rich African peasants from buying European land, a worry to some settlers.

The Native Land Act did not reverse the separation of the African peasantry from the land. One year later, in 1914, missionaries were reporting that 'the reserves were utterly dependent on the earnings remitted home by migrant miners and that the reserves were, in effect, being turned into mining villages'.[28]

The situation has grown much worse since. In 1955 the

government's Tomlinson commission investigated the economic problems of the Reserves. The basic cause was the scarcity of land which, combined with the migratory labour system and the continuance of traditional agricultural methods, led to overpopulation, soil erosion and overstocking. Many holdings were completely uneconomic - 2 hectares or less - and many families were landless. In the Ciskei in 1948 nearly 30 per cent of the families were without land and cattle.[29] The commission calculated that over 500,000 men - about 40 per cent of the men between 15 and 65 - in the Reserves, were away working in industrial areas, and that all men migrated to work at some time in their lives. Most agricultural labour was done by women and children.[30]

Despite the policy of separate development aimed at turning the Reserves into politically independent Homelands, little has changed in the twenty years since the Tomlinson report. In 1975 the Homelands could feed less than one-quarter of their population from home production.[31] In 1954 per capita income in the Reserves was R25.80 per annum, or R48 including remittances from migrant workers. In 1969 the equivalent figures were R22 and R53.[32] Even in money terms income generated in the tribal areas had fallen; the total income, boosted by migrant workers' remittances, had also fallen in real terms.

Not only did the Land Act of 1913 forbid the purchase and sale of land to Africans outside the Reserves, it also provided for the removal of African tenants or squatters from white farms. Moreover, since the establishment of the Union of South Africa in 1910, the state had begun to provide massive aid to white farmers who progressively abandoned their old feudal traditions and produced for the market. By 1913 yields per capita on African farms were falling and after the 1920s the absolute yields fell as well.[33]

In this manner, the black working class was created in South Africa. Perhaps it would be a mistake to overemphasise the uniqueness of this process. After all, from the sixteenth century onwards the English peasantry was expropriated and forced to sell its labour-power through the enclosure of the common land, bloody legislation aimed against the 'idle' and 'slothful' unemployed, statues fixing a minimum working day, and so on. But the political freedom that the English working class won also grew during the same process - from the seventeenth century revolution to the electoral reforms of the nineteenth century. The African working class that gathered in the mining compounds and townships of South Africa at the beginning of this century was free in Marx's sense - free from any control over the means of production and from any restrictions preventing them from selling their labour-power; indeed they were forced to do so in order to live. But the political freedoms that workers in Western Europe and North America had won were denied to them.

Afrikaner Nationalism, State Capitalism and the White Working Class

In the quarter-century between the discovery of gold in 1886 and the establishment of the Union of South Africa in 1910, mining capital, backed by British imperialism, established its dominance over South African society. The main obstacle in its path was provided by the two Afrikaner republics of the Transvaal and the Orange Free State, ruled by feudal landowners who were largely unsympathetic to British capital and the skilled English-speaking workers invading their territories (the main gold deposits were in the Transvaal).

War broke out between the British imperial government and the Afrikaner republics in 1899. A number of factors played a part in bringing things to a head - conflicts between the republics and the mineowners, differences of interest between the Transvaal in particular and the British colonies of the Cape and Natal over railways, Whitehall's fear of a link-up between the republics and Germany, which had already conquered neighbouring South-West Africa.

For three years (the Boer War of 1899-1902) the Afrikaner republics resisted the full weight of the British onslaught. The settlers' farms were destroyed, their families herded into the first concentration camps, where 26,000 women and children died in a series of epidemics. The brilliant use of guerilla warfare by the Afrikaner citizen levies - the commandos - denied the British troops complete military victory and the Vereeniging Agreement that ended the war in 1902 made considerable concessions to the Afrikaners. Self-government was to be granted to them and it was left to them to decide whether to enfranchise the Africans.

In 1910 the Union of South Africa was established, merging the four provinces of the Cape, Natal, the Transvaal and the Orange Free State into a single, self-governing state. The basis of union was an alliance of mining capital and the big Afrikaner landowners represented by the Boer War generals Botha and Smuts, who formed the first government of the Union. The alliance, personified by Jan Christian Smuts, was to dominate white South African politics for a generation. Yet it was to face continual challenge, not only from the oppressed and exploited African majority, but also from the mass of Afrikaners, and it was this latter challenge that led finally to Smuts' displacement in 1948.

The development of the gold-mining industry transformed settler agriculture. A large internal market for agricultural commodities was created in addition to the export markets that were growing for commodities like wool. Market relations spread in agriculture. The various systems by which African tenants worked the land in exchange for paying the farmer rents in cash, kind or labour-services were gradually replaced by wage-labour. The farmer's hand was strengthened by separating the peasant from the land, enabling him to pay very low wages - an important consideration given the very low productivity of agriculture.

The state intervened to back up the farmers. The Native Land Act of 1913 abolished certain types of feudal rents and forced African 'squatters' off the land, thus increasing the supply of landless labour. By the early 1930s labour tenancy, although it survived, was disintegrating,[34] and the Native

Trust and Land Act of 1936, which speeded the transition to wage-labour, provided an almost final blow. The increasing dominance of wage-labour on the white farms is shown by figures for the late 1960s and early 1970s; they show the number of labour tenants as 16,350, the number of semi-proletarianised squatters as 462,000 (many of them women and children), the number of registered wage-labourers as 420,600 and the number of domestic servants as 150,000.[35] Since 1947 the state has also built a series of farm gaols in agricultural areas to provide farmers short of cheap labour with convicts to work on their farms. There are about 8,000 convict workers.

Hand in hand with the proletarianisation of the peasantry has gone the concentration of settler land ownership in the hands of a small minority. In the years after the Boer War, many Afrikaners lost their land because of their inefficiency and inability to compete, a succession of droughts, land speculation, the devastation caused by the war and the parcellisation of the land through inheritance. The *bywoners*, white tenant farmers traditionally permitted to squat on the under-utilised settler land, were gradually shifted off. In 1960 one quarter of the farms accounted for 77 per cent of the total land area.[36]

The result was a tremendous influx of landless whites into the towns. Between 1904 and 1911 the number of whites living in urban areas grew by 7 per cent; in the Rand it grew by 42 per cent - 70,000. Most of this increase was of Afrikaners.[37] In 1900 there were barely 10,000 Afrikaners living in the ten big cities; by 1959 there were about 600,000,[38] concentrated in the Rand. Lacking skills, they were unable to compete with the British trade unionists imported from Cornwall and Northern England to do the skilled work in the mines. Equally, they were excluded from the market for unskilled labour by the existence of a mass of black workers prepared to work for lower wages and by their own reluctance to do manual labour, which, after all, was Kaffir's work.

This mass of proletarianised Afrikaners - 'poor whites' - was to provide the social base of the Nationalist Party, which, first under Hertzog, and then, after Hertzog's alliance with

Smuts in the mid 1930s, under Malan, was the focus of settler opposition to the mineowners and British imperialism.

The opposition went through two main phases. After a brief reversion to the days of the Boer War and the commandos, when a group of Boer War veterans organised an uprising in protest at South Africa's entry into the First World War on Britain's side, and were unsentimentally and firmly crushed by their old comrades-in-arms, Smuts and Botha, Afrikanerdom on the whole concentrated upon the peaceful conquest of the state.

The first phase, which lasted until the 1930s, was dominated by the struggle between the Afrikaner rural interest backed by white workers and the mineowners.

The constitution had laid down a system for delimiting constituencies for the all-white parliament that favoured rural as against urban districts. During the early years of the Union the settler farmers tried to use their electoral advantage to control the state with the aim of taxing the mining revenues in order to subsidise agriculture. They found ready allies among the white skilled workers, who were as eager as the farmers to use state intervention against the employers whom they confronted as workers and against the black workers whom they feared as competitors.

The South African Labour Party was formed in 1910 to organise the white working class (black workers, with the exception of some in the Cape, did not vote). When the Native Land Act of 1913 was introduced in parliament, Creswell, the Labour leader, criticised it because it aimed at 'an abundance of cheap Kaffir labour' and argued for the partition of South Africa among the races - an early version of separate development.[39] The Labour Party naturally supported the Mines and Works Act of 1911, under which the colour bar was legally entrenched in the mines.

Equally naturally, the mineowners were less enthusiastic about the colour bar, since it made skilled labour scarce and expensive. They did not, however, press the point until after the first world war, when it led to a major crisis.

Wartime inflation drastically increased the costs of mining. At the same time the war led to a shortage of skilled labour, as many of the white mineworkers volunteered for military service. They were replaced by proletarianised Afrikaners, who by the end of the war formed 75 per cent of the white labour force in the mines compared to 40 per cent in 1914.[40] The white miners took advantage of their improved bargaining position - white wages rose by 60 per cent between 1914 and 1920, while African earnings remained static.[41] In addition, the white miners won the Status Quo Agreement of 1918, which banned the displacement in the mines of whites by blacks. This reflected the pressure of the Afrikaans miners, who, relatively less skilled than the English-speaking workers they replaced, were threatened by the introduction of black workers into semi-skilled jobs. On the employers' part it represented a strategy of accommodation in face of the growing strength and militancy of the white miners.

The crunch came after the war. Rising costs, falling output and the anticipated fall in the gold price that would arise from the return of Britain to the gold standard, caused an acute crisis.[42] By 1921 over two-thirds of the mines could not operate at a profit under normal conditions. The mineowners went on the offensive, demanding the abolition of the Status Quo Agreement so that they could take on blacks as semi-skilled workers, a wage-cut and a reorganisation of underground work aimed at raising productivity and reducing the number of white miners, 2,000 of whom were to be sacked.

The miners' response was militant. They struck in January 1922. The Rand Revolt, as it became known, was fought in defence of the colour bar. As the legal defence committee, formed after the strike, explained: 'The Strike was fought throughout on the question of the Colour Bar, including the Status Quo Agreement.'[43] The more radical, including the Communist Party, sought to turn the strike into a general challenge to the employing class. They were even prepared to justify the slogan 'Workers of the World, Fight and Unite for a White South Africa', under which the strikers marched.[44] The miners' union secretary promised that they would deal with any attempt at a black uprising during the strike.[45] Reverting to the traditions of the Boer War, the miners formed armed commandos all over the Rand, and so 'transposed the traditional fighting formation of the Afrikaner farmers to a new setting, that of the urban, industrial class conflict'.[46]

Smuts sent in 7,000 troops, backed by bombers, artillery, machine guns, armoured cars and trains, and tanks. The miners' attempt to call a general strike met with little response even on the Rand. By 14 March the government and the mining houses were in control: probably about 200 people had been killed and about 500 or 600 wounded; 5,000 people were arrested and four of the strike leaders were eventually executed.[47]

The Rand Revolt cemented the alliance between the white working class and the Nationalist Party, which had backed the strike. The mineowners' victory was short-lived. At the election of 1924 Smuts was turned out and replaced by Hertzog, Prime Minister of the Pact Government of the Nationalist and Labour Parties, a coalition of rural Afrikanerdom and white industrial labour whose common interest was in state intervention to defend themselves against the mining capitalists and the black masses.

The Pact Government, and its successors, over which Hertzog presided, passed the Industrial Conciliation Act of 1924 which created a system of registered trade unions and employer-employee industrial councils that cut down on industrial disputes and speeded up the formation of a white trade-union bureaucracy integrated into the machinery of the state. African workers were denied the right to form registered unions. The Wage Act of 1925 introduced minimum wage standards aimed at pricing black workers out of jobs considered suitable for whites. The Mines and Works (Amendment) Act of 1926 restored the colour bar in the mines. Hertzog issued a circular shortly after coming to office requiring government departments to substitute 'civilised' for 'uncivilised' labour possible. An uncivilised person was one 'whose aim is restricted to the bare requirements of the necessities of life as understood among barbarous and undeveloped peoples' while a civilised person was one whose standard of living was one 'generally recognised as tolerable from the usual European standpoint'.[48]

These measures, aimed at protecting the position of the white working class and providing jobs for the mass of 'poor whites', were combined with others aimed at shoring up settler agriculture. A series of laws, culminating in the Marketing Act of 1937, set up commodity control boards with powers to fix government-subsidised prices for agricultural products. The Afrikaner farmers, who dominated the control boards, were given state backing to raise domestic prices above world levels, and incidentally above prices that could be afforded by the impoverished African workers and peasants, in order to protect them from the agricultural price instability of the inter-war years.[49]

The mineowners' profits were heavily taxed to provide the revenue necessary to subsidise farm prices, to give white farmers easy loans, finance agricultural research, etc. The rate structure of the state-owned railways also favoured agricultural as against mining interests.[50]

The Pact Government's policies were in conflict with the mineowners at an even deeper level. A few weeks before the outbreak of the Boer War the settler government in the Transvaal had issued a statement to the effect that the republic's aim was 'to build up other industries on the back of the gold mines'. This, it explained, was already being achieved by taxing the mines, giving specific encouragement to manufacturing industry and by the introduction of other industries,

> round which it has created a semi-protective wall... All men cannot be gold-miners, nor can the state live by gold-mining alone. Somehow or other ... manufacturers have to be encouraged if the ultimate condition of the state is to be sound. Monopolies (in the form of protective tariffs and monopoly concessions) have their weak points: but they come most conveniently to Pretoria's hand.[51]

Twenty-five years later this strategy of creating manufacturing industry financed by the mineowners' profits and protected and encouraged by the state was initiated by the Pact Government. The mining capitalists opposed it. They were part of the international capitalist system; they did not need a domestic industry to confirm it. Moreover, protection would force up prices and hence increase costs.

The policy was implemented nonetheless. A general protective tariff was introduced in 1925. The Act was integrally linked to the policies of the Pact Government aimed at protecting white labour, since it also gave the Government 'discretionary power to apply a minimum instead of a maximum duty, and so reduce the protection afforded by the Act to any industry which maintained "unsatisfactory labour relations"'. [52]

From the start the state played a major role in the manufacturing industry built up behind the tariff wall. The railways were already in its hands. The South African Railways and Harbours Administration to this day is the biggest single employer and one of the pillars of the white labour policy, with about 229,000 people employed - 111,073 white and 117,889 black.[53] The state-controlled Iron and Steel Corporation (Iscor) was set up in 1928 despite the mineowners' bitter opposition, and played an important part in building up the South African economy.

The international crisis that began in 1929 caused a reorganisation of the ruling white power bloc. The Nationalist Party refused to follow Britain's example in coming off the gold standard in 1931, since the devaluation of the South African pound would have meant a rise in the price of gold, to the exclusive benefit of the English-speaking mineowners. The resulting flight of capital was running at £1 million a day when the government reversed its position in December 1932, and formed a coalition with Smuts' South Africa Party under Hertzog's premiership. In 1935 the two parties merged as the United Party. It appeared that Afrikanerdom had surrendered to mining capital and British imperialism.

In fact, the diehard Nationalists marshalled themselves under the leadership of D.F. Malan, representing a new group of urban intellectuals which replaced the Boer War generals as the leaders of Afrikanerdom. These realignments were speeded by the second world war. Hertzog, with the traditional Afrikaner sympathy for German imperialism, opposed Smuts' policy of going into the war on Britain's side. Overruled, Hertzog resigned from office, to be replaced by Smuts. His followers joined Malan's in a united National Party. Hertzog was rapidly displaced by Malan as party leader, and a new phase in the history of Afrikaner nationalism had begun.

In order to understand the new Nationalism we have to remember the circumstances in which it developed. The consequence of the government going off the gold standard was an inflationary boom fuelled by the rise in the gold price that led to a huge increase in manufacturing industry. Between 1933 and 1939 the manufacturing workforce grew by 77 per cent, from 133,000 to 236,000, while the number of black workers in manufacturing grew by 88 per cent, from 76,000 to 143,000. The value of gross output grew by 108 per cent. The boom was accelerated by the war: between 1939 and 1945 the value of gross output grew by 116 per cent; the total manufacturing work force grew by 53 per cent, while the number of black workers employed in manufacturing grew by 74 per cent to 249,000 (out of a total workforce of 361,000) in 1945.[54]

This development of manufacturing took place partly in mining-related industries like those processing new materials, and among light industries producing consumer goods whose creation was stimulated by protective tariffs. But it was also more solidly based. State cartels like Iscor, Escom (Electricity Supply Commission) and IDC (Industrial Development Corporation, set up in 1940) played a major part in laying the foundations of a developed capitalist economy. By 1951-52 the contribution of manufacturing to gross output had overtaken that of mining, producing 25 per cent of the GNP compared with 13 per cent.[55] Moreover, although there was a big influx of foreign capital in the 1930s, when, for example, ICI set up the massive chemicals complex African Explosives and Chemical Industries together with De Beers, much of the investment in manufacturing was by the South African commercial bourgeoisie. Even in the mining industry the share of South African investors grew - from less than 15 per cent in 1913 to 40 per cent in the 1930s.[56]

The world that Afrikanerdom found itself in from the 1930s onwards was that of a growing industrial capitalist economy in which more and more of the Afrikaner population were becoming urban workers. It was also a world in which a sizeable black urban proletariat had developed.

One sign of change in the Nationalists was, as we have seen, the emergence of a new leadership of urban intellectuals drawn largely from the Afrikaner professionals. Of the four Nationalist Prime Ministers since 1948, Malan had been a clergyman and journalist, Strydom and Vorster lawyers, and Verwoerd an academic and journalist. This new leadership reflected the changed nature of Nationalism's social base. The Afrikaners were no longer united by a common, apparently natural relation to the land (only apparently natural because the relation presupposed the exclusion of the Africans from their land). Although the farmers remained an important section of the Nationalist Party's base (the latter owed its victory in 1948 to the unequal weighting of rural and urban constituencies) and their interests have been looked after under successive Nationalist governments, they were no longer the dominant group in the Afrikaner coalition. The core section which the new leadership represented was now the Afrikaner urban petty bourgeoisie - professionals and small capitalists - whose aspiration was to establish themselves as the dominant section of South African industrial capital.

However, as private capitalists this aspiring Afrikaner bourgeoisie could not compete with mining capital and its interlocking network of links with British capital. In order to establish a position of hegemony the Nationalist petty bourgeoisie needed to win control of the state. In order to do that they needed the voting power of the mass of Afrikaner workers (during the second world war most Nationalist politicians hoped for a German victory that would lift them to power on Nazi bayonets, but this dream did not last long).[57]

The locus of power in the new Nationalism was the *Broederbond* (Band of Brothers), a secret society, founded ostensibly as a cultural association, grouping together the Afrikaner intelligentsia. In 1952 it was thought to consist of 357 clergymen, 2039 teachers, 905 farmers, 159 lawyers, and 60 MPs.[58] For a generation, until the early 1970s, the *Broederbond* dominated Afrikaner politics, with cells throughout white South Africa. The Nationalist Prime Ministers since 1948 have all been members.

Under the aegis of the *Broederbond* the Afrikaner intelligentsia in the 1930s and 1940s developed an ideology aimed at strengthening their hold over the white working class. They harked back to the Great Trek, the Boer War, and the other great moments of Afrikaner history, in order to assert the unity of the Afrikaner *volk* in the face of its enemies - 'Anglo-Jewish' big capital and the African masses. With its stress on the Afrikaner nation as possessing a reality that transcended both class divisions and the individual, it had distinctly fascist overtones:

> To Afrikanerdom belong only those who by virtue of blood, soil, culture, tradition, belief, calling, form an organic unitary society...
>
> This nation is by nature an organic wearer of authority with the patriarchical leader as the chief bearer of authority of the nation, and with the members of the nation as active and co-operative workers.
>
> The national Afrikaner state of the future is therefore the political embodiment and ordering of the whole of Afrikanerdom as an organic articulation of authority, and is in this sense also a medium of Afrikanerdom to protect and promote its own fulfilment of calling...
>
> The future Afrikaner national state will be a leadership state, an authoritative state, and a corporative state.[59]

They set up a number of institutions to bind the Afrikaner workers to the Nationalist petty bourgeoisie in its struggle for political power: the *Reddingsdaadbond* (RDB) was set up during the centenary celebrations of the Greak Trek in 1938 in order to raise money to 'redeem' the mass of impoverished landless Afrikaners. Dönges, a future cabinet minister, explained the function of the RDB:

> The foreign influences must be removed from our trade unions, and they must take their place foursquare on a national basis... It is the task of the RDB to keep the Afrikaner worker, in the midst of foreign elements, in his Church, language, and national environment.[60]

The *Blankewerkersbeskermingsbond* (White Workers' Protection Society) was founded and used to organise the Afrikaner workers, particularly in those unions where the Nationalist influence was small and where the leadership sometimes included socialists and communists.

Hand in hand with the attempt to shackle the Afrikaner worker to the Nationalist leadership, went the attempt to develop an Afrikaner capitalist class. As Malan had put it in 1950:

> The enormous upsurge in the emotions of our people should not be allowed to evanesce like the morning dew. The mighty stream of reborn love for the nation, the feeling of unity must not be allowed to disappear unused in desert sands. It *must* ever be converted to permanent, self-perpetuating values; and the necessary machinery must be created. The trek must continue.[61]

An *Ekonomiese Volkskongres* (people's economic congress) was held in 1939 under the auspices of the RDB.

A number of major Afrikaner enterprises had already been established - the insurance companies SANLAM and SANTAM in 1918, the burial society AVBOB in 1921, the banking house Volkskas in 1934 (significantly, with *Broederbond* backing). But the overall share of Afrikaner capital in the private economy was derisory - five per cent in the total private economy and only one per cent in the mines.[62] M.S. Louw, managing director of

SANLAM, explained to the *volkskongres*:

> If we want to achieve success, we must make use of the technique of capitalism, as it is employed in the most important industry of our country, the gold mining industry. We must establish a financial company which will function in commerce and industry like the so-called 'finance houses' in Johannesburg.[63]

As a result of the economic congress the Afrikaner investment company, *Federale Volksbeleggings* (FVB), was established in 1939. It was followed by the establishment of the *Afrikaanse Handelsinstituut* (Afrikaner Chamber of Commerce and Industry) with financial backing from the RDB. But when the second *volkskongres* met in 1950, the total share of Afrikaner capital in the private economy had grown from 5 to only 11 per cent: in industry it had grown from 3 to 5 per cent, in finance from 5 to 6 per cent, in mining it remained at one per cent; only in commerce had it risen from 8 to 25 per cent.[64] The attempt to mobilise the savings of the Afrikaner *volk* had raised little more than £100,000.[65]

The second congress met two years after the Nationalist Party came to power. Since then they have systematically used their control of the state apparatus to develop Afrikaner capitalism. State intervention in the economy has increased enormously. A whole number of parastatals have been set up in addition to Escom, Iscor, IDC and SAR&H: Armscor (armaments), Ucor (uranium), Nufcor (uranium processing), Soekor (oil exploration), Sasol (oil, coal, gas and chemicals), Foskor (fertilisers). Through the IDC the state is involved in mining, aircraft manufacturing, shipping, textiles, leather and printing. Between 1960 and 1970 public sector fixed investment grew at an average annual rate of 13.3 per cent compared to 11 per cent in the private sector. By 1970 the public sector share of total fixed investment was 46 per cent.[66]

The growth of state capitalism in South Africa since 1948 has also been the growth of Afrikaner capitalism. Government departments are expected to bank with Volkskas or other

Afrikaner banks. The personnel of the parastatals is largely Afrikaans-speaking:

> Of the Industrial Development Corporation's nine direct-ors, only one is English-speaking. Foskor has not had a single English-speaking board member in all the years of its existence. The language in which most board meetings of the corporations are conducted is Afrikaans.[67]

Decisions about government contracts and the siting of public utilities favour Afrikaner private firms.

The result has been a phenomenal expansion of the Afrikaner private sector. Let us take the most important example. Between 1962 and 1967 the assets of FVB grew from R15 million to over R84 million.[68] Fed Chem, set up by FVB jointly with African Explosives and Chemical Industries, dominates the chemicals industry. In 1953 FVB set up a mining company, Federale Mynbou, jointly with the Afrikaner investment company, Bonuskor. Company assets were worth about R2 million. Attempts to take over Rand Mines and then Johannesburg Consolidated Investments were blocked by Anglo-American. Then, in 1963, with Anglo-American's agree-ment, *Federale Mynbou*, took over the General Mining and Finance Corporation, with assets in gold and uranium mining worth about R250 million. The takeover was described by the Johannesburg *Sunday Times* 'not only as a personal triumph for Mr Harry Oppenheimer chairman of Anglo-American, but also as an important step forward in his proposals for closer business co-operation across the South African language barrier'.[69] By 1967 Federale Mynbou controlled 37 per cent of South Africa's uranium, 20 per cent of its coal, and 32 per cent of its asbestos, as well as 9 per cent of gold mining. In 1976 it crowned its efforts when its subsidiary General and Mining took over Union Corporation, making the Afrikaner company the third largest of South Africa's mining finance houses, with assets worth R750 million. Afrikaner capitalism has arrived.[70]

The state capitalist policies of the Nationalist governments since 1948 have altered the balance of power within the white ruling bloc. Not only is Afrikaner private capital now able to deal with English-speaking capital on equal terms so that increasingly the two groups collaborate; but thanks to its control of the state via the Nationalist Party and the complex of interests linking it to the parastatals and the government, the Afrikaner bourgeoisie has become the dominant section of South African capital.

2. Black Resistance and White Oppression

Black resistance to white rule in South Africa is almost as old as the first colonial settlement in 1652. The Bantu peoples first fought a series of bitter and heroic wars against the white invaders. Then, after the Afrikaner and British colonial armies had succeeded in conquering the country, black resistance took the form of struggles against expropriation and proletarianisation and against their exploitation as workers.

The Making of the African Working Class[1]

In 1906 there was a widespread uprising in Zululand - the Bambata rebellion, as it was called after its main leader. It is often regarded as the last of the tribal wars against white rule. Yet the cause of the uprising - the imposition of a poll tax of £1 on every adult male in Natal - showed that already the focus of the struggle was becoming the use by the settlers of state power to force the African peasantry to become workers. The uprising was suppressed by troops armed with machine guns. 4,000 blacks and 25 whites were killed.

The Natal Indian community, led by M.K. Gandhi, a young lawyer, supported the suppression of the African uprising, even providing medical auxiliaries for the colonial troops. But when the Transvaal government introduced a law requiring Indians to carry passes Gandhi was stirred into action. He pioneered the methods of mass passive resistance which he was later to make famous during the struggle for independence in India itself. The government was forced to back down, although the wave of strikes by Indian coal miners in Newcastle, Natal, proved more effective than pass-burning.

The foundation of the Union of South Africa in 1910, under a constitution which reserved the vote for whites except in the Cape, where a franchise based on property and educational qualifications meant that there was a significant black minority vote, stirred into being the first nation-wide expression of African nationalism.

The South African Native National Congress was set up in 1912. In 1925 it changed its name to the African National Congress (ANC). It was the product of an alliance between the African petty bourgeoisie - lawyers, professionals, traders, rich peasants - and the chiefs, the traditional leaders of African society. In its early years Congress included an Upper house of 'Princes of African Blood'. Until the late 1940s the ANC concentrated its efforts upon appeals to the British government (which had washed its hands of 'the Native problem' the moment it handed over self-government to the settlers) and upon attempts to win the support of white 'liberal' opinion. The latter, to be found mainly within the circles of English-speaking capital, was often prepared to lend a sympathetic ear, but since the core of English-speaking capital was in mining, which depended on the migrant labour system and the pass laws in order to survive, white liberalism did not strike deep roots.

The first world war led to rapid growth in the number of black factory workers and, following the example of the militant white workers of the time, in militancy as well. In 1918 black sanitary workers in Johannesburg went on strike for an increase of sixpence (6d) a day. Although the 'bucket strike' was rapidly crushed, the surge of black rebellion continued. The ANC was stirred to organise a campaign against the pass laws. More important was the foundation of the Industrial and Commercial Workers Union of Africa in 1919. Under the leadership of Clemens Kadalie, an inspired demagogue from Nyasaland, the ICU sparked off a strike of black dockworkers in Cape Town that swept the whole country with a strike fever. But even the ICU's activities were swamped by a great spontaneous strike of 40,000 black mineworkers in 1920.

The Communist Party of South Africa (CPSA) was

founded in 1921. It was to play the central role in the development of the black working-class movement during the inter-war years. It had originated in 1915 as the International Socialist League (ISL), an anti-war breakaway from the white Labour Party. Almost all of its members were white trade unionists and professionals, heavily influenced by syndicalist ideals, who saw the organised and, to an extent, militant white working class as the vanguard of the South African revolution. Although the ISL had leafleted white miners during the strike of 1920 - 'DON'T SCAB! DON'T SHOOT' - the CP inherited its neglect of African workers. It supported the Rand Revolt of 1922 and even by some twist of logic backed what it called the 'anti-imperialist front' in the election of 1924 - the alliance of racist white labour and Afrikaner Nationalism that defeated Smuts.[2]

However, in December 1924, the third conference of the CP, at the urging of Sidney Bunting, a white lawyer, adopted a policy of mass work among the African proletariat. Initially, the party worked within the ICU, but conflicts rapidly developed.

The ICU was not really a trade union:

> Its strength lay in its loose but appealing amalgam of economic and political demands, attracting support from the ill-defined groups of dissidents characteristic of early industrialisation. Landless peasants, rural squatters, domestic servants, unemployed migrants and other *lumpens*, even aspirant rural and urban entrepreneurs, were its bases, as well as workers *per se*.[3]

The failure to build the ICU around the economic struggles of black workers led, paradoxically, to the attribution of magical powers to the general strike as a weapon. Kadalie once said: 'I will simply go from dockyard to factory and with a single word "STOP" the white people will be held to ransom, the railways will lose over £2,000,000 and while the trouble is on I will be looked upon as Prime Minister.'[4] This syndicalist strain in South African black nationalism, which persists to this day,[5] was the rock on which the CP's attempts to turn the ICU into a black trade union foundered. In December 1926, Kadalie, on the advice of white liberal sympathisers, banned CP members from holding office in the ICU. Rebuffed, the CP set out to build trade unions on its own. In March 1928 the South African Federation of Non-European Trade Unions was formed representing about 10,000 African workers, mainly in the laundry, tailoring, engineering and baking trades. The African membership of the CP grew from 200 in 1927 to 1600 (out of a total of 1,750) the following year.[6]

The Sixth Congress of the Communist International took place in 1928. It confirmed the strategy, developed by Stalin and Bukharin during their battle against Trotsky and the Left Opposition, of an alliance between the Soviet Union and the national liberation movements in the colonial countries. Designed to weaken the war threat to the USSR represented primarily by British imperialism, the strategy represented the Russian leadership's abandonment of the Bolshevik perspective of international working-class revolution. It required that the interests of workers in the colonies be subordinated to those of a class alliance led by petty bourgeois nationalists.[7] In China the Comintern's insistence on an alliance with the Kuomintang led to the virtual destruction of the Chinese Communist Party.[8]

Applied to South Africa, the strategy implied that workers' struggles be subordinated to the struggle for 'a democratic independent Native republic'. The new policy was approved by the Congress despite Bunting's confused opposition. He argued that the white working class should not be written off as part of the revolutionary vanguard in South Africa. However, he also pointed out that 'the ANC is a moribund body. The Communist Party is the actual or potential leader of the native national movement.'[9]

Initially, the 'Native republic' line served as a useful corrective to the CP's remaining illusions in white workers: it encouraged the party to embrace the struggles against all forms of oppression of the black population. Bunting loyally formed a League for African Rights which won mass support in campaigning for minimal democratic demands. He also took the campaign to the unemployed migrant workers of the Transkei during the 1929 general election.

However, in 1930 the line changed. The Comintern imposed upon the party an ultra-left policy of confrontation with the state at any price. At its insistence the CP adopted a strategy of hyperactivism - strikes, demonstrations, and general all-out resistance to the state - in order to lead as rapidly as possible to the revolution which the Comintern saw as round the corner. The League for African Rights was dissolved; Moscow considered its demands 'reformist'.

This 'third period' policy delivered the CP into the hands of the regime. The Nationalists had been re-elected in 1929 in a pogrom atmosphere as the world economy drifted into slump. The pro-Nazi Minister of Justice, Oswald Pirow, initiated a wave of repression. The Riotous Assemblies Amendment Act of 1930 gave him dictatorial powers of banishment and of control over public meetings. Pirow personally led 700 policemen armed with machine guns, tear gas and fixed bayonets on a tax-collecting raid in the Durban African townships. The ANC refused to resist and the CP was left isolated and exposed. One of the party's leading African members was murdered by the police in Durban. Party branches in Natal and the Western Cape were smashed. Blacks once attracted towards the CP began to shun it. One African communist explained: 'I find the general idea of Zulus in Durban is that it is no use joining the Party, as people are sent to gaol.'[10]

The ultra-left turn was accompanied by the 'Bolshevisation' of the Party on Moscow's orders. Stalin's agent in these matters was Douglas Wolton, known to African members as 'deepening economic crisis' because of the frequency with which he used the phrase. He purged Bunting and most of the best African trade union activists as 'Right opportunists'. The low point was reached in 1934, when Wolton's co-thinker, Lazar Bach, anticipated separate development by calling for a 'voluntary association of national republics ... Sotho, Tswana, Swazi, Zulu, Xhosa ... in a federation of independent native republics'.[11]

In 1935 the CP dropped the ultra-leftism of the third period for a Popular Front against fascism and war. The move was once again the result of orders from Moscow. (Bach was recalled to Russia and executed soon afterwards.) Stalin hoped to stave off the Nazi military threat through an alliance with the 'democratic' imperialist powers - Britain and France. Nonetheless, although the absurdities of the third period were abandoned, the CP remained committed to the fundamental assumption underlying the 'Native republic' period - the idea that national liberation would precede, and be separate from, socialist revolution.[12]

The boom stimulated by South Africa's abandonment of the gold standard and the fusion of Smuts's and Hertzog's followers into the United Party did not stem the wave of repression. In 1935 Hertzog introduced a Bill to deprive African voters in the Cape of the qualified franchise they had previously enjoyed. This move stimulated a temporary revival of ANC. An All African Convention (AAC) met in December 1935 to protest against Herzog's proposals. Despite the widespread support given the convention, a delegation led by Professor D.D.T. Jabavu accepted a compromise with Hertzog under which a separate African electoral roll would be introduced and a Native Representative Council ('a toy telephone', as one of its members was to call it) would be set up.

The Communist Party accepted the agreement. Its adoption of Popular Frontism had led it to make a complete U-turn, from denouncing the ANC as reformist to collaboration, not only with the black petty bourgeoisie but also with the 'anti-fascist' white liberals, who had persuaded the ANC leadership to participate in the elections to the Native Representative Council (NRC).

The disasters resulting from the CP's ultra-leftism during the third period, and the surrender of the AAC leadership to Herzog in 1936, did not mean that there was no mass resistance to white supremacy. In the reserves, there had been widespread revolts even before the passage of the 1936 Native Trust and Land Act as part of Hertzog's package of racist measures. The

Act, which completed the work of the 1913 legislation by applying it to the Cape, stimulated further resistance in the reserves. Between 1937 and 1943 half a million peasants are reported to have been involved in militant activity in the northern Transvaal alone. It was rumoured that bombers were used to crush the rising.

In the towns, there was a major revival of the black workers' movement. We have seen how in the 1930s and 1940s the expansion of the South African economy created an African urban proletariat. African workers were increasingly becoming a settled urban class. Between 1921 and 1945, the urban African population trebled, so that one in four Africans were in urban areas by the end of that period, while the ratio of African women to men rose from under 1:5 in 1921 to 1:3, indicating the extent to which the migrant labour system was being undermined.[13]

The new strength of the African working class expressed itself in the spread of unionisation and strike militancy. The CP's orientation on the Popular Front meant that independent socialists played the leading role in building many of these unions, particularly in the Transvaal. Gana Makabeni, an expelled party member, set up a new group of unions under entirely African leadership. Max Gordon, a white member of the Trotskyist Workers' Party, built up the Joint Committee group of unions to a membership of 20,000 by 1939.[14] CP members also played a part in the new unions. Ray Alexander (R.E. Simons) organised at least a dozen unions in the Cape. J.B. Marks, an expelled party member, took perhaps the most important step of all when he founded the African Mine Workers Union (AMWU) in 1941.

The unions suffered from many problems. Lack of resources forced Gordon and Makabeni into financial dependence on white liberals. Strong collaborationist pressures on union leaders arose from the fact that they spent a lot of time presenting their members' cases to the government Wage Boards responsible for determining minimum wages.

Nonetheless, the black trade unions grew. At the end of 1942 the largest and most comprehensive strike wave in African working-class history began. It involved in the main previously unorganised workers - confectionery workers, coal miners, dockers, dairy workers, brick workers, railway labourers and municipal employees - on the Rand and in Natal. Between 1930 and 1939, 26,254 black workers had struck, costing industry 71,078 working days; between 1940 and 1945 the corresponding figures were 52,394 strikers and 220,205 working days lost. African workers' real wages rose during the war for the first time since before 1896.[15] By 1945 there were over 150,000 members of the Non-European Trade Union Council (NETUC) and at least 40 per cent of African workers in commerce and private industry had been unionised, as intermittent subscribers if not paid-up members.[16]

The war-time boom caused a huge influx of Africans into the cities. The failure of the authorities to provide housing for these workers and their families resulted in tremendous overcrowding. In 1944 thousands of Africans left the Johannesburg township of Orlando to squat illegally on nearby vacant municipal ground. The squatting movement that resulted was on such a scale that the municipality was forced to provide the squatters with housing.

There were other struggles as well. Two huge bus boycotts by the residents of Alexandra township near Johannesburg, one in August 1943 and the other, which lasted seven weeks, beginning in November 1944, forced the postponement of planned fare increases. The first boycott gave birth to a new organisation, the African Democratic Party (ADP). Its emergence helped to stir Congress and the CP, both busy backing the war effort, into action. An anti-pass campaign was launched in 1944. However, its main activity, a monster petition, fell far short of its target of one million signatures.

During the early part of the second world war, when a Japanese invasion seemed likely, Smuts adopted a conciliatory approach. He even said: 'Isolation has gone and I am afraid segregation has fallen onto evil days.'[17] The Communist Party reciprocated once Hitler had invaded Russia:

During that whole period, beginning at the time when the Soviet Union entered the war, the CP was indistinguishable from General Smuts' Party. In the 'Friends of the Soviet Union' and allied bodies the members of the CP and the Bishop Lewises, etc., were all of one fraternity. With equal zeal they mobilised man-power, labour, industry in one grand war effort. From pulpit to social club, from factory to rural village they were busily engaged recruiting the oppressed to join the army - even as baggage warriors - in order to defend 'their country'. At this time their favourite argument was that nothing must be done to embarrass the Government in the prosecution of the war, and General Smuts was proclaimed as the greatest leader in the 'fight against Fascism'.[18]

Once the military situation had improved, Smuts felt safe enough to clamp down. In 1943, War Measure 145 banned all African strikes. Nonetheless there were over 60 illegal African strikes in that and the following year.

Smuts attempted to exploit the tensions between the different black groups produced by the massive influx of Africans into Coloured and Indian districts. In Natal, he was comparatively successful: the Natal Indian Congress, dominated by the Asian merchant class, succeeded in diverting Indian workers from their previous involvement in the African strike movement to a general campaign in defence of Indian trading, investment and residential rights. Smuts' divisive tactics failed in the Cape. There revolutionary Coloured school teachers used a successful boycott of the Coloured Affairs Council (equivalent to the stooge NRC) as the starting point for an attempt to draw all blacks into opposition to white supremacy. Under the leadership of I.B. Tabata, a fiery African Trotskyist, they revived the All African Convention and founded in 1943 the Non-European Unity Movement (now Unity Movement of South Africa) on a ten-point programme of democratic demands and a strategy of non-collaboration with the regime. Their efforts, under the slogan 'the battle of the African is the battle of us all', drew into the Unity Movement the main African organisations in the Transkei Reserves.

The decisive battle came in 1946. The leadership of the African Mine Workers Union, headed by J.B. Marks, who had now rejoined the CP, was under heavy pressure from its 25,000 members to join the wave of strike militancy. In August an emergency conference of the AMWU voted, against their leaders' pleas, for an all-out strike for a ten shilling basic wage and housing for their families.[19] These demands threatened to undermine the very foundations of the migrant labour system and turn the miners into a settled urban work force. But the strike came at a time when postwar unemployment was growing fast, undermining the workers' bargaining power.

Smuts hit back hard. The leaderships of NETUC (which had voted full support to the miners), of the AMWU and of the Johannesburg CP were arrested. Despite an impressive turnout - 70,000 on strike out of the Reef's 308,000 African mineworkers - affecting 32 out of the 45 mines on the Rand by the second day, armed police were able to force the miners back to work. At City Deep the workers responded with a sit-down strike underground and were baton charged and driven up, stope by stope, level by level, to the surface and back into the compound.

Apartheid

The miners' strike and the war-time struggles of which it was the culmination, represented a turning point in South African history. A settled urban African working class had emerged and was laying claim to trade-union rights, to higher wages, to an end to the pass laws, to better housing. The miners' strike had been based on demands which, if met, would have turned the most important single section of the black proletariat into a stable urban group, ending their status as migrant workers.

South African capitalists were well aware of the dangers. The Board of Trade and Industries said in a report on South African manufacturing industry in 1945:

Racial and class differences will make a homogeneous Native proletariat which will eventually lose all contact with their former communal rural relations which had previously given their lives a content and meaning. The detribalisation of large numbers of Natives congregated in amorphous masses in large industrial centres is a matter which no government can view with equanimity. Unless handled with great foresight and skill these masses of detribalised Natives can very easily develop into a menace rather than a constructive factor in industry.[20]

The South African ruling class were in a dilemma. The migrant labour system was central to the profitability of mining and agriculture. However, there were strong arguments for scrapping it in manufacturing industry. There a settled and stable black working class would be better trained and more productive than one composed of migrant workers. And since the ruling United Party represented the interests of both mining and manufacturing capital, the contradictions inherent in the situation were reproduced within it. The mineowners pulled one way, the manufacturers another. On the one hand Smuts would tell Parliament in 1945, at much the same time as he was helping to set up the United Nations: 'All South Africans are agreed ... except those who are quite mad ... that it is a fixed policy to maintain white supremacy in South Africa.'[21] On the other hand, his government was prepared to concede something to integrate the African working class into the system; it was even suggested by the Fagan Commission in 1948 that the migrant labour system be gradually abolished.

These latter ideas were anathema to the Nationalists. All sections of the Afrikaner *volk* were opposed to the economic and political advancement of blacks. The workers feared that they would be displaced by cheaper black workers. The farmers and the industrial capitalists needed the migrant labour system and the white monopoly of political power in order to establish their economic and political dominance. They responded to the challenge presented by the new African working class and to the shift in government policy with *apartheid*.

Apartheid is the Afrikaans word for separation. It originated as a policy among the Nationalist ideologues in the 1940s. Its aim was to perpetuate the migrant labour system and extend it to the African working class as a whole, and to block all attempts to recognise and adapt to the existence of a settled African working class in the cities. Africans were to continue as 'temporary sojourners' in urban areas and the whole weight of the pass laws would continue to hold them down.

Apartheid was systematically implemented by the Nationalists once they came to power in 1948. The Africans' right to national political representation was denied; the NRC was scrapped; and Coloured voters were put on a separate roll which was later abolished. The Group Areas Act of 1950 gave the government sweeping powers to remove people from their homes and expropriate their property in order to enforce the physical separation of the races. Legislation systematised the pass laws and influx controls, applying them to women for the first time, as part of the policy of extending the migrant labour system.[22]

These and other measures were implemented under the direction of Hendrik Verwoerd, Minister of Native Affairs after 1948, and Prime Minister from 1958 until his assassination in 1966. Verwoerd justified his programme by invoking the doctrine of separate development. He explained:

> South Africa is a white man's country and ... he must remain the master here. In the reserves we are prepared to allow the Native to be the masters; we are not the masters there. But within the European areas, we, the white people of South Africa, are and shall remain the masters.[23]

This implied, and Verwoerd drove coldly towards the conclusion, that the regime should concede independence to the various reserves as sovereign nation states. This it did: the establishment of self-governing tribal authorities in the Reserves, renamed the Homelands (although they came to be known as Bantustans) was explicitly provided for by the

Promotion of Bantu Self-Government Act of 1959.

Indirect rule via tribal leaders went back a long way. Rhodes' Glen Grey Act of 1894 had set up *Bungas*, or tribal councils, in the Transkei. If there was novelty in separate development, it lay in the promise of independence to the Homelands. Its major function, however, was to serve as an ideological and political mechanism for perpetuating the migrant labour system. Denying rights to urban African workers could be justified on the grounds that they, like Turkish, Spanish and Greek *Gastarbeiter* (guest workers) in West Germany, were foreigners temporarily living in the country while working there. The tribal rulers of the Bantustans would present little threat to Pretoria: like the Protectorates of Basutoland, Bechuanaland and Swaziland, they would remain effective South African colonies, exchanging migrant labour for South African capital and manufactured goods. As Verwoerd said:

> I take as a comparison ... the British Commonwealth of Nations, where the various constituent members ... are not represented in the Mother Parliament, but within which organisation there are still links - economic and otherwise - by which cooperation is possible without a mixed Parliament or government, whether of the country itself or of the federation, ever being established.[24]

The police had other advantages. African political aspirations could be canalised via the Homeland leaders, themselves reflecting the interests of the rich peasants and the African commercial class. Investment in the 'border industries' adjacent to the Bantustans could be encouraged, permitting South African capitalists to use the unemployed labour in the reserves. Investment by whites in the Homelands themselves was permitted after some hesitation. But above all apartheid perpetuated the migrant labour system and the atomisation of the black proletariat and so hindered it from developing into a general challenge to the system.[25]

English-speaking capital, hitherto dominant in mining and

manufacturing, was in two minds about the policy. The more advanced and capital-intensive sectors had an interest in concessions to urban African workers, but the mining industry remained dependent on the migrant labour system and they all benefited from measures aimed at destroying the black workers' ability to resist. The United Party, English-speaking capital's traditional representative, adopted a policy of opposition to petty apartheid - segregated park benches, buses and so on - but did not oppose apartheid as such. A section of the party, impatient with its subservience to the Nationalists, split off in 1959 to form the Progressive Party, on a platform of a non-racial but qualified franchise. Its main backer was Harry Oppenheimer of Anglo-American, whose interests include the most advanced sections of South African industry as well as investments in many African countries that were to become independent states in the 1960s, and was therefore much less dependent on the migrant labour system.

In general, however, South African capital was quite happy to share in the benefits of apartheid once the Nationalist regime proved its ability to smash all black resistance. It was only in the late 1960s and the 1970s that doubts about the effectiveness of apartheid began to reappear among large numbers of South African businessmen.[26]

Defiance and Defeat

One of the most serious obstacles to the implementation of apartheid was the series of rural revolts that shook the reserves from the 1930s onwards. Partly the work of the local peasantry and partly of unemployed migrant workers and their rural dependents, they both had an impact in the towns and reflected developments in them.

One such wave of revolts was triggered by Smuts' wartime Rural Rehabilitation Scheme, which aimed at weakening the bargaining power of migrant workers by depriving them of what was left of their stock and good grazing land in the Reserves. In Pondoland in the Transkei the people took to the hills and formed the *Konga* resistance organisation in opposition to the quisling *Bunga*. When Tabata and other Unity Movement activists were arrested in 1945 for agitation in the Transkei, People's Committees were spontaneously formed throughout the area in their defence. Resistance spread to Zululand, to Witzieshoek in the Orange Free State and then to the Sekhukhuniland and Zeerust Reserves in Transvaal. Unemployment in the towns and the employers' offensive against the black unions after the defeat of the miners' strike in 1946 fuelled the rural revolt with a stream of sacked urban militants. Influenced by the Unity Movement, the Transkei Organised Bodies mounted a highly successful boycott of the elections of the NRC and the white Native representatives to Parliament in 1948.

The resistance on the Reserves fed back into the towns. In 1948 the dockers' leader Zulu Phungula led a general strike of African workers in the Durban area to demand a £1 a day minimum wage aimed at ending the migrant labour system. Armed police drove the strikers back to work.

The Nationalist electoral victory had a radicalising effect on the ANC. Its December 1949 conference adopted a Programme of Action against the government which called for 'immediate and active boycott, strike, civil disobedience, non-cooperation and such means as may bring about the accomplishment and realisation of our aspirations'.[27]

The programme was the work of the ANC Youth League, formed in Johannesburg in 1943 in order to counter the new African Democratic Party. The programme reflected the experience of the wartime bus boycotts, and perhaps also of the Unity Movement's boycott tactics in the Transkei. The dominant influence in the Youth League was Anton Lembede, who fathered the ideology of Africanism, according to which the struggle was one of the national liberation of the African people as a whole, rather than a class struggle or a multi-racial fight against apartheid. One of the Youth League's main centres of influence was Fort Hare College, traditional nursery of the African elite. Its leading members included, apart from Lembede, Oliver Tambo, Nelson Mandela, Robert Sobukwe and Walter Sisulu.

1950 saw the beginning of mass action against the regime. A stay-at-home on 1 May won mass support in the Johannesburg townships, even though it had been initiated by the CP against the ANC Youth League's opposition. It was followed by another on 26 June in protest against the murder of at least 13 people by the police at meetings in the Rand during the first stay-at-home.

The stay-at-home was to become one of the main weapons in the Congress armoury:

> It was easy to organise such a campaign in the compact crowded townships where thousands of workers were concentrated. By closing a few entrances (or stationing pickets appropriately) an entire town's population could be organised into mass defiance. The working force of a town could be withheld by stopping labour at its very source...
>
> Even more particularly, as Trade Unions were weak (and often non-existent) and as industrial strikes were illegal ... this new industrial action in the residential areas seemed to offer a solution to the problem of effective working-class action.[28]

Use of the general political strike coincided with an offensive against black trade unions: in 1950, for instance, the police put 66 African unions out of operation and African trade-union membership fell to just over 38,000.

The other tactic adopted by the Congress Alliance was passive resistance. In 1952 it launched a Defiance Campaign against seven unjust laws like the Group Areas Act and the Suppression of Communism Act:

> The philosophy of passive resistance is one that flows from a middle class leadership which places no reliance in the masses and their ability to pursue militant tactics. It is a glorification of the leaders and elevates them as political martyrs. Its stress is on the leaders surrendering themselves to the police in protest against bad laws, without at the same time calling for mass action in support of the campaign, for

in this way the tactic assumes that it can lead to a change of heart by the ruling class.[29]

The ruling class showed a clarity wanting in its opponents; it passed new draconian laws that broke the back of the Defiance Campaign.

The ANC responded with a rally in June 1955 at which a Freedom Charter was adopted. It called for the introduction of political democracy without specifying how these demands were to be won. The preamble to the Charter infuriated Africanists like Robert Sobukwe: it stated 'that South Africa belongs to all who live in it, black and white' (as distinct from 'Africa for the Africans'). The incipient anti-communism of the Africanists was fuelled by the activities of white Communists apparently intent on tying the Congress Alliance to Russian foreign policy. It was also fuelled by the infiltration tactics adopted by the Communist Party.

The party had never recovered from the loss of African members during the third period and remained a predominantly white organisation. It was so preoccupied with legality (its members sat in parliament as white Native representatives) that when the Nationalists passed the Suppression of Communism Act of 1950, the party Central Committee voted to dissolve with only two dissenting votes. Although reconstituted by 1953 as the South African Communist Party (SACP), with its predominantly white membership in the Congress of Democrats (COD), it has not engaged in mass work since 1950, not even illegally. Instead it has concentrated upon operating as a ginger group within ANC, either through the COD as part of the Congress Alliance embracing the ANC, the Natal Indian Congress, the Coloured People's Organisation, or through the presence of leading members like Moses Kotane and Govan Mbeki in the ANC leadership, or through allies like Nelson Mandela, effective leader of the Youth League in the years of the Congress Alliance, who was won over from Africanism.

The result was a bitter battle between the 'Charterists' led by Mandela and backed by the CP, and the Africanists. This dispute, along with the long trial of 156 Congress Alliance leaders for treason which began in 1956 (they were finally acquitted in 1961), debilitated the resistance and diverted its attention from the struggle against the regime.

Nonetheless there was a general revival of the mass movement in 1957. A successful bus boycott by Alexandra residents forced the bus company to drop a penny fare increase. The boycott was led jointly by a number of groups, amongst which the ANC did not play a distinguished role - it attempted to persuade the boycotters to accept a compromise proposed by the bus company. There were other signs of revival - a stay-at-home called on 26 June by the Congress Alliance won massive support.

The revival prompted a campaign for £1 a day minimum wage. It was proposed by the South African Congress of Trade Unions (SACTU), a pro-Congress federation formed in 1955 in response to the predominantly white Trade and Labour Council's decision to expel black unions. However, at the CP's insistence, the £1 demand was thrust into the background and the campaign was transformed into a demonstration aimed at the 1958 general election around the slogan 'The Nats must go'. The protest was to culminate in a stay-at-home in April 1958. The stay-at-home was a fiasco, partly because of the ANC's initial opposition to the call. There were other reasons as well:

> Whereas an economic struggle can get a response when the demand has the support of the workers, a political strike, directed at affecting an all-white election cannot get the response that was needed to keep the workers at home. And the workers said quite openly that they failed to see how a strike called for one day, or three days, could win them their wage demands. [30]

Recriminations within the ANC over the stay-at-home which the Africanists had opposed all along, led to Sobukwe and his followers splitting off to form the Pan-Africanist Congress in April 1959. Pure and unadulterated African nationalism and anti-communism made up the Africanists' diet. Despite their understandable hostility to the white communists who pulled so many strings behind the scenes in ANC, the PAC found their own white friends, prominent amongst whom was Patrick Duncan of the Liberal Party, a predominantly white group which supported universal adult suffrage.

There was little to choose between the two Congresses. Neither saw mass action as more than a means of putting pressure on the regime; neither saw that only armed insurrection could overthrow the regime. In 1958 Michael Harmel, a leading CP member, could still write after ten years of Nationalist rule:

> Revolution need not involve violence. There have been plenty of examples in history where a combination of factors have been compelling enough to make a ruling class give way for urgent and overdue changes, without dragging the people through the agony of civil war.[31]

In 1960 the PAC launched a campaign of passive resistance to the pass laws. The regime responded by slaughtering African demonstrators at Sharpeville and Langa. The great national stay-at-home that followed was crushed by mass arrests, a state of emergency and the mobilisation of white national servicemen. In Cape Town the striking townships were cordoned off and terrorised by the army. ANC and PAC were banned and driven underground.

Even then the nationalist organisations did not break with their traditional methods. Mandela called for a three-day national stay-at-home starting on 29 May 1961 to demand a multi-racial national convention. The response was disappointing and concentrated mainly among Coloured workers in the Cape and Indian workers in Natal. People were tired of being called out on ineffectual strikes that were ruthlessly crushed by the regime. Even an ANC sympathiser could write:

> The ANC's main weakness lay in concentrating on nationwide protests and strikes — however successful in some places - rather than in action affecting the daily lives of the people. The bus strikes proved people would *act* when it was a question of pence.[32]

Meanwhile, a bitter and bloody struggle was being waged in the reserves largely independently of PAC and ANC.[33] It began in 1957 in response to the extension of the pass laws to women. In Zeerust women led mass pass burning protests that were joined by busloads of miners from the Rand at weekends. The campaign developed into violent resistance to the Mobile Watch regiment specially drafted in to crush the unrest. A people's tribunal was set up to try government collaborators. Eventually the mobile columns of armed police succeeded in crushing the uprising.

But the struggle spread. In Sekhukhuniland the *Feta Khomo* resistance organisation emerged to lead the opposition to the newly introduced Bantu authorities and to end all collaboration with the regime. The Mobile Watch had to be moved in to give the reserve 'the Zeerust treatment'.

In Zululand the rebellion developed around a number of issues - the application of the pass laws to women, the Rural Rehabilitation Scheme, the introduction of Bantu authorities. The struggle led to solidarity strikes by Durban dockworkers in 1956 and deported dockers played a leading role in the rural revolt. It was not until 1970 that the KwaZulu territorial authority was established under the leadership of Gatsha Buthelezi who has been remarkably successful in concealing from his white liberal admirers both at home and abroad the fact that his position depends on white terror in the African countryside.

But the greatest struggle took place on Pondoland, where another rising had taken place against the Rehabilitation Scheme in 1953. This was followed from 1957 onwards by a bitter fight against the imposition of Bantu authorities. In 1958 4,000 Mpondo shouted down the Minister of Bantu Administration, yelling: 'To hell with it - we shall never accept it till slain to a man'.[34] The old resistance organisations of the 1940s, the Hill Committees, were revived. Collaborators were tried by these bodies and their huts burned down. Once again the Mobile Watch was called in. In June 1960 helicopters and armed police were used to disperse a mass meeting at one of the centres of the resistance, Ngquza hill in Lusikisiki district. Thirty people were killed when police fired at the backs of the fleeing crowd.

The resistance continued. The rebels launched a boycott campaign aimed at taxes, white traders, and labour recruiting agents for the miners and sugar plantations - the very foundations of the migrant labour system.

The regime had to crush this challenge. In November 1960 under Proclamations R400 and R413 a state of emergency giving the police dictatorial powers was introduced. It is in force to this day. The Mobile Watch surrounded the region, cut all the roads and then moved in to crush the rising. 4,769 Africans were arrested and 2,067 were brought to trial.[35]

Although open resistance was finally crushed, Pondoland continued to seethe with disaffection. In late 1970 and early 1971 about fifty people were killed in clashes in the Lusikisiki district. Even on the eve of Transkei independence in October 1976, the tribal quisling regime of Kaiser Matanzima was forced to gaol most of the leading members of the opposition Democratic Party.

The political organisation that claims to have been most involved in the Pondo revolt was the Unity Movement. Unfortunately, it has never been able to transcend this experience: it continues to focus upon the struggles of employed and unemployed migrant workers in town and country, failing to appreciate the central role of the settled black urban working class in the South African evolution.[36] Moreover, it shares many of the assumptions of the Congress Alliance, and stresses above all else the boycott tactic that it had helped to originate. Its propagandism - campaigning for adherence to the ten-point programme - prevents it from offering an agitational lead in workers' struggles around partial economic demands, demands that could develop the consciousness, confidence and organisation necessary to crush the regime.

Victory over the rural revolts gave Verwoerd and his Minister of Justice, John Vorster, the confidence necessary to press ahead with the decapitation of the urban movement. They were greatly aided in this by ANC's decision in June 1961 to launch a campaign of sabotage aimed at government property, and mounted by ANC's secret armed wing, *Umkonto we Sizwe*, Spear of the Nation (MK), in December 1961. PAC for its part was heavily involved in *Poqo*, a frankly terrorist organisation that concentrated on killing whites. Another group that opted for armed struggle at this time was the National Committee for Liberation (NCL), renamed African Resistance Movement (ARM), which united several groupings, including former members of the ANC Youth League in Soweto and white radicals from the Liberal Party.

The result was complete disaster. In July 1963 the security police captured the MK leadership at their secret Rivonia headquarters. The ensuing trial ended in Mandela, Sisulu and Mbeki receiving life sentences. A reign of terror mounted by Vorster and the chief of security police, General Hendrik van der Bergh, an old friend from the fascist *Ossewa Brandwag*, destroyed the underground resistance.

Ben Turok who participated in the sabotage campaign as a member of the Congress of Democrats, recalls:

> While sabotage provided the government with every excuse for unleashing a brutal wave of terror it failed to mobilise the mass of the people who seemed to be left outside the arena from the time of the first blasts. Sabotage remained the weapon of an *elite* corps in the liberation movement. As a consequence, sabotage had the effect of isolating the organisation from the mass who felt unable to join in this new phase or even to defend the actionists when they were seized.
>
> Many were inevitably caught and forced, under systematic torture, to give away their contacts. Here too, the movements revealed their unpreparedness. Having talked of fascism for a decade and more, the movements were nevertheless caught by surprise when the police behaved like fascists. Under torture, many victims found to their regret that they knew too much and that the police knew that they knew. The process of extraction of

information was carried out in all its horror of vicious torture, murder and suicide. Remorselessly the police uncovered the networks and suppressed the organisations. Those who were not caught either went into hiding or fled abroad.[37]

The failure, however, was not one of organisation or of courage (courage is something the South African resistance has never lacked) but a political failure. By the time of the last stay-at-home in 1961 the black working class was exhausted and demoralised. Demonstrative protest after demonstrative protest had been called and had failed. Each protest was crushed more brutally than the last. A vast engine of repression - the Suppression of Communism Act, the Unlawful Organisations Act, the Sabotage Act, the 90-day Detention Act, the 180-day Detention Act, the Terrorism Act - was erected to destroy all opposition to the regime.[38] With the masses in retreat, the nationalist organisations launched into a course of armed struggle whose conclusion could only be either their complete destruction or the overthrow of the regime. Members of the Congress Alliance have stressed the educational and demonstrative role of the MK campaign.[39] Yet this was not how the campaign was presented at the time; for example a 1963 Communist Party statement called for every economic struggle by black workers to be transformed into a general strike and concluded with a summons to armed insurrection.[40]

A strategy of insurrection could only have succeeded if the masses had been mobilised and drawn into the armed struggle, as had happened in the rural revolts. In the towns, this strategy would have required an abandonment of the demonstrative protest actions of the 1950s and instead the use of every economic struggle by black workers in order to build up their confidence and organisation. As it was, the sabotage campaign simply increased the isolation of the resistance and the passivity of the masses. The armed actions were the work of small, elite secret groups. To quote Turok again:

> *The sabotage campaign failed on the main count - it did not raise the level of action of the masses themselves.* Although it seems that the masses supported and even welcomed the resort to force, they could find no way of joining in and expressing their support. They were left on the threshold, frustrated bystanders of a battle being waged on their behalf. Perhaps the over-sophisticated methods used in sabotage was itself the political consequence of the outlook of the movement... Sabotage was seen as another vehicle of protest.[41]

The survivors fled into exile. Both the PAC and ANC made abortive efforts to infiltrate guerillas into South Africa, via Mozambique and Rhodesia respectively. Exile exacerbated the old division, PAC lining up with China and ANC with Russia after the split between Moscow and Peking. Exile reinforced the dependence of the ANC on the white Communists who were the source for Russian material aid. The ANC's 1969 Conference at its Morogoro headquarters near Dar-es-Salaam revealed the CP's influence. A document (on strategy and tactics) that reproduced the SACP's 1962 programme was adopted.[42] A Revolutionary Council was set up that included Joe Slovo, a white Communist. Meanwhile PAC toyed with Maoism and squabbled with the Zambian government.

Events were to leave both PAC and ANC behind. When a new challenge developed to the apartheid regime in the 1970s, it was to emerge as a result of new forces.

3. The Contradictions of South African Capitalism

The last two chapters showed how there has emerged in South Africa a powerful complex of capitalist interests organised under the hegemony of Afrikaner capital through the latter's control of the state and resting upon the atomisation of the black working class. This chapter will deal with the way in which this peculiar society obeys the laws of motion of the capitalist mode of production.

South Africa and Western Capitalism

The first point to make is simply to record the sheer *scale* of Western capital's involvement in the South African economy. The crisis of 1960-61 caused a huge outflow of capital, at a rate of R12 million a month. The government slapped on a series of restrictions on the flow, raised interest rates and tightened import controls. The critical move, however, was to crush the black opposition, which restored Western capital's confidence in the South African government's control of the situation and encouraged it to invest in an economy which had already been recovering from the recession of 1958-59 at the time of Sharpeville.

Between 1960 and 1970 the South African economy clocked up a real annual growth rate of 7 per cent.[1] Foreign capital poured into the country: between 1960 and 1970 South Africa's total foreign liabilities grew from R3024 million to R5818 million. Direct foreign investment grew faster, more than doubling from R1819 million to R3943 million, so that its proportion of total foreign investment grew from 60 per cent in

1960 to 68 per cent ten years later.[2] Although its share of the total fell from 63 per cent in 1960 to 58 per cent in 1970, the sterling area remained the main investor. Western Europe's share grew in the same period from 14 per cent to 24 per cent.[3]

The rate of inflow accelerated in the late 1960s and early 1970s, rising from £93 million in 1965-67 to £235 million in 1968-70. In 1970 it was £328 million and in 1972 £447 million.[4]

Part of this tremendous inflow was induced by the West's need for raw materials, and in particular for strategic minerals.

In August 1971, the African Affairs Advisory Council submitted a study, *Africa's resources*, to the State Department, in which it pointed out that:

> Africa contains a major proportion of the world's reserves of a few commodities important to US strategic or economic needs. In the future, the US will probably have to look to Africa for, among other products, its chromite, platinum group metals, tantalite, petalite, gold, long-fibred amosite and crocidolite asbestos, natural industrial diamond stones and phosphate rocks.

In a later section of the report - 'Commodities Most Urgently Needed by the US' - all the above minerals are mentioned as the most important minerals in this category. Excluding tantalite, industrial diamonds, and phosphate rock, they 'are found primarily in almost unique concentrations in southern Africa'. Under the category 'Resources Most Important to US', in 1968-69 the US depended on African sources for 40 per cent of its antimony (almost entirely from South Africa). That same year, South Africa was 'virtually the only recorded African supplier to the US' of chromite (38 per cent) and supplied the US with over one-third of the US needs of platinum group metals, as well as 85 per cent of its uranium oxide imports. In regard to other minerals such as manganese and vanadium South Africa and South-West Africa was thought to be the future source for the US.[5]

But South Africa is by no means simply a producer of raw materials. In 1970 the value of manufacturing output was 27.1

per cent of the gross domestic product, compared to 11.7 per cent for mining and 9.5 per cent for agriculture.[6] Similarly, out of an economically active population of 7,040,000 in 1970, manufacturing and construction employed 1,539,000 (336,000 whites, 882,000 Africans and 321,000 Coloureds and Asians) while mining employed 676,000 (63,000 whites, 606,000 Africans and 7,000 Coloureds and Asians), and agriculture, forestry and fishing 1,980,000 (115,000 whites, 1,680,000 Africans and 185,000 Coloureds and Asians).[7]

Foreign investment in the South African economy has reflected the shift towards manufacturing industry. In 1960 mining still got the lion's share (33 per cent), although its position was a lot weaker than in 1936, when its share was 66 per cent. By 1966 manufacturing had overtaken mining - 29 per cent compared with 28 per cent.[8] Between 1965 and 1971 US direct investment in manufacturing fluctuated between 48 and 112 per cent (i.e. net disinvestment in other sectors) of its total direct investment in the South African economy; the equivalent share of British investment fluctuated between 43 and 65 per cent.[9]

Figures alone do not tell in full the part Western capital has played in the development of South Africa's economy. As one group of commentators write:

> Its strategic role has been even more important than its volume. At each stage of the country's development since the last war, foreign investment has provided the capital equipment and technological skills which have enabled South Africa to build up new sectors of its economy. In the 1940s and 1950s the key growth sector was engineering, and British companies exported the capital, the machinery and the knowledge which gave South Africa this sector. Other firms went into partnership with the Government to provide South Africa with a modern textiles industry. On the base of the explosives industry British technology helped to build up a sophisticated chemicals sector, and also moved into food-processing and canning, chiefly for the export market. In the 1960s the sectors expanding most

rapidly were the production of motor vehicles and automobile accessories, and oil prospecting and refining, in which American corporations played a major role. Foreign capital has been crucial to South Africa's economic development because of the technology and skills which it has brought with it. In computers, electronics, chemicals and even nuclear energy this technological 'bridge-building' is linking South Africa with the latest Western trends.[10]

Foreign capital collaborates closely with both the private and state sectors. In 1974 a project involving the investment of R1 billion over ten years for the expansion of the South African energy and chemicals industries was announced. The project is the result of a link-up between Sasol, the South African Coal, Oil and Gas Corporation, set up by the Nationalist Government in 1950, and African Explosives and Chemical Industries. (AE & CI is jointly owned by ICI and De Beers, Rhodes's old company, now controlled by Anglo-American, and is linked to the huge Afrikaans investment company FVB through their jointly owned chemicals firm, FedChem).[11] This project illustrates the way in which the different interests involved in South Africa's industrialisation - English-speaking capital, Afrikaner capital, state capital and Western capital - interlock. It is also characteristic that the project is carried on under the direction of the state.

There is a qualitative difference between Western capital's involvement in the South African economy and in the rest of Africa, where the 'classic' pattern of extractive investments still largely hold sway. South Africa's highly industrialised economy and her mineral wealth has resulted in a concentration of Western investment that has been critical in making available to South Africa's capitalists the technology and skills that are the prerogative of the advanced capitalist countries. The result is, as we have seen, that South Africa today possesses many of the features of an advanced capitalist country, and is closer in structure to the western economies than to the ex-colonial stereotype.

Uneven and Combined Development in the South African Economy

However, that is not the end of the story. South African capitalism is not an exact replica of Western capitalism. Its development has been uneven, a result of its position in the world economy and of the peculiar configuration of classes within South Africa itself.

Compared with levels in the advanced capitalist countries, productivity of labour in South Africa is very low. Between 1964 and 1974 it grew 1.7 per cent a year on average in manufacturing. In mechanical engineering it actually fell. The equivalent figures were 2.6 per cent for Australia; 2.9 per cent for the US; 3.5 per cent for Canada; 4.2 per cent for Britain; 5.1 per cent for West Germany; 5.8 per cent for France; 10.1 per cent for Japan.[12] It is low not only because of the inefficiencies and bottlenecks produced by the colour bar and the migrant labour system, but also because of the very low wages black workers receive. They do not receive enough to cover the cost of the training involved in acquiring the skills necessary to maintain high productivity or to sustain a greater intensity of work. This does not necessarily mean that they are more exploited than, say, British workers; on the contrary, their lower productivity may mean that they spend a larger portion of each working day replacing the value of their labour power and hence are *less* exploited.[13]

Low productivity was far less serious during the earlier phases of South Africa's industrialisation, when the emphasis was on replacing the imports kept out of the South African domestic market by government-imposed tariff walls. Now, however, the technology and scale of investment in major South African industries like chemicals and engineering are, thanks to the link-up provided by Western capital, of the sort that require larger markets than South Africa can provide in order to be profitable. The low incomes of the mass of the population, black workers on very low wages and their dependants, simply makes the problem worse.

The alternative is to export. But then South African capital finds itself competing for markets with the advanced capitalist economies, which enjoy much higher levels of productivity and hence are able to sell their products at lower prices.

The effects of this situation can be seen in the economic slow-down of the late 1960s and early 1970s, when the real rate of growth fell from 7.1 per cent in 1969 to 3.3 per cent in 1971.[14] The growth rate of several manufacturing industries, most noticeably the engineering industry, which had been in the vanguard of the post-war boom, fell drastically: from an incredible 43 per cent per year in the machinery industry between 1945/46 and 1963/64 to 2 per cent and less in the late 1960s.[15] It can also be seen in the structure of South Africa's trade. Although the share of manufactured goods in South Africa's exports grew from 35 per cent to 49 per cent between 1959 and 1971, the country remains critically dependent on nine raw materials, including gold, and five agricultural products, as earners of foreign exchange. Meanwhile, the expansion of industry has led to the share of capital goods in total imports growing from 30 per cent to 45 per cent between 1957 and 1970.[16]

The result is that every major period of growth since the war has led to balance of payments crises for the South African economy. These crises have been alleviated by gold exports - about 37 per cent of total exports since the war[17] - but not cured. On the contrary, the continued dependence of the South African economy on the gold-mines simply adds to the problems of South African manufacturing industry.

The role of gold in the international monetary system has been at the root of a bitter and prolonged struggle in the 1960s and 1970s between US capitalism on the one hand and the Europeans and Japanese on the other. Successive American administrations have tried to supplant gold with the dollar, while the Europeans and the Japanese have resisted a situation in which they would always have to accept dollars in payment of American debts. In 1971 the Nixon administration suspended the convertibility of the dollar into gold. In the resulting chaos caused by the abandonment by most major capitalist countries of fixed exchange rates and the devaluation of the dollar, the gold price shot up, reaching a high of 195.50 dollars an ounce in December 1974.

The world recession of the mid-1970s strengthened the position of US capitalism. By 1975 its main competitors were dependent on an American economic revival for their own economic recovery. The American balance of payments was in surplus. The US Treasury was once again in a position to take the offensive. The result was an agreement by the International Monetary Fund in August 1975 to demonetise gold. Official gold prices were abolished, although European pressure ensured that the metal would still be exchanged for currency and vice versa. The IMF was to sell off one-sixth of its gold reserves, 25 million ounces, over the following four years and the proceeds were to go to the hard-pressed semi-colonial countries to help pay off their huge debts to Western bankers. The effect on the first gold auctions in mid-1976 was to push the gold price down to, at one point, little more than 100 dollars.

The effect of the falling gold price on the South African economy was devastating. In the years after 1971, the constantly rising gold price had led to such huge increases in government revenue that the regime doubled its expenditure between 1973 and 1976. Imports also doubled between 1972 and 1976. By mid-1976 the current account deficit was running at 2 billion dollars a year.[18] Since every 5 dollar drop in the gold price costs South Africa R100 million per annum,[19] the fall in the gold price caused by the announcement of the IMF agreement had drastic consequences: it led to an 18 per cent devaluation of the rand against the dollar in September 1975. The further fall caused by the IMF auctions combined with the outflow of capital as a result of the Angolan debacle, forced Pretoria to increase interest rates, impose import deposits and borrow about R150 million from the IMF. The conditions of the loan were a tight ceiling on domestic credit, a rapid end to the import deposit scheme and a commitment to half South Africa's foreign debt (17 per cent of GNP in 1975).[20] The fall in the price of gold also put sections of the gold-mining industry in jeopardy - there are 16 mines which cannot operate profitably if the price is below 110 dollars.[21]

It is, of course, quite possible that the gold price will rise again as and when the international capitalist economy recovers and renewed inflation and intensified competition once again threaten the dollar. This, indeed, is what the South African ruling class is looking for. As the Johannesburg *Financial Mail* put it: 'The main hope for a big lift in the gold price ... remains the inflation rate in the US.'[22] That is to say, South Africa, because of its reliance on gold as a source of foreign exchange, has an interest in the instability of the international capitalist system. Yet it is an instability which can do it extensive damage. Combined with the political instability caused by the black challenge inside and outside South Africa, it can make it difficult for South Africa to attract the foreign capital which provides the technology and foreign exchange the economy needs. A recent survey by the *Financial Mail* argued that South Africa needs at least R1 million per annum of foreign investment to cover her traditional current account deficits and maintain an economic growth rate that can keep up employment. But the South African government is finding it much more difficult to borrow abroad - a 25 million dollar Eurobond loan floated during the Angolan adventure failed dismally, while a 30 million dollar Foskor loan among a group of US banks also failed.[23] The Angolan war also led to a steep fall in the price of South African shares - on the London stock exchange they fell by 25 per cent between October 1975 and March 1976.[24] The Union Bank of Switzerland decided to sell all its South African shares.[25]

The long-term problems are equally serious. One wing of South African capital advocates a drastic improvement in the status of black labour - the abolition of job reservation and general increases in black wages:

Not only would there be enormous gains from the develop-ment of skills and increases in motivations [as a result of such measures] but the resulting growth in Black incomes would so expand our domestic markets as to magnify the scope for applying greater economies of scale in our manufacturing industry.[26] (Sir Albert Robinson of Johannesburg Consolidated Investments)

There are major obstacles in the way of this strategy. The first is the white trade-union movement. Its members have a vested interest in job reservation because of the huge wage differentials they enjoy as a result of it. As the mass of white manual and white-collar workers provide the Nationalist Party with its base, major changes are very difficult.

But a more important obstacle is the structure of South African capitalism itself. A firm's ability to absorb general wage increases depends on the proportion of wages to its total costs: if the wage bill is relatively small it can afford higher wage increases than if the opposite is the case. Now, while the more advanced sections of the South African economy like chemicals and engineering are in a comparatively easy position to afford wage increases for black workers, this is not true for industry as a whole. South Africa's policy of import substitution has been most successful in the sphere of consumer goods production, and these industries are relatively labour intensive. The majority of South African manufacturing firms are quite small: in 1967-68 the average firm produced net output worth R182,000, employed 80 workers and had fixed capital worth R172,000.[27] These firms are not in a position to absorb big wage increases. In the gold-mines, moreover, wages are 50 per cent of industry's working costs.[28]

As a whole, South African industry is not in a position to grant large wage increases to the black working class. Improvement in their economic position is only feasible when directly tied to increases in productivity. Thus, the chairman of Volkskas told the bank's last Annual General Meeting that 'There was no objection to narrowing the [wage] gap providing it was done on merit. However, it could mean playing with fire if the country allowed non-economic considerations to set the pace'.[29] Similarly, a South African economist writes: 'Any increase in the incomes of the poorer section must ... be related to over-all increases in productivity because, unless this were so, unit costs of production would rise and impair the position of exports to world markets.'[30]

South African capitalism is caught in a vicious circle: to increase productivity and thus improve its competitive position it must raise black wages. But, if wages are to be raised, they must be raised in line with productivity, or else South Africa will price itself out of the international market.

The only way to break this vicious circle is to rely on the West to provide the capital and technology needed to improve productivity and with it the competitive position of South African capital. As we have seen, this is becoming more difficult. But, even if it does take place and wages are raised as a result, the increasing productivity necessarily means replacing workers with machines. Already black unemployment is rising fast in South Africa. A recent study by a University of Cape Town economist predicted total unemployment of 1,995,000 - 20 per cent of the labour force - in 1976. In 1961 - a year of economic difficulty - unemployment was only 573,000 (9 per cent of the labour force). The rate at which unemployment grows has also speeded up: between 1961 and 1970 it grew by 4,000 per month; between 1970 and 1975 by 11,000 a month; in 1976 by 22,000 a month. 1976 was admittedly a year of recession, but the study estimates that a secular growth rate of nearly 7 per cent per annum would be required simply to *stabilise* unemployment at just above the 2 million mark.[31]

Thus even a very high growth rate would mean a growing mass of unemployed blacks, who would present a formidable threat to the regime. Already unemployment has played a major part in fuelling the black youth rebellion in Soweto (where unemployment is estimated to be over 50 per cent) and Cape Town.

South African Imperialism

Increased investment in South African industry will not solve the problem of markets either. The domestic market for South African goods is small. At 25 million, the country has a comparatively small population, most of whom are extremely poor. Already the white market for South African cars is near saturation point.[32]

The obvious market is in the rest of Africa. As early as 1957, Eric Louw, the South African Foreign Minister, said:

> As far as South Africa is concerned, we naturally welcome any development on the continent of Africa ... provided no impediment will be placed in the way of South Africa's access to these markets. The territories to the north of the Limpopo are the natural markets for our large and expanding industries.[33]

Unfortunately for Louw, such an impediment did exist in the boycott of South African goods by independent Africa. To take one example, Zambia, the biggest market in Southern Africa apart from South Africa itself: when Zambia became independent in 1964, 22 per cent of her imports came from South Africa. By 1973 the proportion was down to 15 per cent.[34] South Africa's success in doubling her share of the Rhodesian market, stagnant after UDI, and of the tiny Malawian market, did not compensate for the drastic fall in sales to Zambia.[35]

Nonetheless, South African capital and commodities did flow into the rest of Southern Africa in the 1960s and early 1970s. South African capitalists were able to dominate the captive markets of Lesotho, Botswana and Swaziland, the former British protectorates which, although formally independent states, are in effect South African colonies. The opening of the Portuguese colonies to foreign investment in 1965 provided South African capital with an important opportunity. South African parastatals like Escom and private companies provided much of the finance for the Cabora Bassa dam in Mozambique

and the Cunene dam in Angola, with the aim of providing South Africa and Namibia with additional sources of cheap electrical power.

The Anglo-American Corporation epitomises the expansion of South African capital into the rest of Africa. Apart from controlling De Beers and thus having a virtual monopoly of world diamond production,

> The Anglo-American group produces roughly twenty-eight per cent of the gold mined in South Africa annually, twenty-two per cent of South Africa's uranium and forty-four per cent of South Africa's coal. It also produces fifty-seven per cent of Zambia's copper, and controls investments worth hundreds of millions of rand in South-West Africa, Swaziland, Rhodesia, Angola, Mozambique, Tanzania, Congo (Kinshasa) and other West and East African territories, Australia, Malaysia, Canada, Britain and the USA ...

> It is the sheer scale of Anglo-American operations which gives the group its enormous power on the African continent. Through a system of inter-locking directorates, Anglo-American and De Beers are linked with the Société Générale de Belgique, Union Minière du Haut Katanga, Tanganyika Concessions, Roan Selection Trust, American Metal Climax, and other groups. In the sphere of banking, it now has links with the Banque de Paris et des Pays Bas, the Deutsche Bank, the Union Bank of Switzerland, Banca Commerciale Italiana, Rothschilds, Morgan Grenfell, the First National City Bank of New York, and Morgan Guaranty.

At the end of 1975 Anglo-American's total interests were worth R3,400 million; that year its profits totalled R450 million.[36]

The need for much larger markets for its manufactured goods has led to calls in South Africa for a common market embracing South Africa, Namibia, Lesotho, Botswana, Swaziland, Malawi, Angola, Mozambique, Rhodesia, Zambia and Zaire. As one South African journal, *Africa South*, put it:

Our economic and political objectives in Southern Africa are to harness all natural and human resources from Table Mountain to the border of the Congo river... There is already a Resources Planning Council for Southern Africa which has to investigate and advise all countries in Southern Africa to avoid duplication of certain industries, which duplication could lead to extravagance and unnecessary competition between countries. Member-countries of the Common Market could complement one another. For example, the Republic of South Africa could manufacture machinery, chemicals and electrical appliances - while the Transkei could produce jute, Swaziland sugar, Botswana beef, and Lesotho water.[37]

South African investment in the rest of Africa will be decisive in the battle for African markets between South African capitalists and their European competitors. In the early 1970s the Afrikaner tobacco tycoon, Anton Rupert, set up a multi-national investment bank, Economic Development for Equatorial and Southern Africa (Edesa), with the aim of raising European finance for South African investment in Africa. Its headquarters are in Zurich and Swaziland. Its president is Karl Schiller, former West German Minister of Economic Affairs, and its shareholders include: South Africa - Anglo-American, and Rothmans; Netherlands - Amsterdam/Rotterdam Bank; Canada - Bank of Montreal; Britain - Barclays, and Union Castle; West Germany - Robert Bosch, Daimler-Benz, Deutsche Bank and Dresdner Bank; USA - Ford, General Motors, IBM and Universal Leaf Tobacco; Switzerland - Union Bank; Japan - Marubeni Corporation.[38]

Increasingly, the South African ruling class have seen their role in Africa as that of an imperialist power exercising economic and political control over black Africa. Vorster, soon after becoming Prime Minister in 1966, said in an interview:

We do not at all fear these developments - the establishment of African governments in those states. It is a natural development as far as we are concerned... We want to work with them as independent black states, to their advantage and to our advantage... We wish to avoid the dangers of neo-colonialism in any pattern of assistance which may be agreed upon...

In many respects we have, in respect to much of Africa south of the Sahara, a responsibility which the United States has undertaken on a much larger scale with respect to the underdeveloped areas of the world as a whole. Although we do not publicise it, we are already doing quite a lot in this field.[39]

In pursuit of his imperial mission, Vorster launched a policy of 'dialogue' with black Africa after coming to power, but with little success initially, and this among states peripheral to the main thrust of South African expansionism like the Ivory Coast, the Malagasy Republic and Malawi. A decisive shift came with the inauguration of Vorster's detente policy in 1974, when for the first time South Africa appeared to be offering major concessions like support for majority rule in Zimbabwe and independence for Namibia. In reality the aim of the policy had not changed; it was to open up the economies of black Africa, and in particular the comparatively large markets of Zambia and Zaire, to South African capital and commodities. The Johannesburg *Star* spelled out the potential rewards:

With a huge market all over the subcontinent eagerly waiting to soak up South African exports of cars, mining machinery, textiles and a host of other manufactured and primary products, the conviction is dawning that a golden era could be dawning ... for South Africa.

Boosted sales in South Africa's 'natural' markets would bring down unit costs of production and improve the viability of local industry.[40]

Thus the stakes in the policy of detente are high. The continued expansion of South African capitalism depends on a political settlement with the black African states.

The Black Working Class

The tremendous growth of the South African economy since the second world war laid the basis for the apartheid state. But it has also created a massive black working class. By 1971 there were about 6.1 million black workers employed in mining, manufacturing and services. [41]

The apartheid system consolidated since 1948 greatly speeded up the proletarianisation of the black population. African peasants living in the countryside outside the Homelands, whether as labour tenants or 'squatters' on white farms, or in 'black spots', pockets of land reserved for African ownership under the native Land Acts, have been removed and dumped in resettlement camps in the Bantustans - 1,393,000 people between 1960 and 1970 alone. [42] Deprived of their land, with nothing to sell but their labour-power, these Africans have been forced to work for very low wages.

At the same time, government policies stimulated the expansion of manufacturing industry. The result has been a very rapid growth in the demand for black labour, particularly since many of the new industries were, as we have seen, labour-intensive. Not only did the black workforce grow very quickly, but also many more black women became wage-labourers. The number of economically active whites grew by about 50 per cent between 1951 and 1970 and the number of wage-earning blacks by 80 per cent, the number of black women workers grew by 230 per cent. In 1951, 24 per cent of black women were wage-earners; by 1975, 46 per cent were. The ratio of black women workers to all black workers rose from 1:5 in 1960 to 1:3 in 1970. Although the great majority of black women work in agriculture or as domestic servants in white homes, the number working in manufacturing grew tenfold between 1951 and 1970, from 7,000 to 70,000. [43]

However, contradictions have begun to develop. Apartheid was intended to extend the migrant labour system to all black workers, turning them into *Gastarbeiter* (guest workers) in the white areas. The problem is that the migrant labour system increasingly does not fit the interests of that section of South African industry involved in technologically advanced manufacturing. These industries require a trained and stable labour force which it would be prohibitively costly to renew every 18 months or so. At the same time, there are not enough white skilled workers for the jobs that are reserved for them. The shortfall may be 2 million by 1980.[44]

Naturally, the white working class has a vested interest in maintaining job reservation, that is, in a situation aimed at keeping the mass of South African workers as rightless, unskilled cheap labour. The 'wage-gap' between black and white earnings is growing. Between 1965 and 1970 the ratio of white to black wages grew from 5:1 to 6:1 in manufacturing; from 5.5:1 to 6.5:1 in construction; and from 17:1 to 20:1 in gold mining.[45]

The official trade-union movement is committed to defending the privileges of white workers. Three quarters of the 587,242 members in the 182 registered trade unions in 1970 are classified as white.[46] At its founding conference in 1954, the main trade-union federation, the Trade Union Council of South Africa (Tucsa) with about 200,000 members in 1971,[47] decided to exclude Africans. Although this decision has since been reversed, Tucsa operates within the limits of the Industrial Conciliation Act of 1956, which forbids the registration of new racially mixed unions and bans Africans from holding office. Its slogan 'equal pay for equal work' simply entrenches the white workers' privileges, since black workers are denied the opportunities for equal work. Tucsa is also under pressure from the right, since there is a pro-government South African Confederation of Labour, with 119,000 members in 1967.[48]

The privileged position of white workers is reflected in the job structure. In 1971, of the economically active population outside agriculture, 80.7 per cent of working whites were concentrated in the following categories: professional, with degree or equivalent qualification (8.1 per cent of working whites, 93.0 per cent of those employed in this category); lower professional (16 per cent, 67.9 per cent of the category); clerical

(38 per cent, 76.5 per cent of the category); skilled manual (18.1 per cent, 77.6 per cent of the category). Only 13.2 per cent of working whites were in the semi-skilled manual category (12.5 per cent of the category) and 2.2 per cent were unskilled manual workers (2.2 per cent of the category). By contrast, only 1.4 per cent of African workers were skilled manual workers (11.0 per cent of the category), while 40.3 per cent were semi-skilled manual workers (69.2 per cent of the category) and 47.2 per cent unskilled manual workers (87.0 per cent of the category).[49]

Thus there is an apparent paradox. White workers are workers in the sense that they do not control the means of production and continue to be exploited by the capitalists who employ them. Yet their wages are not simply skilled workers' wages. They are kept artificially high by job reservation, which excludes black workers from skilled jobs and creates a skilled labour shortage. Because this privileged position enjoyed by white workers depends on settler control of the state, they can be expected to resist any concessions to black interests. The liberation of the black majority in South Africa will take place against the opposition of the mass of white workers.[50]

That the apartheid system has been successful in holding down black wages is shown by the fact that 80 per cent of African employees in British and South African controlled firms in South Africa were being paid below the Poverty Datum Line, the minimum subsistence level, in 1972.[51]

But it is also under strain. The survey on which this figure is based was undertaken at a time of rocketing inflation: the official figure for price increases, at 8 per cent, understated the increase in food prices caused by the devaluation of the rand in 1971 and rising world food prices. The result was a tremendous wave of strikes in the Durban area in January and February 1973 which, at their height, involved nearly 100,000 workers, mainly in the textile industry, but also in rubber, iron and steel, chemicals, and the electrical services industries. These took place after a decade of relative quiescence among black workers, during which the number of African workers involved in officially reported strikes had not risen above 2,000 a year (between 1962 and 1969).

The strikes were spontaneous explosions. One report says:

Typically, the stoppages seem to have followed spontaneous mass meetings at the workplace; wage demands were
not normally specified at the outset, but once formulated
these involved ambitious increases. Serious bargaining did
not occur, for no worker representatives were prepared to
come forward and risk victimisation; works committees
were ineffectual; while the textile union (the only one to
operate in any of the undertakings affected) was weak and
discredited. Commonly the employers offered increases of
up to R2 a week which, though usually rejected initially at
mass meetings, were normally accepted when it was clear
that no further improvements were forthcoming.[53]

The employers and the government did not respond with
wholesale repression such as they used during the Durban
dockworkers' strike in 1969, when most of the 3,000 strikers
were sacked and deported. Wage increases of between 20 and 25
per cent were granted, although the 20 per cent increase in food
prices during 1973 left the strikers no better off in real terms.[54]
The black industrial workers' bargaining power had clearly
advanced.

The Durban strikes represented a turning point in the
history of the black working class of South Africa. Hyman
compares them to the wave of strikes that laid the basis for
unions like the Transport and General Workers' Union in
Britain at the turn of the century:

Labourers in docks and road transport, municipal services,
and a range of factory industries, long considered beyond
the pale of effective collective organisation and action,
became involved in a series of dramatic and spontaneous
disputes. The strike wave won important improvements in
wages and conditions, provided an impetus towards stable
trade unionism, and - perhaps most important of all - gave
the submerged strata an ineradicable sense of their own
collective strength.[55]

The strikes gave a tremendous impetus to the black workers' movement generally. The *Financial Times* could write in February 1975:

> Two years ago news of the strikes in Durban was blazoned across the South African press. Now African strikes have become commonplace, and hardly a day goes by without a brief newspaper report about a wildcat strike somewhere in the country, hardly the most fitting present for the Department of Labour's fiftieth birthday.
>
> According to the most recent official figures, in the 18 months up to June last year there were 300 strikes involving nearly 76,000 workers. Ninety per cent of them concerned wages, and the iron, steel and metallurgical sector was the most strike-prone, with 39 strikes. Textiles suffered 30, clothing 22 and the building industry 18.[56]

The strike wave also stimulated rapid growth in the unofficial black trade-union movement. In 1969 there were 13 African unions with 16,000 members; by 1974 there were 22 African unions with 40,000 to 45,000 members.[57]

The response of the ruling class in South Africa to the black workers' movement was ambiguous. Vorster refused to recognise the right of African workers to organise trade unions and to strike. However, other measures were announced, although not implemented, to improve the position of black workers and integrate them into the industrial relations system that already embraces white workers - the government would permit employers to set up under its supervision and with its financial assistance public centres for the training of African workers; and African workers were to be allowed to form 'industrial committees' to negotiate with employers on an industry-wide basis. (During the Durban strikes, the employers were unable to find anyone to negotiate with because the strikers refused to appoint representatives for fear of victimisation.)

There are other trends within the South African ruling class which favour unionisation of black workers. Reacting to the shortage of skilled labour, some employers have favoured 'dilution' or 'fragmentation', by means of which the colour bar is gradually shifted upwards, and black workers are introduced into jobs previously reserved for white workers. One advantage of this strategy is lower labour costs, as can be seen from this example taken at random from the *Rand Daily Mail*:

> Africans are to get their chance to drive tractors, previously a 'White' job, for the Pretoria Municipality, and the relaxation will mean a big saving for the municipal coffers.
>
> The Pretoria City Council decided at its monthly meeting last night to initially convert 18 White lorry driving posts, and this includes driving tractors, into posts for Black drivers. A further seven posts will be opened to Black drivers later.
>
> White lorry drivers ... are paid on the wage scale R320 a month...
>
> The Africans will receive R19 a week...
>
> Conservatively, this will mean a wage bill for the Black tractor drivers for the City council of less than a third of the present Wage bill for whites.[58]

The capitalists who support black trade unions are also responding to a long-term process which is leading to the growth of the technologically advanced, capital-intensive sector of South African industry. Since wage costs in this sector are a comparatively small proportion of total costs, wage increases for black workers are much less of a threat to profitability. Most notable in expressing this sector's interests is Harry Oppenheimer of Anglo-American. In 1974 he said:

> There comes a time when, for economic as well as moral reasons, this type of industrial organisation, a system which is highly labour-intensive, making use of large numbers of undifferentiated units of labour with low wages and low productivity, must come to an end. For it there must be substituted a high productivity, high wages, capital intensive organisation such as exists in the advanced industrial countries of the world.[59]

Supporters of black trade-union rights like Oppenheimer hope that the unions will enable them to control and integrate black workers - through Tucsa, the white-dominated trade union council, the British Trade Union Congress, and the International Confederation of Free Trade Unions (ICFTU), all of which already have a major influence in the black trade-union movement.

The largest existing black trade union is the National Union of Clothing Workers. It is part of Tucsa and its leader, Lucy Mvubelo, has shown herself ready to collaborate with the regime on a number of occasions. In April 1975, she issued a statement jointly with Arthur Grobelaar of Tucsa and Attie Niewoudt of the openly racist Confederation of Labour, pledging support for the government 'in stopping Communist infiltration into the country's labour force'.[60] She has also declared her public support for detente and called on foreign companies to invest in South Africa. Her efforts did not, however, persuade the predominantly white delegates at the Tucsa conference in September 1976 to elect her a Vice-President, despite Grobelaar's backing.[61]

Other black trade unions have fallen into other traps. The Trade Union Advisory and Co-ordinating Council (TUACC) was set up in late 1973 to co-ordinate the unions formed as a result of the Natal strikes, like the National Union of Textile Workers, the Metal and Allied Workers Union, the Union of Clothing and Allied Workers, and the Chemical Workers' Industrial Union. Estimates of total membership vary between 10,000 and 50,000.[62] TUACC is linked to the Institute for Industrial Education (IIE), a trade-union correspondence college heavily influenced by radicals from the anti-apartheid English-speaking white student movement, National Union of South African Students (NUSAS), and in receipt of a grant from the British TUC in 1974 for 'straightforward trade union training - no frills and no politics'.[63] TUACC has concentrated entirely on economic issues like wages, conditions, etc, ignoring the directly political character that each strike takes in a country where African strikes are illegal and the employer calls in the police as a matter of course. Despite that, TUACC unions have not won recognition from employers predominantly hostile to black trade unions.

The group of unions in the Transvaal associated with the Urban Training Project (UTP) have taken the same line. The Black Allied Workers Union (BAWU), an organisation linked with the black consciousness movement, issued a statement shortly after its formation in 1972 according to which it did not intend to 'hold the economy of the country to ransom by organising illegal strikes and making unreasonable demands for political reasons'. In 1973 D. Koka, the then leader of the union, claimed that BAWU was receiving donations for transport from Ford. The UTP has received a grant of R20,800 from the TUC.[64]

The gold mines have also been shaken by labour struggles. A major black strike for higher pay broke out in Western Deep Levels mine at Carletonville near Johannesburg in September 1973. The Johannesburg *Star* pointed out that Western Deep Levels is 'one of the wealthiest mines in the world. Last year it achieved a total working profit of R46,339,000 and paid out R20,000,000 in dividends'.[65] The owners, Anglo-American, called in the police the day the miners came out, on 11 September. Eleven miners were shot dead and the strikers went back to work the next day.

Nonetheless, disturbances continued. 162 black miners died violently between September 1973 and March 1976. A suppressed government report admitted that 'the fundamental cause was the migrant labour system itself, which herds thousands of men into the psychologically unhealthy and explosive environment of barrack-like compounds'.[66] These events took place at a time when, according to the *Financial Mail*, 'It is known that the police are under orders to handle mine violence with kid-gloves because government - and industry - fear another Sharpeville, which is about the last thing South Africa can afford'.[67]

Meanwhile, a fundamental change in the structure of the mine labour force has been taking place. In February 1974 only

22 per cent of all black workers in the mines were from South Africa.[68] The rest were recruited in neighbouring countries - Mozambique, Lesotho and Malawi. But in April 1974 the Malawi government suspended mine labour recruitment. Lesotho also imposed restrictions on recruitment and the coming to power of Frelimo in June 1975 put a premium on attempts to reduce the mines' reliance on 100,000 Mozambican workers. The resulting drive to recruit mineworkers in South Africa forced up wages, previously held down at very low levels because of the mines' ready access to a huge pool of captive migrant labour in neighbouring countries. An increase in June 1976 brought the minimum wage rate for black mineworkers to R65 a month, which, miserably inadequate though it was, nevertheless was six times the minimum in 1971.[69] By July 1976 the Chamber of Mines was claiming that 43 per cent of the black mineworkers were from South Africa and that its target of 50 per cent was in sight.[70]

The Chamber of Mines' success in dealing with the labour shortage (black jobs were filled to nine-tenths of requirements by July 1975[71]) was made possible by two factors. First, the huge rise in the gold price meant that the mines could afford to pay out large wage increases so as to make its rates for black workers competitive with wages in manufacturing industry. Second, there is a huge pool of underemployed and miserably low paid black labour - anything up to 2 million - in the inefficient farm sector.

In an effort to reduce labour costs, the Chamber of Mines demanded of the white unions that they accept black teams underground without supervision by white miners in exchange for a five-day week. Opposition, particularly among the white artisan unions, pushed the white Mineworkers Union to threaten strike action in 1975 and 1976, which was averted only by government intervention on both occasions.

The last few years have seen a dramatic increase in the mines' dependence on black labour, which, given the pressure exerted by the fall in the gold price to cut costs, will mean dramatic struggles by black mineworkers.

The Crisis of Apartheid

The great boom in the South African economy has immeasurably increased white capital's dependence on black labour. A large and increasingly self-assertive black working class has flexed its muscles in the last few years. In attempting to respond to this challenge, the white ruling class is faced with a dilemma.

Separate development offers nothing to the mass of black workers. The Bantustans remain little more than reservoirs of black labour and dumping grounds for the dependents of black workers. In the Transkei, the most important of the Homelands, which became 'independent' in October 1976, one third of the economically active population work in white areas. Of those economically active within the Transkei itself, 78 per cent are involved in traditional subsistence agriculture, which does not produce enough to feed its population. Staple foods have to be imported. 51 per cent of the 1.74 million residents are dependent on others for their income. Manufacturing industry employs less than 4,000 people. Black entrepreneurs funded by the government Xhosa Development Corporation employed little over 2,000 people mainly in retail and wholesale trading, catering and accommodation. There are 285 children to every 100 adults (as opposed to 180.9:100 for all black South Africans).[72]

The attempt to make the 1.3 million Xhosas living outside the Transkei citizens of the independent state and to deprive them of South African citizenship will not alter the fact that they live and work in the white areas. As we have seen, the migrant labour system is becoming less and less appropriate to the needs of South African industry, which require a stable and skilled black labour force.

Yet it is not possible for South African capital to demolish the apartheid system and give black workers the same rights as white workers. First, the dominant fraction of South African capital, the Afrikaner bourgeoisie, derives its position of hegemony from its control of the state. This, in turn, depends on its mass base among white workers. Yet, as we have seen, white workers derive their position of privilege from the settlers' monopoly of political power. Second, the less advanced sections of South African capital, as well as the gold-mines, depend on the migrant labour system to keep down black wages, the most important component of their costs. Third, the transition from apartheid to 'normal' bourgeois democracy would threaten an upsurge among black workers that could bring down capitalism in South Africa. Under apartheid South African capital dispensed with the various ideological and political mechanisms used to contain workers within bourgeois democracy in western Europe and North America - principally, the reformist political parties and the bureaucratic trade union machine. There are at present no intermediaries between the ruling class and the mass of black workers and, given the poverty of black people and their dependence on wage labour, there is little likelihood of developing such intermediaries at a time of economic and political crisis.

To some extent, the Homelands policy of turning the Bantustan rulers into representatives of urban black workers has worked. Gatsha Buthelezi, chief executive of KwaZulu Bantustan, and other KwaZulu representatives, were able to play a mediating role in the Natal strikes, where many of the workers involved were Zulu in origin. Buthelezi has also launched a Zulu separatist movement, *Inkatha Ye Sizwe* (Power is Ours), which has a following among Zulu migrant workers and which played a strike-breaking role during the Soweto stay-at-home of August 1976. But the hold of tribal leaders on the increasingly urbanised black working class is weakening, and a policy of 'domestic detente' aimed at involving the small but growing black middle class in the townships in containing the black working class is being promoted. Blacks will be permitted to buy 30-year leasehold rights in the townships, cutting across the policy of treating them as 'temporary sojourners'. Other measures have been introduced aimed at encouraging the development of a black middle class. In November 1974 the first black bank was set up with branches in Soweto and Garakya.[73]

Promoting the black middle class is unlikely to succeed. T.J. Makhaya, the chairman of the Soweto Urban Bantu Council, and Richard Maponya, the Soweto millionaire, were forced into hiding and their homes placed under police guard to protect them from the anger of young black militants after the Soweto uprising in June 1976. The embryonic black trade-union leadership is also far too weak to act as a brake on the militancy of black workers. There is very little to prevent the black workers' struggle against starvation wages and the denial of political and trade-union rights from developing into a struggle against capitalism itself.

4. Rhodesia: the Crisis of White Power

On 25 April 1974 the Portuguese dictatorship was overthrown by the Armed Forces Movement (MFA). More than any other single event it brought to the surface the contradictions in South African society.

The colonial wars in Africa provided the immediate cause of the Lisbon coup. The dictatorship presided over for more than 40 years by Antonio Salazar and then by his successor Marcello Caetano, had sought to prop up feeble and backward Portuguese capitalism by making the colonies a captive market for the metropolis' uncompetitive manufactures and by using them as a source of raw materials which Portuguese capitalists bought at prices below the world level and then re-sold at a profit. The burden of forced or 'contract' labour, compulsory cash-crop production and *palmatorio* - the beatings inflicted on Africans for minor offences - sustained the great rebellion in Portuguese Africa which began in Angola in February 1961 and spread to the other colonies of Mozambique and Guinea-Bissau.

By early 1974 the colonial regime was in serious difficulties. In Mozambique Frelimo (the Front for the Liberation of Mozambique) and in Guinea-Bissau PAIGC (the African Party for the Independence of Guiné and Cape Verde) had succeeded in liberating large parts of the countryside. Although the military situation was more favourable to the regime in Angola, where it faced three bitterly divided liberation movements, MPLA (the Popular Movement for the Liberation of Angola), FNLA (the National Front for the Liberation of Angola), and Unita (the National Union for the Total Independence of Angola), the burden of the wars was crushing. There were about

160,000 troops in Africa eating up nearly half the Portuguese budget.

Although the new government in Portugal was bitterly divided over the pace and nature of decolonisation, it rapidly became clear that Mozambique would quickly become independent under a Frelimo government, and since Mozambique shares a long common border with South Africa and Rhodesia, that the settler regimes would be profoundly affected.

The most directly threatened of the two by the collapse of Portuguese colonialism was Rhodesia. Subject to economic sanctions since its unilateral declaration of independence (UDI), the Rhodesian regime was extremely vulnerable to blockade by Mozambique, whose ports of Beira and Lourenco Marques (now Maputo) provided it with its most direct means of access to the sea. Moreover, in 1974 the regime was already seriously threatened by a guerilla campaign in the north-east of the country, itself a result of Frelimo's victories.

The Nature of the Regime

The white colony of Rhodesia was a by-product of the South African gold-mining industry. Cecil Rhodes, the dominant figure among the first generation of Randlords, believed that the interests of mining capitalism in South Africa, and indeed of British capitalism as well, were intimately connected with the expansion of the British colonial empire into Africa. In 1895 he explained to the journalist W.T. Stead:

> I was employed in the East End of London yesterday and attended a meeting of the unemployed. I listened to the wild speeches, which were just a cry for 'bread! bread!' and on my way home I pondered over the scene and I became more than ever convinced of the importance of imperialism... My cherished idea is a solution for the social problem, i.e., in order to save the 40,000,000 inhabitants of the United Kingdom from a bloody civil war, we colonial statesmen must acquire new lands to settle the surplus population, to

provide new markets for the goods produced in the factories and the mines. The Empire, as I have always said, is a bread and butter question. If you want to avoid civil war, you must become imperialists.[1]

There were two obstacles to Rhodes's plans. The first was the Afrikaner republics which, as we have seen, were eventually reduced to British colonies during the Boer War of 1899-1902, although Rhodes did not live to see the final victory.

The second obstacle was the rivalry of other imperialist powers. German armies were conquering Tanganyika and South-West Africa. It was suspected that Portuguese moves to occupy Zimbabwe and Zambia in order to link up Angola and Mozambique were encouraged by the German government, which, like Rhodes, had its own designs on these territories with their vast mineral wealth (Zimbabwe, in particular, was believed to be a 'second Rand').

Rhodes decided to forestall the Germans and Portuguese, cutting off the Afrikaner republics' rear at the same time. He tricked Lobengula, King of the Ndebele in Zimbabawe, into signing a mineral concession over to the British South Africa Company (BSA), which led to the occupation of Zimbabwe by a Pioneer Column of white settlers and police in 1890. Three years later the Company found a pretext to invade the Ndebele kingdom. The warrior *impis* were mowed down by machine guns and Lobengula died in hiding in the bush. In 1896 the entire country, both the Ndebele and the Shona, the majority tribe, rose against the settlers who were taking their land and forcing them to work on the white farms. Rhodes personally intervened to secure a negotiated peace with the Ndebele.

The settlers' real ferocity was reserved for the Shona. A Catholic missionary wrote: 'It seems to me that the only way of doing anything at all with these natives is to starve them, destroy their lands and kill all that can be killed.'[2] (Rhodes encouraged missionaries to settle in Zimbabwe, saying that they were cheaper and more efficient than policemen.) This formula was scrupulously followed by the settlers. Despite a long and heroic resistance, the Shona rebellion was gradually crushed - crops were destroyed and *kraals* besieged tribe by tribe. The rebels often took refuge in caves. Dynamite was thrown in after them by the settler forces. The leaders of the uprising were executed, most of them shot out of hand.[3] The colony of Southern Rhodesia was founded.

Whatever promises were made to the Ndebele were not kept. The pattern of the South African mines was reproduced, although in a more vicious form because the gold deposits were scattered and of variable quality, unlike those in the Rand. Moreover, the Rhodesian mines had to compete for African labour with the South African mines, where wages and conditions were generally better. African wages were forced down and the compound system introduced. 30,000 black mineworkers died as a result of accidents and 'occupational diseases' between 1900 and 1933.[4] In the early years of the colony, before the African economy began to disintegrate and the peasants came to sell their labour-power to the settlers in order to survive, brute force was used to make Africans work in the mines. Contracts with the Rhodesian Native Labour Bureau, largely responsible for recruiting to the mines during these years, were called by the Africans *chibaro*, which means slavery.[5]

The conquest and suppression of the uprisings helped strengthen the white settlers vis-a-vis both the British South Africa Company and the Imperial government. In no other colony in Africa had settlers been directly responsible for colonising the country. As a result, 'From the beginning the settlers were deeply involved in the processes of administration; they had no control over policy and no representation politically but their armed support was essential to the success of the colony.'[6]

Moreover, since Rhodesia turned out not to be the 'second Rand' which the Company had dreamed of, and the small and scattered nature of the gold deposits did not allow the concentration of ownership that was quickly achieved in South Africa, the BSA Company had a direct interest in the economic wellbeing of the settlers. It hoped to recoup the money it spent in conquering and administering the country through sharing in the profits of settler agriculture.

The result was that Southern Rhodesia became a self-governing colony, with power vested in the hands of the settlers, in 1923. This move took place against the wishes of both the British government and the BSA Company, who wanted the incorporation of the country in the Union of South Africa.

The pattern of colonisation followed the South African example closely. By 1902 three-quarters of the land had been taken from the Africans.[7] The Land Apportionment Act of 1931 limited land purchases by Africans to the Native Purchase Areas. In 1969 the Land Tenure Act entrenched a 50-50 division of the land between black and white, although the ratio of blacks to whites is about 24 to 1. By 1970, 98 per cent of the land suitable for afforestation, fruit growing and intensive beef production lay in the European areas, as did 82 per cent of the land suitable for intensive farming, while 100 per cent of the land unsuitable for any agricultural purpose lay in the African areas.[8]

Mining and agriculture formed the basis of the settler economy before the second world war. Settler farmers producing for export received generous help from the state. Labour was provided by the African peasantry, with whom the settlers established semi-feudal relations, permitting them to remain on the land in exchange for rent in money or labour services:

> The moment a man had pegged his farm, he regarded the African villagers on it as his serfs, who would have to work for him. The chief means of mobilising this pool of labour in the first years was the *sjambok* or hippo-hide whip, and after 1908 labour agreements which committed tenants to work several months, usually three, for the privilege of remaining on their ancestral land.[9]

In the early years the mines also recruited labour through the *chibaro* system of often forcible enrolment. But other methods were used. Hut taxes and then poll taxes imposed in the early years of the colony, forced Africans to become at least part-time wage labourers. The ruin of the comparatively large group of African farmers producing for the market during the slumps of 1921 and 1929 swelled the labour force. Labour services drove Africans off the white farms and into the Reserves set aside exclusively for them. As in South Africa, the extensive methods of agriculture appropriate to the African communal economy wrought devastation when restricted to the Reserves, which presented the same face as the South African Bantustans - overpopulation, overstocking, soil erosion, malnutrition. In 1956 annual African rural income was estimated to be £15 *per capita*; by 1968 it had fallen to £11.[10]

The destruction of the pre-capitalist African economy provided the settlers' farms, mines and factories with a large pool of cheap labour. The second world war provided both the finance, through increases in the prices of Rhodesia's exports - primarily raw materials - and the stimulus, thanks to the need for import substitution, for the development of manufacturing. The settler bourgeoisie, until then based mainly on agriculture, provided state backing for industrialisation, investing where private capital was unwilling, nationalising private steel works and cotton spinners. By 1945 the value of manufacturing output was £14.1 million, having overtaken both European agriculture (9.8 million) and mining (£8.1 million).[11]

The rapid expansion of the Rhodesian economy - an annual rate of growth in gross domestic product of more than 10 per cent between 1945 and 1953[12] attracted large movements of foreign capital and settlers from Britain. In 1953 the Central African Federation, embracing Southern and Northern Rhodesia and Nyasaland, was formed, giving Rhodesian manufacturing industry access to a much larger, protected market, while the revenues from the Northern Rhodesian copper mines were devoted mainly to improving the economic infrastructure of Southern Rhodesia. By 1957 the value of Southern Rhodesian manufacturing output had grown to £105.1 million.[13] Between 1953 and 1965 foreign investment in the colony had grown from £200 million to £550 million. Its share of gross domestic capital formation in 1964 was 27.9 per cent, quite a low figure compared to its 67.7 per cent share in 1953.[14] A cautious estimate suggests that foreign capital was dominant in beverages, tobacco, chemicals and chemical products and finance, and more important than domestic capital in mining (non-gold), basic metal and metal products, building and construction.[15] Its share of gross profits was 68 per cent in 1963.[16]

Industrial development created an urban black working class. By 1960 African wage-earners numbered 640,000, 17.8 per cent of the African population.[17] As in South Africa, industry required a stable and comparatively skilled working class, which led settler governments in the 1950s and early 1960s to pursue a policy of 'partnership' between the races, with the aim of encouraging the development of a black middle class that could be politically and economically integrated into the existing system and be used to contain the African proletariat. The Native Land Husbandry Act of 1951 aimed to create a layer of African small capitalist farmers owning fixed plots of land that could be sold but not subdivided. The Act also encouraged the proletarianisation of the African population: it replaced communal by individual tenure thereby depriving the urban blacks of all links with the land, and outlawed subdivision of the land, thereby increasing the number of landless peasants forced to become wage-labourers. The 1961 Constitution, introduced under pressure from Whitehall, provided for a limited African franchise.

These measures did not contradict the settler bourgeoisie's overriding aim - to preserve white supremacy. Godfrey Huggins, dominant figure in white Rhodesian politics from the 1930s to the 1950s, described the policy of partnership as 'the partnership of the rider and the horse'. Garfield Todd, who was removed as Prime Minister in 1958 for being too enthusiastic in his concessions to black interests, had not scrupled to use troops and emergency powers to break an African railway workers' strike. Nonetheless, the policy of drawing the African petty bourgeoisie into the circle of power, combined with the growing assertiveness of the mass nationalist movement, detonated the most tenacious settler rebellion in the history of colonialism. The mass of the settlers - farmers, small businessmen and wage-workers - could not accommodate themselves to a black government. Even the most moderate black government would threaten their monopoly of skilled and white-collar jobs and of fertile land. The settlers' rebellion led to the victory of the Rhodesian Front in the 1962 general election, the appointment of Ian Smith as Prime Minister, ousting the more conciliatory Winston Field, in 1964, and the unilateral declaration of independence (UDI) by the white regime on 11 November 1965.

The rebellion won support even from Rhodesian capital. The Federation of Rhodesia and Nyasaland had broken up in 1963, and the other two territories became independent black states, Zambia and Malawi, in 1964. Without the large protected market provided by the Federation, Rhodesia alone became a much less attractive proposition, and in 1964 there was a net outflow of capital.

> The prospects, therefore, were for stagnant or negative foreign investment coupled with rising profit [out]flows, with little remedy inside a free enterprise, open economy. UDI and sanctions came as a blessing in disguise, foreseen neither internally nor externally. As a debtor nation Rhodesia had far more ability to retaliate by freezing payments than Britain had to withhold capital. So Rhodesia in blocking payments due jeopardised only poor prospects of new investment. Equally important it had as a hostage a body of foreign capital which was too large for the local market in absence of protection, and which was therefore beginning to rationalise its geographical distribution in Rhodesia's disfavour.[18]

Thus, despite the imposition of economic sanctions by Britain and the UN, and encouraged by the need to produce goods previously imported, real gross domestic product grew at an annual rate of about 8 per cent between 1966 and 1974.[19] Tight state controls blocked the repatriation of profits on foreign investment and the outflow of capital. Foreign-controlled firms were 'Rhodesianised', although their executives, often themselves white Rhodesians or South Africans, were left in control. The new industries tended to be labour intensive and so, wages being a comparatively high proportion of their costs, relied on cheap black labour. Hence capitalists in these industries were likely to be less favourable to black advancement than those linked to Western companies.

Two factors enabled the Rhodesian settlers to survive. First, the British government, fearful of jeopardising British capital's massive investments in Southern Africa, decided not to send in troops to put down the rebellion. Wilson made two abortive attempts to reach a settlement with Smith: on the HMS *Tiger* in 1966 and the HMS *Fearless* in 1968. In both cases he offered the settlers terms that would give them independence without black majority rule, but even that failed to satisfy Smith's *ultras*.

Second, the regime received large-scale economic support from South Africa. Although Verwoerd and his successor Vorster were not opposed to the idea of a neo-colonial black regime in Rhodesia, the Nationalist government set out to break the sanctions, since their success in Rhodesia might encourage their application to South Africa. The first guerilla offensive in 1967, organised jointly by the Zimbabwe African People's Union (ZAPU) and the South African ANC, hardened South African support for the Smith regime. UDI also had the welcome effect of opening the Rhodesian market, which had been protected during the Federation era, to South African goods. These now make up about 50 per cent of all Rhodesian imports.[20]

South Africa has also penetrated the Rhodesian economy with direct investment. Even before UDI South African capital dominated agriculture and mining. But between 1964 and 1974 South African investment doubled, to about £200 million.[21] In 1970, 5 out of the 10 largest Rhodesian industrial companies were partly or wholly South African controlled. In 1971, 4 of the top 10 manufacturing companies were South African controlled.[22] South African firms like Anglo-American, Huletts

Corporation (sugar), Barlow Rand (investments) and South African Breweries, have a huge share in the Rhodesian economy.

In the early 1970s the Smith regime, backed by the Nationalist government in South Africa, appeared impregnable. But the revival of the African resistance was to threaten the foundations of white power in Rhodesia.

Black Resistance

It was the struggle of the African proletariat created by the industrialisation of the country that gave the real impetus to black nationalism in Rhodesia. In 1944 and 1948 strikes by black workers in Bulawayo shook the white establishment. The 1948 strike engulfed the city and won the support of workers in every town and mining centre in the country. The strikes revived the old petty bourgeois Southern Rhodesia African National Congress, whose Bulawayo branch fell under the control of Joshua Nkomo, the black railway workers' leader. Meanwhile, young black radicals in Salisbury, influenced by the South African example, formed the City Youth League in 1955; the following year they led a successful three-day bus boycott against fare increases in Salisbury's Harare Township.

In September 1957 the Youth League and the Bulawayo ANC came together to form a countrywide African National Congress. Joshua Nkomo was elected President. The ANC took to mass action in support of its demands for independence and African majority rule. It won rural support by campaigning against the Native Husbandry Act.

Edgar Whitehead's 'liberal' white government responded ruthlessly. In 1959 a state of emergency was declared, the ANC was banned and 500 of its members arrested. Whitehead rammed through a mass of repressive legislation modelled on that of the South African regime. This policy was continued and extended under the Rhodesian Front government, which imposed mandatory death sentences for certain acts of political violence.

In 1960 violent mass demonstrations - called *Zhii*, or crushing[23] - in the major towns led to 18 blacks being shot dead by police. The ANC was renamed the National Democratic Party (NDP). When this in its turn was banned, the Zimbabwe African People's Union (ZAPU) was formed. Under Nkomo's leadership ZAPU pursued a policy of relying on the British government to pressurise the settlers into granted majority rule. Nkomo had been the only African nationalist leader in the Rhodesias and Nyasaland to have taken part in the negotiations leading to the formation of the Central African Federation. He had formed his approach out of the experience of decolonisation in the rest of Africa, where Britain had peacefully handed over independence to the black nationalist leaders, and where mass action had served only to improve the nationalists' bargaining power. Nkomo believed that he could follow the same course in Rhodesia. He took part in the negotiations on the 1961 Constitution and agreed to the result, even though it left the settlers in control. Only pressure from the rest of the NDP leadership and the nationalist rank-and-file made him reverse his position and call for the boycott of the elections held under the new Constitution.

Nkomo made the mistake of not realising that Rhodesia was unique among Britain's African colonies. The metropolitan government had never directly administered the colony; an armed settler minority had entrenched itself in power from the start. Moreover, Britain's investments in the region meant that no government, Labour or Tory, would take the risk of using armed force to make the settlers accept majority rule.

Nkomo's continued reliance on the British government and the UN led to a split in ZAPU in 1963. Nkomo formed an 'Executive-in-Exile' with the aim of winning a negotiated independence. Various ZAPU leaders, most notably Ndaban-ingi Sithole and Robert Mugabe, broke away to form the Zimbabwe African National Union (ZANU), arguing that the main task was to organise the opposition within the country.

Helped by the bitter factional fighting in the townships between ZANU and the People's Caretaker Council (PCC), a front for the banned ZAPU, the regime exploited the nationalist divisions during the run-in to UDI. In August 1964 ZANU and PCC were banned. Nkomo and Sithole were detained without trial. A massive show of force enabled the regime to weather UDI without serious mass opposition.

UDI was a watershed for the nationalists. The old methods had clearly failed - mass action and negotiations aimed at pressurising liberal whites and the British government had not prevented the triumph of the Rhodesian Front. UDI crystallised the nationalists' decision to fight. But before looking at the record of armed struggle, it is first worth examining the nature of the nationalist movement in Zimbabwe.

Rhodesian society is, as we have seen, identical with South African society in essential respects. The back of the peasant economy has been broken, 37 per cent of the African population live in the towns, and since 1946 the proportion of blacks who are wage earners has fluctuated between about 15 and 19 per cent. In 1974 there were 933,000 African wage earners.[24] Allowing for the fact that half of the population is under 16 years of age, and that most workers are adult males, it can be estimated that up to 70 per cent of African households are dependent upon wages for basic subsistence.[25]

It is these workers who form the basis for the nationalist movement in Zimbabwe. However, the leadership of that movement has always been petty bourgeois, a class of African clerks, traders, clergymen and teachers. Of the major contemporary nationalist leaders, Abel Muzorewa and Ndabaningi Sithole are clergymen and Robert Mugabe an alumnus of Fort Hare College, breeding ground of the black elite in South Africa. The African trade-union movement reflects the same pattern. Although black trade unions may register under the Industrial Conciliation Act, they are subject to a structure of industrial councils embracing employers and employees, binding agreements, and government-imposed arbitrators that effectively bans strikes. A minute proportion of black workers are members of trade unions. According to its president, Phineas Sithole, the African Trades Union Congress (ATUC), one of the two main black trade union groups, has a total membership of 18,000.[26] The structures of the unions are top-heavy and bureaucratic with very little rank-and-file participation, and the two largest groups of workers - farm workers and domestic workers - are unrepresented and largely unorganised.

The black trade-union movement has not been united. The two main groups - ATUC and NATUC (the National African Trades Union Congress) - originate from a split in the early 1960s that reflected to some degree the ZANU/ZAPU split, ATUC being linked with ZANU and NATUC and its predecessors with ZAPU. There have been other factors as well. NATUC has received financial backing from W.G. Lawrence, Rhodesian representative of the International Confederation of Free Trade Unions. Lawrence is accused by ATUC of perpetuating the split and controlling a number of black trade unions through financial hand-outs to individuals.[27]

The nationalist movements have all set as their target independence under black majority rule, i.e. independence of the sort won in countries like Ghana, Tanzania and Zambia. They split, as we have seen, ostensibly over methods. ZANU opposed Nkomo's orientation towards Britain and the UN or, as Ndabaningi Sithole put it:

> African politics in Zimbabwe, as well as in European-ruled Africa, began as 'reformist politics', but now we have entered the phase of 'take-over' politics, as it is impossible for the present white minority to rule Zimbabwe for the benefit of the voteless African majority. We have entered the period of political CONFRONTATION. ZANU represents the fighting spirit which began with an imposed rule in 1890 and shows the unity of spirit between those who have gone on and those who are still living. We have a duty to ourselves and to unborn generations of Zimbabwe, and that duty is to free Zimbabwe. 'WE ARE OUR OWN LIBERATORS'.[28]

ZANU certainly represented a more radical mood among the African masses. However, the mood was not translated into a strategy different from that of ZAPU and indeed was expressed in terms of the continuity between the *chimurenga* - the great Shona uprising of 1896-97 - and the struggles of the present. ZANU did not abandon Nkomo's methods of lobbying Whitehall. Soon after the split in 1963, Robert Mugabe, its Secretary General, hurried off to London to meet R.A. Butler, the British cabinet minister responsible for Rhodesia. Both ZANU and ZAPU saw mass action simply as a way of putting pressure on the regime.

Other factors played a part in the split. Personal squabbles were certainly involved, and perhaps also tribal divisions - although Nkomo is not himself Ndebele, his support has tended to come from that tribe, while ZANU's support has traditionally been mainly Shona. In exile, the rhetoric of both parties became much more overtly socialist. Each found a backer among the 'socialist countries': ZAPU was supported by Moscow and lined up with the pro-Russian alliance of Southern African movements headed by ANC; ZANU was backed by China and imbibed large doses of Maoist politics along the way, as well as a genuine political radicalisation among those of its members who left the country to undertake military training.

It was ZANU that initiated guerilla operations inside Rhodesia, in 1964, even before UDI.[29] However, the first major phase in the armed struggle was opened at the end of July 1967, when a joint force of guerillas from ZAPU and the ANC of South Africa crossed the Zambesi from Zambia. The decision by ZAPU to take the offensive was a result in part of final disillusionment with the Wilson government after the *Tiger* talks with Smith.

The guerilla offensive took the regime by surprise. In August 1967 the South African government sent a force of paramilitary police into Rhodesia to give the hard-pressed settler security forces the backing and additional manpower they needed in the initial stages.

The ZAPU offensive lasted until 1970, and although fought

with great courage, it did not dent the regime's armour. And this for two reasons: first, the fighting took place in the Zambesi valley, whose barren terrain made it difficult for the guerillas to live off the land. Second, the nationalists' tactics of using comparatively large units and inviting confrontation with the security forces, gave the advantage to the settler troops, who possessed much greater firepower and mobility.

The failure of the Zambesi offensive encouraged bitter internal bickering within both the ZAPU and ZANU leaderships in exile in Zambia, mainly over nationalist reunification. The Kaunda regime intervened, deporting 129 ZAPU guerillas to Rhodesia, where they were gaoled and some even executed. A Front for the Liberation of Zimbabwe (Frolizi) was formed in 1971 by some ZAPU and ZANU dissidents, but it failed to unite the nationalists, simply adding a third, much smaller, party to the other two.

Events within Rhodesia transformed the situation. In November 1971 the new Tory government in Britain reached a settlement with the Rhodesian settlers which, according to one estimate, would delay majority rule until 2035 at the earliest.[30] The agreement hinged on the preparation of a report by the Pearce Commission, set up to 'test African opinion'. In the event, both supporters and opponents of the regime were confounded by what happened. The Zimbabwean people took advantage of the comparative freedom permitted them during the Pearce Commission's visit in early 1972 to show their opposition to the regime. Mass demonstrations swept through every major city and were only crushed by police gunfire, which took the lives of scores of Africans. The African National Council (ANC) was set up by the nationalist parties in alliance with a group of unaligned middle-class blacks like Bishop Abel Muzorewa, who became President of the new organisation. Faced with this tremendous African political revival, the Pearce Commission was forced to conclude that the proposals were unacceptable to the black majority.

The British government abandoned its efforts to reach a settlement. It laid down a precondition for further negotiations with the settlers that there be an 'internal settlement' between them and the ANC. The result was a series of desultory and ineffective negotiations between Smith and Muzorewa, during which the latter agreed to terms little better than the ones Home had proposed, only to be overruled by his Executive.

Meanwhile ZANU was preparing to open a new front in the north-east of the country, bordering on Mozambique's Tete Province where Frelimo was expanding its operations. Using Frelimo bases and supply routes, ZANU began infiltrating guerillas. They took to the offensive in December 1972. Unlike ZAPU in the Zambesi valley, ZANU avoided direct confrontation with the security forces on terms that would favour the latter. Herbert Chitepo, the ZANU chairman, explained:

> The strategical aim ... is to attenuate the enemy forces by causing their deployment over the entire country. The subsequent mobilisation of a large number of civilians from industry, business and agriculture would cause serious economic problems. This would have a psychologically devastating effect on the morale of whites, most of whom had come to Zimbabwe, lured by the prospect of the easy, privileged life promised by the regime.[31]

The guerillas concentrated on winning the support of the African peasantry. Their attacks were aimed mainly at the farms of settlers, picking out those who were especially unpopular among the local blacks. This strategy has met with much success. The campaign took on the aspect of a people's war, with ZANU stressing the link between their struggle and the *chimurenga* of 1896-67.

Once again, the regime was taken largely by surprise, and once again South African military support was important in rescuing the situation. Then, a variety of measures were taken to force the local peasants to stop helping the guerillas. Security fences were built along the Rhodesia-Mozambique border; the villagers were herded into 'protected villages'; the rest of the countryside was turned into 'no-go areas' - free fire zones where those breaking curfew could be shot on sight. Collective fines were imposed on villages suspected of helping guerillas. Those accused of sympathising with ZANU were beaten up and sometimes killed.[32]

Yet the regime's hold was unsure. Its most spectacular failure was when Smith closed the border with Zambia temporarily in January 1973 in retaliation for Kaunda's support for the guerillas. Kaunda responded by closing the border permanently. Smith's blunder infuriated Vorster. The burden of increased conscription on the settler population exacerbated industry's shortage of skilled labour and encouraged whites to emigrate.

Meanwhile, the Africans grew in confidence, especially after the fall of the Caetano regime. The elections to the Rhodesian Parliament took place in July 1974, more or less coinciding with Spinola's announcement of independence for the African colonies. For the third time in a decade the Rhodesian Front swept all 50 white seats. A cartoon in the pro-Nationalist African paper *Moto* commented:

'This will be the last election in Rhodesia - the next one will be in Zimbabwe.'

5. Zambia: the Failure of State Capitalism

Until 1974 the major black states presented a solid united front towards the minority regimes. Whatever cracks there were in this front - for example, the collaboration of the Banda regime in Malawi with Vorster's 'outward' policy, which culminated in Banda's visit to South Africa - did not represent any major victories for Pretoria. This situation changed dramatically in 1974. The lynchpin of the black states' united front against the white South, Zambia under Kenneth Kaunda, dropped out in support of Vorster's policy of detente.

The Prisoner of the White South

Northern Rhodesia became an independent state in 1964, taking the name of Zambia. The new state had been shaped in the colonial period by two principal factors: the domination of Northern Rhodesia by the white minority regimes to the south, and the dependence of its economy on the copper mines.

It had been conquered by force and fraud in much the same way as Zimbabwe, although less brutally. In 1890, Lewanika, king of the Lozi (Barotse), gave the British South Africa Company the same sort of mining concession they had won from Lobengula in Zimbabwe. Once again the concession was used to give validity to the conquest, not only of the Lozi, but of surrounding tribes. The casual way in which the fate of entire peoples was settled during the 'scramble for Africa' is brought out by the settlement of the border dispute between Britain and Portugal in the area:

In 1903 the British and Portuguese decided to invite the King of Italy to draw the boundary. A thoroughly independent arbitrator, living in blissful ignorance of the people of the Zambesi valley, King Emmanuel took up his pen on May 30, 1905, and drew what is now the Zambia-Angola border down the line of longitude twenty-two degrees east.[1]

In the late 1920s the huge deposits of the Copperbelt were discovered, and almost at once integrated Zambia into the network of interests which wove together the multinationals and the South African regime. The copper industry was controlled by two huge mining companies - Anglo-American and the Rhodesian (now Roan) Selection Trust, itself controlled by American Metal Climax Inc (Amax). The mines reproduced the South African system - skilled jobs were reserved for whites through an informal colour bar, the mass of unskilled black miners, driven to the mines by land shortage and taxation, were paid very low wages and kept in compounds.

Although not directly controlled by the settlers, the colony was run in their interests. Settler agriculture, with backing from the state, supplied the mines with food. No efforts were made to develop the African agricultural sector. The best land from the point of view of the market - that along the railway line - was reserved for the whites. At the time of independence about 70 per cent of the population were largely dependent on pre-capitalist African agriculture for their subsistence, with an average annual cash income of £10.[2]

The country became more dependent on the white South during the period from 1953 to 1963, when it was part of the Federation of Rhodesia and Nyasaland. The Federation was dominated by the settlers of Southern Rhodesia who used revenues from copper to develop their own economy and expanded their manufacturing industries at the expense of the other two territories, which were reduced to captive markets.

Unlike Southern Rhodesia, Northern Rhodesia was never settler controlled. There was no armed occupation of the country by large numbers of white adventurers; when the BSA Company was displaced in 1924, a British colonial regime took control. The result was that the settlers in Northern Rhodesia were never in a position to defy Britain and take control of the country as the whites under Ian Smith did on the other side of the Zambesi. When decolonisation gathered pace, the Tory government in Britain was prepared to give way to the demands of the African nationalists for independence. There was nothing the settlers could do but accept black rule or emigrate.

The main African nationalist force during the last years of the Federation was the United National Independence Party (Unip) led by Kenneth Kaunda, and based primarily on the black mineworkers of the Copperbelt. Unip played a prominent part in breaking up the Central African Federation and in blocking attempts to sabotage independence by the settler leaders, principally the Prime Minister of the Federation, and one-time trade union leader from Northern Rhodesia, Roy Welensky. The other main black party, the African National Congress led by Harry Nkumbula, and at one time the main nationalist party, degenerated into the role of a collaborator with the settlers. Unip swept to power in the pre-independence elections and Kaunda became the first President of Zambia in 1964.

Independent Zambia remained closely integrated into the economic complex dominated by South Africa. The copper mines owned by Anglo-American and RST dominated the economy. In the year of independence, 'copper accounted for ninety-two per cent of the country's exports, contributed fifty-three per cent of the total government revenue and supplied forty-seven per cent of the net domestic product'.[3]

Although the Kaunda government nationalised the BSA Company's royalty rights over the mines shortly before independence, this did not alter the structure of economic power. The BSA Company was replaced by a new and much more powerful investment company, Charter Consolidated, headquartered in London but controlled by Anglo-American.

The rest of the economy was run by companies based on South Africa or Rhodesia: Northern Breweries was owned by

South African Breweries, itself linked with Anglo; the major banks were Barclays, the Standard Bank and the Netherlands Bank of South Africa. Lonrho was rapidly buying its way into the Zambian economy, taking over breweries, newspapers, construction and road transport companies. Many Zambian firms were run from Salisbury, the capital of Rhodesia. The coal for the Zambian mines came from the Wankie Colliery in Rhodesia, owned by Anglo-American. Zambia's main source of cheap power was the Kariba Dam, which it shares with Rhodesia and which runs along the two country's borders. Zambia's two main routes to the sea were the Benguela railway, running through Portuguese-ruled Angola and owned by a British company, Tanganyika Concessions, and the connection with the Mozambique ports of Beira and Lourenco Marques, running through Rhodesia. In 1964, 60 per cent of Zambia's imports came from South Africa or Rhodesia.[4]

The Drive Towards State Capitalism

Now that Kaunda has clearly emerged as an ally of South African and US imperialism in their efforts to stabilise the region, he is often criticised for having failed to break out of the economic stranglehold exercised over Zambia by the white minority regimes. Thus *Chimurenga*, ZANU's London newsletter, speaks of 'the lack of self-reliance in the economy and administration' of Zambia.[5] However, while it is true that Zambia remains heavily dependent on Western capital and on South Africa, it is also true that Kaunda's policies since independence have been aimed at lessening this dependence.

Immediately after independence Kaunda sought to encourage industrialisation, partly through investing the copper revenues in state-directed manufacturing industry, partly through attracting foreign investment. The instrument of this policy was the state-run Industrial Development Corporation (Indeco).

There was not much to show for this effort: foreign companies had as little interest in investing in a small and economically backward African country as they had in any semi-colonial country in the Third World. Added to this was the effect of UDI in Rhodesia on the Zambian economy, since Zambia took the brunt of Britain's policy of economic sanctions against the Smith regime.

Moreover, internal divisions were shaking the regime. Real wages rose dramatically after independence. Between 1964 and 1970 average wages doubled while the cost of living index rose by 50 per cent.[6] In part this was a result of 'Zambianisation' - blacks replacing whites in managerial and administrative jobs. In part, it was a product of the militancy and power of the miners on the Copperbelt. In 1966 a series of unofficial strikes in the mines forced the union leaders to press for a wage increase of 22 per cent, which the government conceded, and which encouraged other workers to demand and win similar wage increases. Higher wages encouraged the drift off the land, where the collapse of the communal economy continued, swelling the vast number of unemployed.

The failure of economic development led to squabbling among the new black ruling class over political office and the patronage, power and bribes that went with it. Even within Unip these divisions went along tribal lines, polarising the party between the Bemba, who made up the mass of the urban population in the Copperbelt, and the Lozi, and often leading to violence, even at meetings of the Unip national council.

When Kaunda launched his 'Mulungushi Economic Revolution' in April 1968, one of his aims was to strengthen his hand in the factional struggle. The 'revolution' involved three sets of measures. First, steps were taken to break the dominance of retail trading by Asian traders, replacing them with Africans. As elsewhere in Africa, the Asian commercial bourgeoisie had served as an intermediary between the colonial power and the African masses, and used their position to exploit the latter; from the standpoint of developing an African capitalist class, eliminating the Asian middleman made sense.[7]

The second set of measures was aimed at stopping the outflow of capital and the repatriation of profits by foreign businessmen, which had developed into a huge problem after independence.

Finally, Indeco took a 51 per-cent share-holding in 25 leading foreign-controlled companies, in retail trade, breweries, transport and construction. No steps were taken in relation to the mines.

When Kaunda did finally act against the mineowners, it was again as part of the factional struggles within Unip. The general election of December 1968 had intensified divisions within Unip: the opposition ANC, which disagreed with Kaunda's policy of confrontation with the settler regimes, not only remained dominant in its Southern Province stronghold, but swept to victory among the Lozi in Barotseland, where Unip's Lozi leaders like Arthur Wina were humiliatingly defeated. At the same time, Kaunda's position was threatened by the growing power of Simon Kapwepwe, leader of the Bemba on the Copperbelt and Vice-President.

Kaunda attacked at the Matero meeting of the Unip national council on 11 August 1969. He abruptly announced that the government would take 51 per cent of the mining companies' shares, and dissolved the national council, taking direct control of the party. He followed this up by isolating and humiliating Kapwepwe. Two years later Kapwepwe resigned to set up his own United People's Party (UPP), which looked for a time as if it might become a major threat to Kaunda's position in the Copperbelt towns, as unemployment grew more and more serious. In December 1971 Kapwepwe won the Copperbelt seat of Mufulira in a by-election. That was the high point. Reversing his old radical stance and lining up with Nkumbula to conciliate the settlers and criticise Kaunda's policy of confrontation with the white South, Kapwepwe failed to capitalise on his potential support among the copperminers and urban unemployed. In February 1972 Kaunda was able to ban the UPP and gaol Kapwepwe and many of his supporters. He followed this up by introducing a one-party state in 1973. ANC dissolved itself into Unip, only to find that Kaunda reneged on his promises of parliamentary seats and ministerial positions for most of Nkumbula's followers.

Kaunda took other steps apart from the Mulungushi and Matero reforms to strengthen the Zambian state. The most important were aimed at reducing the country's dependence on South Africa, Rhodesia and the Portuguese colonies. In 1970, 15,000 skilled Chinese engineers began work on the Tanzania-Zambia railway (the Tanzam railway or Tanzara), whose aim was to provide Zambia with an outlet to the sea which did not go through white-ruled territory. The railway opened in 1976, and it is expected that about 65 per cent of Zambia's foreign trade will be routed via Dar-es-Salaam, the Tanzanian terminus of the railway. [8] Moreover, the Kafue and Kariba North dam projects are aimed at reducing Zambia's dependence on electricity from the Kariba dam, which it shares with Rhodesia.

Kaunda justified these policies in terms of an ideology which he called 'Humanism', and which in turn was heavily influenced by Julius Nyerere's theories of African socialism. The Mulungushi 'revolution' bore the marks of Nyerere's Arusha declaration of February 1967, when he nationalised the banks and took a 60 per cent shareholding in Tanzania's basic industries. Both Kaunda and Nyerere stressed the continuity between the pre-capitalist communal African societies and the societies they were attempting to build. They argued that socialism could be built in Africa without a class struggle within African society, but rather on the basis of a united and self-reliant nation. Economic growth would be the result not of encouraging foreign investment, although neither were in favour of expelling Western capital, but of building up a strong national economy under the *aegis* of the state.

These theories reflected the interests of the nationalist petty bourgeoisie that had led the struggle for independence. Too weak to compete with Western capital, this group, drawn from the clerks of the old colonial order, required the backing of the state to embark on the sort of economic development that would establish it as a national capitalist class or to buy out foreign capital. The normal avenues for private capital were very narrow, and concentrated in the commercial sector; and even there the new ruling class required the backing of the state to squeeze out the Asian merchants.

The one-party state, implemented by Nyerere immediately after independence and by Kaunda with a nine-year delay, was essential for the new black bourgeoisie. Economically weak, torn by tribal divisions that reflected regional disparities and the anomalies resulting from the imperialist division of Africa, threatened by the mass of workers and peasants below them and by external enemies - in Zambia, the South African and Rhodesian regimes which were extremely active in organising espionage, sabotage and subversion especially in the immediate post-UDI period - the black bourgeoisie required unity at any price. Of course internal divisions persisted within the single party, which explains the peculiar position of Kaunda and Nyerere, as Presidents who embody the unity of the ruling class.

Kaunda's policies in Zambia reflected the need of the black bourgeoisie to establish its economic position through control of the state. How far they went in establishing Zambia's economic independence is another matter. The most important aspect of the programme was, of course, the takeover of the mines: the government-run Mining Development Corporation (Mindeco) became the majority shareholder in the mining groups, which were renamed Nchanga Consolidated Mines, and Roan Consolidated Mines, for the Anglo and RST groups respectively. However, management and service contracts were signed with Anglo-American and RST, who also kept a minority 49 per cent shareholding.

Management and service agreements have also been a feature of nationalisations in Tanzania and other semi-colonial countries. In no way do they represent a threat to the power of the multinationals, whose world-wide sphere of operations, monopoly of technology and access to far larger amounts of capital than the states they are dealing with, guarantee their dominant position quite independently of the degree to which they own the means of production which they manage.

The Vice-President of the Chase Manhattan Bank explained in 1965:

Most successful projects have been achieved without hard and fast requirements for certain rigid percentages of stock ownership. The important element is that there be a meeting of minds at the beginning as to who does what - *who manages and controls*. Under these circumstances, a minority shareholder can in fact functionally not only manage but also control the enterprise.

And *The Economist* wrote at the time of Kaunda's takeover of the mines:

It will be a tragedy if potential investors in Africa are mistakenly led to believe that there is no longer a place for them there. Although doing business in independent Africa now calls for a high degree of political acumen, the opportunities available to those who possess it are good. The risks are greater than in more settled parts of the world but so are the returns...

The shrewdest businessmen in that part of the world have argued for some time that a 49 per cent stake in a business whose success is underwritten by government participation may be more valuable than 100 per cent of a concern exposed to all the political winds that blow.

Finally, the chairman of Lonrho in Zambia said:

We welcome Government participation in our businesses for, in our view, the very fact that government will be a substantial shareholder should assist in their future stability and expansion.[9]

The multinationals in Tanzania and Zambia have benefited greatly from government participation. They have mobilised and used large quantities of local capital provided by the government in exchange for quite limited investments on their part. They have received official backing for their expansion, priority in gaining government contracts and protection from strikes. (When Kaunda took over the mines, he banned strikes and froze wages.) When the copper mines were nationalised, the companies were released from the Mulungushi restrictions on the repatriation of profits and, under the compensation agreement, enabled to transfer far more money out of the country than before nationalisation.[10] Finally, the multinationals remain in an excellent position to determine investment decisions, which therefore naturally reflect the overall interests of the Western companies and, thanks to their management and service agreements, to manipulate foreign currency accounts.[11]

Kaunda's reforms were meant to provide the Zambian bourgeoisie with a secure economic base by introducing a measure of state capitalism into the economy. Too weak to accumulate capital in competition with the West as individuals, the Zambian ruling class would do so collectively through the medium of the state, a path followed by many semi-colonial countries, Egypt, Brazil and Argentina, among others.[12] However, even collectively, the Zambian bourgeoisie was too weak to expropriate foreign capital. It would have involved them in mobilising of the mass of Zambian workers and peasants against the copper companies, which would have threatened their own positioon. Moreover, Kaunda and his fellows could see no way of reducing Zambia's dependence on international capitalism, both as a market for copper and as the only source of the technology and skilled labour-power the country lacked. The result was that the Zambian bourgeoisie entered into a partnership agreement with Western capital that left it still in a junior position, but with a larger share of the profits extracted from the Zambian working class.

The Failure of Humanism

The birds came home to roost in the mid 1970s. Zambia's economic development strategy after independence had rested on the copper industry. Copper is a commodity peculiarly sensitive to the fluctuations of the world economy: its price rose in the 1960s under the stimulus of the Vietnam war, fell during the post-Vietnam recession, zoomed to record levels during the boom of the early 1970s and then came crashing down. By 1975 copper had become almost uneconomic to produce: its price fell from a record K1,953 a tonne in April 1974 to an average of about K800 a tonne in 1975; breakeven point for the Zambian copper mines was estimated at between K780 and K830 a tonne.[13] Copper has never accounted for less than 90 per cent of Zambia's export earnings.

Other factors exacerbated the crisis of the Zambian economy. The post-independence economic reforms had failed to affect agriculture at all. 500 white farmers remained responsible for 80 per cent of Zambia's agricultural output. Production of milk, beef, groundnuts, tobacco and milk *fell* in the decade after independence because many settlers emigrated to Rhodesia and South Africa.[14] The development of African agriculture was given low priority by the government, which was content to use the foreign exchange earnings of agriculture to cover the bill for food imports; its rural development programme was not coherently thought out and implementation was incompetent and often corrupt. Peasants drifted off the land into the towns.

The result was that Zambia became increasingly dependent for food imports on neighbouring countries - South Africa, Botswana and, humiliatingly, Rhodesia. The commodity boom and the oil crisis forced up prices dramatically, importing world inflation into the Zambian economy. By July 1975 Zambia's import bill for foreign foodstuffs was R50 million per annum, while the government was spending R100 million per annum to subsidise the prices of basic commodities like sugar, soap, cooking oil and mealie meal (maize flour). Fertiliser bills had gone up by 333 per cent since 1972, wheat by over 200 per cent, oil by 400 per cent.[15]

Meanwhile, the money to pay for these imports was shrinking rapidly with the fall in the copper price. The shortage of foreign exchange involved other factors as well. The balance of the compensation owed to the copper companies, about K150 million, was paid off in September 1973, although full repayment did not fall due until the 1980s.[16]

The closure of the border with Rhodesia blocked one of Zambia's routes to the sea and tripled transportation costs. Then in 1975 the Angolan war closed off Zambia's access to the port of Lobito, which had previously handled about 50 per cent of its foreign trade. Tanzara did not become operative until 1976 and in any case the port of Dar-es-Salaam was heavily congested. The result was that by August 1975 the foreign exchange reserves had fallen to K40 million, barely enough to cover a month's imports, while it was predicted in South Africa that the 1975-76 shortfall would total R1 billion.[17]

The economic crisis brought political convulsions in its wake. The old tribal divisions, fuelled by popular discontent at rising unemployment and prices, revived. By 1974 food prices had risen 90 per cent above their 1967 level.[18] Real wages fell by at least 15 per cent between 1970 and 1975.[19] A document smuggled out of Zambia in May 1975 described how Unip politicians in Barotseland and the Eastern province were reviving old secessionist ambitions and how the Unip organisation in the Southern province was made up largely of the old ANC. Kapwepwe was out of gaol organising underground in the Copperbelt and the Bemba Northern province. The document summed up the increasingly critical attitude of the Zambian bourgeoisie towards Kaunda's police of confrontation with the white South as follows:

> They believe that Zambia should trade with the cheapest source, i.e. South Africa, and that it is not in Zambia's interest to interfere in the internal affairs of her neighbours. Thus they blame the present economic crisis in Zambia to [sic] Zambia's involvement in the Southern African Liberation struggle and believe that it is in Zambia's interests to refuse any further aid to the liberation movements, and to co-operate with the government of South Africa.[20]

Detente with South Africa would open up the Zambian economy to South African capital and commodities, thus alleviating the immediate crisis. It would also bring about, it was hoped, a settlement with Rhodesia and an end to the border closure (in any case Zambia still imported coke from the Wankie colliery in Rhodesia).

The crisis led not only to detente, but also to a dramatic escalation in the class struggle within Zambia.

The failure of Kaunda's state capitalist policies did not express itself only in soaring inflation. In June 1974 the number of jobs stood at 386,830 compared to 342,970 at the end of 1970. Employment in manufacturing had grown from 38,160 to only 43,170 in the same period.[21] Meanwhile 80,000 school-leavers are added to the labour force every year. Kaunda's solution was the Rural Reconstruction Programme, whereby military recruits, under strict military discipline and paid subsistence wages, were to be trained and work for three years in the countryside, and school-leavers were to be required to work for 20 months in rural reconstruction camps at a rate of 60,000 a year.[22] The solution to mass unemployment and falling agricultural production was to be the formation of rural labour armies.

The regime also launched a direct attack on the living standards of the mass of the people. Until 1976 food subsidies had helped to offset inflation (even so the low income cost of living index went up 18 points between January and August 1975[23]). The subsidies were lifted in February 1976; and the price of the staple, mealie meal, doubled. This coincided with the outbreak of the Angolan war: the government used a demonstration at the University of Zambia in support of MPLA to declare a state of emergency. They then provoked a student strike and a further demonstration by arresting a pro-MPLA lecturer, Lionel Cliffe. The University was closed down and placed under armed guard; 5 lecturers and 17 student leaders were then detained.

A correspondent in Zambia describes the situation at the time of the February 1976 crisis:

> The University was quite clearly used as a smokescreen to cover this situation. The Party was coming apart at the seams - there hadn't been a Central Committee meeting

ending in agreement for months. And there was a budget that doubled the price of mealie-meal. This was done very slyly. The budget was announced on the Friday, amid a great publicity campaign and rumours that mealie-meal would be greatly increased in price, but there were no increases. Great relief, then on the Sunday it was just announced quickly with no fuss that the price was doubled. And the tactic worked. There were one or two riots in compounds - Grey Zulu, the General secretary of Unip, was speaking at one and at the end of the speech, explaining the necessity of the cuts, he shouted to the crowd 'One Zambia' to which the stock chant is 'One Nation'; and the crowd shouted back 'One Starvation' - but that was all.

After February, the economic position improved: South Africa, the World Bank and the IMF granted Zambia loans; the opening of Tanzara improved the transport situation dramatically; copper prices rose with the recovery of the world economy. But there were still huge stockpiles of copper overhanging the market; in May 1976 Zambia still owed R150 million for goods delivered and the reserves were in deficit by about R100 million; the rate of inflation was running between 25 and 30 per cent. Symptomatic of the corruption and incompetence of the Zambian ruling class was the arrest of the Governor of the Bank of Zambia for receiving K100,000 in stolen property.[24] Western Province, bordering on Angola, was terrorised by armed gangs, possibly the defeated followers of the FNLA leader Daniel Chipenda.

Kaunda is still walking the tightrope on which he has found himself in recent years. To his right he is threatened within his own party by those like Arthur Wina, former Minister of Finance, who favour closer collaboration with South Africa and who criticise Kaunda for not reopening the border with Rhodesia. Tribal divisions which mask the grubbing after spoils by different sections of the Zambian bourgeoisie still threaten to tear Zambia apart. And there is the ever-lengthening shadow of an army that has come to exercise an increasing weight in

Zambian politics, and that may follow the example of soldiers in many other African states by seizing power.

The other threat presented to Kaunda's rule is from the workers and peasants who have suffered the brunt of his policies in recent years, and, above all, the 68,000 copper miners, the most powerful and militant section of the Zambian working class. So far, the leadership of the Mineworkers' Union of Zambia (MUZ) has remained closely integrated into the party and the state. They have resisted and smashed every strike by rank-and-file miners in recent years. They have been helped by the fact that the opposition parties, like Kapwepwe's UPP, have appealed to tribalism in their battles with other sections of the ruling class. So far no alternative leadership has emerged that places the interests and struggle of the working class at the centre of its programme.

The Zambian working class is large by African standards, powerful, militant and able to draw together the mass of the population in a struggle against the Zambian bourgeoisie. It is also linked by a million ties - a common position in the productive process, shared tradition, the regional labour system that concentrated workers from all over Southern and Central Africa in the mining towns of Zambia, Zaire, Rhodesia and South Africa - with its fellow workers throughout the region. These links - the links of international working-class solidarity - could break the hold of South African and Western imperialism on the whole subcontinent and set Africa alight.

6. Detente Phase One: the Vorster-Kaunda Alliance[1]

We have seen how the need to penetrate the African market underlay Vorster's 'outward' policy in the late 1960s, when South Africa attempted to use its economic leverage to prise black states out of the united front against the white South.

Although South African businessmen, diplomats and spies were active in many black capitals, the chief prize, Zambia, eluded them. After UDI and the dramatic rise in trade with South Africa that it provoked, Kaunda proceeded to implement a series of measures aimed at reducing Zambia's economic dependence on the settler states. This policy was aided by the fact that for most of the late 1960s and early 1970s the world copper price was riding high.

Kaunda did not rule a dialogue with South Africa utterly out of court. In 1969 he and Nyerere laid down the preconditions for negotiations with the Vorster regime in the Lusaka Manifesto. It distinguished between South Africa itself, which was recognised as a sovereign independent state despite its internal regime, and Namibia, Rhodesia and the Portuguese colonies, whose situation reflected the incompleteness of decolonisation and a failure to hand over independence to the peoples of these countries. If South Africa showed itself willing to accept majority rule in Namibia, Rhodesia and the Portuguese colonies, the black governments would be willing to talk.

At the time Vorster ignored the offer. But then the Portuguese dictatorship fell. The rulers of South Africa were faced with the prospect of a Frelimo government in Mozambique, and much more serious fighting inside Rhodesia, where the ZANU guerillas could expect to enjoy the backing of the Mozambique government. Vorster decided to take up the Lusaka Manifesto's spurned offer: 'the alternative,' he said, 'is too ghastly to contemplate'.

The economic crisis in Zambia guaranteed that Kaunda would be willing to collaborate. Careful negotiations conducted by Mark Chona, Kaunda's special adviser, on the one side, and agents of the much-feared Bureau of State Security (BOSS), including General van der Bergh, its head, on the other, culminated in Vorster's Senate speech on 23 October 1974, in which he declared that South Africa accepted majority rule in the Portuguese colonies. The result was the Lusaka agreement of December 1974, which opened the way for a settlement in Rhodesia.

The agreement had the backing of the US Administration. The Nixon Doctrine had laid the basis for a wider detente between the US ruling class and the Russian and Chinese bureaucracies, which involved the US in withdrawing from direct intervention in the semi-colonial countries. Instead, certain states in key areas of American interest would be given responsibility for keeping order: Brazil in Latin America, Iran in the Middle East, South Africa in sub-Saharan Africa. As Kissinger spelt out in his memorandum on Southern Africa,

> We would take diplomatic steps to convince the black states in the area that their current liberation and majority rule aspirations in the South are not attainable by violence and that their only hope for a peaceful and prosperous future lies in closer relations with white-dominated states. We would emphasise our belief that closer relations will help to bring change in the white states. We would give increased and more flexible economic aid to black states of the area to focus their attention on their internal development and to give them a motive to co-operate in reducing tensions. We would encourage economic assistance from South Africa to the developing black nations.[2]

Another critical factor was the support given to Kaunda by

Nyerere, who enjoyed considerable prestige throughout Africa and the rest of the world as a champion of the liberation struggle and of 'African socialism'. Moreover as chairman of the OAU subcommittee of 'Frontline Presidents' - which, apart from Kaunda, included Seretse Khama of Botswana, and which was extended to include Samora Machel of Mozambique and, in 1976 Agostinho Neto of Angola - Nyerere provided a link between Kaunda and the radical leaderships of Mozambique and ZANU, many of whose fighters were based in Mozambique and Tanzania. Nyerere met Donald Easum, US Assistant Secretary of State for African Affairs and an ardent advocate of detente, in Lusaka during the celebrations for the tenth anniversary of Zambian independence in October 1974 at the height of the build-up to the agreement over Rhodesia.[3] And after the failure of the Victoria Falls talks in August 1975, it was the Tanzanian Foreign Minister who assured reporters that 'the peaceful aims of Mr Vorster of South Africa were serious'.[4]

Rhodesia: the Breaking of ZANU and the Rise of Joshua Nkomo

The crux of the detente operation was a settlement in Rhodesia, for continued fighting between white settlers backed by South Africa and black nationalists backed by the African states could lead to military confrontation between the principal parties.

There were two obstacles to a settlement - the Smith regime and ZANU. Smith's base lay among the white farmers and petty bourgeoisie who would inevitably suffer under majority rule, since even the most moderate black government could not survive without attacking the white monopoly of the best land and without Africanising the public administration (one-third of the white working population are state employees). Only Vorster had leverage on the regime: the settlers' economic survival depended on South African support and on the troops and helicopters supplied by Pretoria.

ZANU's guerillas had waged a successful liberation war

against the regime for two years. Many of its cadres were committed to the idea of a protracted peasant war that would lead to a radical nationalist regime on the Chinese or Mozambican model. Its leaders were reluctant to see the other nationalist parties share in the spoils of a victory which ZANU would have played the main part in winning.

In the event the various nationalist bodies, including ZANU, were drilled into line by the black governments. Nkomo and Sithole were released from prison to sign the Lusaka agreement on 7 December 1974. The agreement united ZANU, ZAPU and Frolizi into a common negotiating front, the African National Council, headed by Muzorewa. Smith's attempts to sabotage the agreement were brought to an end when Vorster flew to Salisbury.

From the start there were disputes over the interpretation of the agreement. ANC claimed that Smith had agreed to release all political detainees immediately; to release all political prisoners as soon as possible; to revoke all death sentences for political offences;to declare a general amnesty; to end the ban on ZANU and ZAPU; to permit free political activity within the country; to halt all political trials; and to end the state of emergency.[5] Smith claimed that a precondition of a constitutional conference was 'the cessation of all terrorist activities'. His security forces exploited the ceasefire agreement in an attempt to disarm the guerillas. The result was that the fighting continued, which was used by the regime as an excuse to stop releasing detainees. By October 1975 there were *more* nationalists detained than before the Lusaka agreement - 664 as opposed to 430 - and more than twice as many as there were in January 1975 when the ceasefire broke down.[6]

Smith also attempted to exploit the divisions amongst the nationalists. In March 1975 he had Sithole detained, accusing the ZANU leader of responsibility for the guerilla war and of plotting to assassinate Muzorewa, the ANC President. Sithole was released only at the insistence of Vorster, who sent Hilgard Muller, his Foreign Minister, to Salisbury to deliver his instructions. The Pretoria regime brought other pressures to bear on the Rhodesian settlers: at the beginning of August 1975 all South African troops were withdrawn from Rhodesia.

The second development during 1975 was the drive by the black governments to crush ZANU. Nkomo had rapidly emerged as the ANC leader most prepared to negotiate a settlement, and most acceptable to Vorster as the potential head of a neo-colonial black government. But for Nkomo to succeed, ZANU, which controlled the bulk of the guerillas outside the country and which enjoyed mass support within the country particularly among the young unemployed in the towns, would have to be eliminated.

The main responsibility for carrying out this task fell on Kaunda's shoulders. He took his opportunity when Herbert Chitepo, the chairman of ZANU, was killed in Lusaka by a car-bomb in March 1975. Over 1,000 ZANU members were arrested at Chitepo's funeral and Zambian troops seized the guerilla transit camps used by ZANU in Zambia. Although 1,220 ZANU political prisoners were released in December, 57 of their leaders were held in gaol while Chitepo's murder was being investigated. In April 1976 the report of the commission of inquiry appointed by Kaunda accused the *Dare* (the ZANU executive-in-exile) and the ZANU military high command of responsibility for Chitepo's death. The root of the affair, it argued, was a tribal division within ZANU between two Shona subgroups, the Manyika, which included Chitepo, and the Karanga, which dominated the Zanu leadership.

Supporters of Robert Mugabe, secretary-general of ZANU, have produced a detailed reply to the Chitepo report, *The Price of Detente*. Although it is not possible to verify or refute the document's claims, it is carefully argued, and we shall try to reproduce its main points.

The document claims that the 1973 elections to the ZANU leadership involved the displacement of the old-timers by a group of radicals. Some of these, Josiah Tongogara, head of ZANU defence, and Rugare Gumbo, were Karanga, but others, like Kumirai Kangai, were not. Tribal origins were transcended by the split between the old and new leadership, which reflected the huge increase in the size of ZANLA, the ZANU military wing, since December 1972 and the resulting growth in influence of the young guerillas. The result, in December 1974, was a revolt against the new ZANU leadership led by Thomas Nhari but backed by Noel Mukono and Simpson Mutambanengwe, conservative members of the *Dare* who had been displaced in the 1973 elections. According to the document, the rebels attempted to kidnap the ZANU High Command and killed 59 loyalists in the guerilla camps, before the mutiny was put down on Chitepo's orders (it should be noted that Chitepo, like Mukono and Mutambanengwe, was a Manyika).

The ZANU document describes the Mukono-Nutambanengwe group as follows:

> These conservatives were financed by multinational companies, which provided money for cars, food and payment of guerillas. The link between the conservative ZANU-based politicians and the multinationals was formed through Cornelius Sanyanga, a Company Secretary of Lonrho, and Nelson Dziruni, an executive of Shell...
> They feared that if a radical leadership took power in an independent Zimbabwe it would irrevocably put Zimbabwe alone on the line of socialist development which they openly opposed.

The document also alleges that there were contacts between the rebels and 'colonels of the Smith forces'.[7]

Another document smuggled out of Lusaka, which we quoted in the previous chapter, puts forward a similar interpretation of the Nhari revolt. It goes further, arguing that the rebels had Zambian support:

> Zambian support for the dissidents arose from the fact that Sanyanga, a close friend and former classmate of Mark Chona, one of the key figures in the Detente exercise, had convinced the Zambians that the dissidents would support Detente if they were allowed to gain control of ZANU, and [that] it was in the interest of the Zambian government to

remove the leaders known to be violently opposed to Detente.[8]

This document claims that when the Nhari coup failed, South Africa, with Zambian complicity, decided to have Chitepo killed in order to blame his death on the ZANU radicals who could then be accused of murdering him because he was a Manyika like Mukono and Mutambanengwe: 'The aim behind the murder of Chitepo was to arouse as much tribal antagonism as possible, as well as to provide an excuse for arresting all ZANU leaders.'[9] It alleges that shortly before Chitepo's death, Mark Chona met a South African emissary, and that the evening before the assassination, there was a violent argument during a meeting between Chitepo, representatives of ZAPU and Frolizi, Muzorewa, and Kaunda, during which Chitepo refused to place the ZANU guerillas under a joint ANC command. (The Zambian commission report confirms the document in this latter claim.)

Whatever the truth of these claims, it was the advocates of detente who profited from Chitepo's death. ZANU was affected not only in Zambia. Tanzanian and Mozambican troops took over the guerilla camps in their countries. The Frelimo regime cut down drastically on the supply of arms and other war materials to ZANU guerillas operating from Mozambique; as a result, in late 1975 Rhodesian security forces were claiming their greatest successes against the guerillas since the ZANU campaign had begun. Robert Mugabe, the secretary-general of ZANU, was placed under 'protective custody' in Mozambique.

The other prong of the strategy for hammering the Zimbabwean nationalists into line involved projecting Joshua Nkomo as leader of ANC. Nkomo sought to exploit ZAPU's long-standing control of the ANC apparatus within Rhodesia to call a congress and install himself as president. These moves were blocked by a curious alliance between Sithole and Muzorewa, representing between them traditional ZANU loyalties and the group of parsons and intellectuals who had led the old ANC between 1971 and 1974.

Things came to a head after the Victoria Falls conference in August 1975. Despite the much-publicised meeting between Vorster and Kaunda, the talks themselves were a fiasco. Smith refused to permit 'convicted criminals' like Sithole back into the country; the conference collapsed within hours.

Muzorewa and Sithole then went to Lusaka, where they formed the Zimbabwe Liberation Council (ZLC) under Sithole's chairmanship, and declared their opposition to future negotiations and their support for an intensification of the armed struggle. Nkomo retaliated by calling a congress in Salisbury in September which elected him president of the ANC. Thus emerged the split between the so-called 'internal' and 'external' wings of ANC. That this was a misnomer is revealed by the fact that in October 1975 supporters of the Muzorewa-Sithole group called a rally in Salisbury which attracted 40,000 people.

Nkomo set out to court the settlers. His advances were to some extent reciprocated. The Johannesburg *Star* commented: 'Rhodesian whites suddenly see "good old Josh", as they affectionately call him now, as a sort of Great Black Hope for their future security of tenure in Rhodesia.'[10] Nkomo appointed a team 'charged with meeting white professionals and businessmen in commerce and industry'.[11]

In December 1975 Smith and Nkomo agreed to start talks on a settlement. However, Smith had no intention of reaching one: South African attention had been distracted by the Angolan war; the guerillas had been severely weakened by the treatment at the hands of the frontline states. For him negotiating with Nkomo was simply a way of resolving the conflicting pressures from Vorster and the Rhodesian Front, and for a time it looked as if the negotiations would go on for ever.

However, time did run out. In March 1976 Nkomo, in response to changes in the policies of both the frontline states and the Western governments which we shall come to in Chapter 9, broke off negotiations. He published the proposals for a majority rule constitution which he had put before Smith. They provided for 3 electoral rolls: 36 seats were to be elected by universal suffrage; 36 elected on a franchise limited mainly to whites; 72 elected on a franchise involving property and educational qualifications that would allow a majority of African seats.[12] It was a constitution that would give disproportionate weight to the settlers and the African petty bourgeoisie - a perfect neo-colonial recipe.

However, detente in Rhodesia had run out of steam. When the operation was revived after the Angolan war, it took a different form, as we shall see.

Namibia

The other major unliquidated colonial problem dividing South Africa from the black states was presented by Namibia. The territory was a German colony, conquered with great savagery before the first world war. The Versailles peace settlement in 1919 handed it over to South Africa, to be ruled under a League of Nations mandate.

Effectively Namibia has been ruled as if it were a fifth province of South Africa. Mining for gem diamonds, copper, zinc and uranium, amongst others, dominates the country's economy. The industry is controlled by a familiar array of companies - Anglo-American, Rio Tinto Zinc, De Beers, Consolidated Gold Fields, FVB, American Metal Climax, Selection Trust, IDC. The mines, along with the fishing industry and commercial agriculture, are concentrated in the southern Police Zone, a white area, in which Africans are permitted to enter only as 'temporary sojourners'; the barren northern areas are reserved for ten 'Homelands'. A contract labour system provides 43,000 migrant workers, mainly Ovambos from northern Namibia and southern Angola, to the 90,000 white settlers (out of a total population of about 750,000) and the mines, on one-year contracts.

There have been three main sources of opposition to the regime in Namibia. The first is the international campaign against South Africa's continued illegal occupation of the country, a campaign mounted by the Third World countries in the United Nations. The International Court of Justice voted for the revocation of South Africa's mandate in 1971 and the UN has set up its own administration-in-exile for Namibia.

The second is the guerilla struggle launched by the South West Africa People's Organisation (SWAPO) in 1966. SWAPO's history is a complex one. Its internal wing is not banned within Namibia, and its external wing has vacillated between reliance on the UN to enforce independence under majority rule and commitment to armed struggle. It has also been divided on policy issues: whether to link up with the Russian-backed ANC alliance embracing ZAPU and the MPLA in particular, and has been attacked by the MPLA for collaborating with Unita.

The third threat to South African rule is that represented by the Namibian working class. The first crack in the white *glacis* in the early 1970s took place in Namibia, before the Pearce demonstrations in Rhodesia, the Natal strikes in South Africa and the fall of the Portuguese dictatorship. A general strike by contract workers from December 1971 to January 1972 involving, at its height, 13,000 workers, demanded the abolition of the contract labour system. Attempts to break the strike by recruiting replacement workers in the Homelands were blocked by an impressive show of solidarity - Africans in northern Namibia refused to scab. Although the contract labour system was not abandoned, the employers were forced to make concessions: wages were raised by between 66 and 100 per cent.[13]

The strikes gave an impetus to the national struggle. Most of the strikers were Ovambos, who form a majority of the African population in Namibia. When elections to the Ovambo tribal authority took place in August 1973, 350,000 voters followed SWAPO's call to boycott the elections. The guerilla war intensified.

One aspect of Vorster's detente strategy was therefore to reach a settlement with Namibia. The terms of the Lusaka Manifesto and the pressure of the UN gave him no alternative.

In September 1975 a conference on Namibia's future assembled at the Turnhalle in Windhoek, capital of Namibia. It consisted of tribal leaders, representatives of the Coloureds and the leaders of the ruling Nationalist Party.

Vorster could adopt one of two policies, either of which would isolate SWAPO. The first involved separate development, permitting the troublesome Ovambos to form an independent state, perhaps embracing southern Angola, whose people are of the same ethnic group. In this way, South Africa would end up in effective control of the Cunene dam scheme in southern Angola, vital as a source of power for the Namibian economy. As against this, partitioning Namibia would run into mass opposition within the country and would be vetoed by both the black states and the Western governments (after MPLA's victory in Angola the EEC issued a statement in support of the independence of Namibia.)

The other option, which Vorster adopted, was to grant Namibia independence under a coalition government of settler and tribal leaders. An agreement to form such a government was reached by the end of 1976 at the Turnhalle conference, against the opposition of most of the Nationalist Party leadership in Namibia. However, Dirk Mudge, chairman of the conference and the most prominent Nationalist leader among the Namibian settlers, won out with Vorster's backing. Mudge was tipped as the Prime Minister of the new state, with chief Clemens Kapuo of the Herero as President. Mudge declared that South African troops would remain in the country (to keep out the Cubans in Angola), and admitted that he thought Namibia 'can never be completely economically independent' of South Africa.[14]

The main obstacle to detente remained SWAPO, which gathered together another group of tribal leaders in the Namibian National Convention and stepped up the guerilla struggle. Its position was strengthened by the MPLA's victory in Angola, and in March 1976 it was reported that its operational headquarters had been moved to Luanda.[15] Detente had not ended the guerilla war in Namibia.

Economic Collaboration Between South Africa and Black Africa

Despite these setbacks, the underlying aim of Vorster's detente policy - penetration of the black African economies - was achieved. The Johannesburg *Financial Mail* could boast in November 1975: 'There's hardly a country in the Dark Continent [sic] whose traders are not doing good business with South Africa - though admittedly some more furtively than others - and almost all with at least the tacit approval of local rulers.'[16]

The economic crisis that underlay Kaunda's adoption of detente extended to all the black African states. The boom of the early 1970s which led to dramatic increases in the prices of raw materials, many of them produced by African countries, also led to the quadrupling of oil prices. And the recession that followed saw a fall in the prices of their raw materials exports, but not in the price of their oil imports. The result was the same for all the semi-colonial countries who were not lucky enough to produce oil: accelerated inflation, balance of payments crises, social unrest, greatly increased indebtedness to Western bankers.

The economic crisis of the black states imposed dramatic limitations on their freedom to manoeuvre. Radical and right-wing regimes alike were forced to borrow from Western bankers and to trim their domestic policies as a result. One example is the Mobutu regime in Zaire. After the October 1973 war and a visit to China, Mobutu had 'Zaireanised' a number of the principal foreign enterprises (although not the American companies). After a second visit to China in December 1974, he decided on 'a radicalisation of our authentic revolution', nationalising the firms that had been Zaireanised the previous year.[17] But the fall in the copper price had a drastic effect on the Zairean economy. Mobutu was forced to default on his massive foreign debts. Inflation in 1975 ran at 40 per cent. The army went unpaid for months (which may explain why Zairean troops distinguished themselves by their looting rather than their fighting during the Angolan war). Finally, Mobutu found himself pushed towards a deal with his Western creditors under which 40 per cent of the commercial and industrial firms he had taken over would be denationalised and the zaire would be devalued.[18]

The crisis led to social convulsions in many African countries. In February and March 1974 a general strike, mutinies in the army and student demonstrations, brought down the decrepit and corrupt regime of Haile Selassie in Ethiopia. The *Derg*, or military junta, that took its place found itself threatened by militant separatist movements, principally in Eritrea, and by the mass opposition of workers and peasants. The Ethiopian example is known to have been a factor in Mobutu's left turn in November 1974, which was aimed at staving off mass discontent in Zaire.

The crisis had its effects on more radical regimes too. Nyerere made a pilgrimage to London to promise compensation for the owners of British property which he had nationalised in 1967. More significantly, he and his colleagues have been increasingly prepared to repress workers' and peasants' struggles in recent years. In 1971 the Western-backed coup that brought Idi Amin to power in Uganda and a Portuguese military attack on Guinea-Conakry for harbouring the PAIGC led the ruling Tanganyika African National Union (Tanu) to adopt the *Mwongozo* guidelines, which encouraged workers' participation in management, in an attempt to strengthen mass support for the regime. Inadvertently, they released a wave of workers' struggles,[19] which they then met with repression. To take an example, when the Mount Carmel Rubber Factory was occupied by the workforce in June 1973, in protest against the appalling conditions, some of their placards read: 'Long live *Mwalimu* and *Mwongozo*' (Mwalimu is the name by which Nyerere is normally known in Tanzania); 'We are ready to work night and day if allowed to take over the factory'.[20] The strikers were arrested and deported to their 'home' areas, as if they were temporary sojourners in South Africa.

In 1976 Nyerere tightened the screws further. In an attempt to cut back public spending and reduce Tanzania's external deficit, 9,500 civil servants were sacked and the workers' councils established in the public sector under the *Mwongozo* policy were abolished; strikes and go-slows were banned.[21]

Hand in hand with the shift to the right in the domestic policies of such diverse countries as Zambia, Zaire and Tanzania, has gone the development of economic collaboration between black Africa and South Africa.

The South African Industrial Development Corporation negotiated a R6 million export credit with two Zairean foodstuff importers. At the time Zaire was reported to be importing from South Africa foodstuffs, fish, steel, pharmaceuticals, building equipment, much of it via Rhodesia and Zambia despite the border closure. South Africa has established itself as Zambia's most important foreign supplier, providing Zambian importers with long-term export credits. At Kaunda's insistence Nyerere has permitted South African goods to pass through Dar-es-Salaam to Zambia.[22] The *Financial Mail* claims that the South African government has instructed exporters to extend credit to Zairean buyers in foreign exchange difficulties.[23] It was also reported that Zambia received a huge loan to cover the cost of petrol imports.[24] In the Central African Republic South African firms won contracts for hotel construction and low-cost housing projects.[25]

These economic links paid off during the OAU's emergency conference on Angola in January 1976. A right-wing coalition led by Kaunda and Mobutu succeeded in blocking OAU recognition of the MPLA and prevented the Organisation from condemning the South African invasion of Angola. Explaining why he was following the Kaunda-Mobutu line, President Bokassa of the Central African Republic said that 'he abhorred apartheid, but had travelled widely in Africa seeking aid from African countries and had received none. South Africa had come to the rescue and nobody was going to make him join in a condemnation that was one-sided'.[26]

Economic collaboration was not seriously affected by the Angolan War. Zaire, its normal route to the sea blocked by the continued closure of the Benguela railway, exported its copper via Port Elizabeth in South Africa,[27] Kaunda having reopened the border with Rhodesia for the purpose. A Zambian businessman succinctly explained the *rationale* behind trade with South Africa:

> South African imports are cheap and we can't ignore the sophistication of South African industry and agriculture in African terms. It makes sense to trade with her. When you are short of foreign exchange reserves, you can't afford to ignore an economic power on your doorstep.[28]

South African economic expansionism in Africa is likely to continue. As Tony Kirk put it:

> Once let economic interaction commence, and South African trade and influence could flow through Rhodesia and Zambia and up the communications network to the African hinterland. The Tanzam railway, constructed to free Zambia from the embrace of white southern Africa, might ultimately bind the region still closer to Pretoria.[29]

Black-ruled Africa is not exempt from the logic of capitalism, whatever Nyerere and Kaunda's theories of African socialism may say. The oil crisis and the international recession of the mid-1970s forced the black states into increased dependence on the West. Nyerere, Mobutu and Kaunda all found themselves with no choice but to clamp down on the living standards of their own workers and peasants and to trade and deal with their hated and ostracised enemy, the apartheid regime in South Africa. An era in African politics had passed.

7. Angola: the Turning-Point

Attempts at a Neo-Colonial Solution

The Lisbon coup in April 1974 was not an outright victory for the colonial liberation movements. Indeed, it seemed at first as if the coup might accelerate the changes that were taking place in Portuguese capitalism to the detriment of these movements.

The Salazar regime had sought to prop up backward Portuguese capitalism through the systematic and exclusive exploitation of the workers and peasants in the African colonies. This policy provoked the great colonial rebellions of the early 1960s.

The rebellions forced Salazar to abandon his exclusive policy. The regime was forced into large-scale foreign borrowing to finance the wars. In 1965 it allowed foreign capital for the first time to invest freely in both Portugal and the colonies. In the metropolis the share of foreign capital in the annual investment figures grew from 0.8 per cent in 1959 to 26.7 per cent in 1966.[1] Even more foreign capital flowed into the colonies:

> The invasion of the 'overseas provinces' by foreign capital involved the South African government and South African-based concerns, such as the Anglo-American Corporation, in projects ranging from both the Cabora Bassa and the Cunene dams to oil and mineral prospecting, together with interests in various other ventures; the Americans in Cabinda Gulf oil; the Germans and Japanese in Angolan iron ore. A host of other non-Portuguese concerns, including British banks, carried the internationalisation of

Portuguese colonialism to the point of actually entering into partnership with Portuguese companies.[2]

Western investment in the Portuguese colonies was not altogether new. Western mining capital had played a major part in Angola and Mozambique since the turn of the century. The ports of Lourenco Marques and Beira in Mozambique were financed by British and South African capital in order to provide a rail link to the sea for the mines of the Transvaal and Rhodesia respectively. Africans from Mozambique provided a large proportion of the labour force in the Rand. In Angola, the diamond mines of the Luanda district were owned by Diamang, in its turn controlled by the Anglo-Belgian mining company *Union Minière* in collaboration with De Beers and Anglo-American. The Benguela railway linking the copper mines of Zaire and Zambia with the Atlantic ports of Benguela and Lobito was built and owned by Tanganyika Concessions, a British company with mining interests in the region.

But it was only after Salazar opened the doors to foreign capital on a systematic basis that the big Portuguese monopolies like CUF and Champanlimaud became closer to Western and South African capital, and began to press for a change in the regime's policies. They hoped that a limited 'normalisation' at home and a political settlement in the colonies would enable Portugal to join the EEC while retaining control of the cheap raw materials produced in the colonies. The man they selected to implement this policy was Antonio de Spinola, who had somehow managed to salvage a glorious military reputation from the defeats he suffered at the hands of PAIGC in Guiné, and whose book, *Portugal and the Future*, called for a Lusitanian federation of Portugal and the colonies, the latter to be granted the right of self-government.

This trend within Portuguese capital converged with the growing opposition to the wars within the colonial army itself, an opposition spearheaded by the Armed Forces Movement (MFA), a group of young army officers inspired by a variety of largely social-democratic political convictions.

When the MFA overthrew the dictatorship on 25 April 1974, they handed over power to Spinola. However, the months of his presidency were to be dominated by a bitter dispute between him and the MFA, on the future of the colonies. The MFA, backed by the Socialist and Communist Parties which had emerged from the underground to take office in Spinola's government, as well as by the Portuguese revolutionary left, supported independence for all the African colonies. Spinola stuck to his plan of a Lusitanian federation, arguing that self-determination for the colonies (which he supported) was not the same as independence (which he did not).

The major stake in this battle was Angola. Guiné was of comparatively limited economic significance to Portugal, while Mozambique was already closely integrated into the South African economy. Angola, on the other hand, is potentially one of the richest countries in Africa. It is the third biggest oil producer in Africa, after Algeria and Nigeria; Gulf Oil's wells in Cabinda were pumping out oil in 1974 at a rate of 7.5 million tons a year, bringing in 450 million dollars a year in government royalties. Angola is also the world's third largest producer of coffee and the fifth largest of diamonds. It also contains rich deposits of iron ore, copper and uranium. Minerals exports doubled between 1965 and 1970, fuelling a boom in the local processing industries that trebled output between 1962 and 1969; in 1973 alone exports went up 37 per cent in value and manufacturing output by 26 per cent.

One factor in particular made a neo-colonial solution in Angola seem possible. In Mozambique and Guiné the Portuguese had faced a more or less united liberation movement. Although there were nationalist rivals to both Frelimo and PAIGC, their hegemony was not seriously challenged. In Angola, however, there were three major nationalist movements. The oldest, the Popular Movement for the Liberation of Angola (MPLA), had much in common with Frelimo and PAIGC. It originated among black urban intellectuals, belonging to the tiny minority of *assimilados*, African professionals and clerical workers granted the same rights as whites because they had reached the stage of 'civilisation', many of them *mesticos*, blacks of mixed race, the equivalent of the South African Coloureds. The MPLA was formed in 1956 by the fusion of a number of small radical groups that had emerged out of the associations petitioning for the reform of the Portuguese colonial administration, the cultural magazines influenced by Pan-Africanism, and, what proved to be the catalyst, the Angolan Communist Party, formed by clandestine members of the Portuguese Communist Party working in the colonial civil service.

The MPLA's programme reveals the Communist Party's influence. It rests on the notion of a broad multi-class popular alliance for national independence, a movement quite distinct from the struggle of workers and poor peasants against capitalism. MPLA's main objectives are:

(a) the elimination by every possible means of Portuguese colonial domination and of all vestiges of colonialism and imperialism;

(b) joint struggle with all patriotic forces in a broad people's movement whose objective is the taking of power by the Angolan people and the establishment of a republican, democratic system based on total independence;

(c) the sovereignty of the Angolan state belongs entirely and solely to the Angolan people irrespective of ethnic groups, race, class, sex, age, political tendency, religious belief or philosophic conviction.[3]

The MPLA leadership has always been very careful to deny that it is a socialist movement. Agostinho Neto, the movement's president, explained in an interview:

MPLA is not a Marxist-Leninist organisation. Also, our leadership is not Marxist-Leninist. Some of us have read Marx and Lenin, but we don't consider ourselves Marxist-Leninists. We are a large organisation with various shades of opinion and different types of groups united solely under the flag of liberation. As a heterogeneous organisation, it contains both Marxist and other points of view.[4]

Assisted by the development of the Angolan economy after the second world war and the rapid growth of the black population in the cities, the MPLA succeeded in sinking roots among urban workers so deep that, particularly in Luanda, the capital, they were to last for nearly two decades, until the war of 1975-76.

In 1959 the Portuguese colonial authorities moved to crush the growing nationalist ferment. The mass arrests that followed decimated the MPLA cadre and prompted the movement's leadership to launch a premature insurrection. On 4 February 1961 MPLA supporters attacked the Sao Paolo prison in Luanda. In retaliation the settlers ran amuck in the shantytowns of the city: according to one estimate, 20,000 blacks were slaughtered. The MPLA withdrew into exile and adopted a strategy of guerilla warfare in the countryside.

The Luanda uprising was followed in March 1961 by a huge and bloody revolt of peasants and contract workers from amongst the Bakongo people of northern Angola. The army and the settlers put down the rebellion with the help of napalm and fragmentation bombs, massacring 30,000 blacks.

This rural revolt was not the work of the MPLA, but of the Union of the Peoples of Northern Angola (UPNA) which began life as a Bakongo separatist movement in 1954.

Holden Roberto, who had spent most of his life in the Belgian Congo, rapidly emerged as the leader of UPNA. In 1958 he attended the first All-African People's Conference in Accra, the capital of Ghana, which had been granted independence the previous year. Under pressure from the leaders of the African nationalist movements whom he met there, Roberto turned UPNA into the Union of the Peoples of Angola (UPA), and set as its target Angolan national independence.

After the failure of the 1961 revolt, UPA was forced into exile in the Congo, along with hundreds of thousands of Bakongo refugees. In 1962 it changed its name to the Front for the Liberation of Angola (FNLA) and formed the Revolutionary Government of Angola in Exile (GRAE). Its part in the 1961 revolt won it support from many African radicals, including

Sekou Touré, President of Guinea-Conakry, and Frantz Fanon, theoretician of the Algerian independence movement, who based much of his strategy of peasant insurrection in *The Wretched of the Earth* upon the Bakongo revolt.

However, Roberto developed other links that were to prove to be more important than his flirtations with Pan-Africanist radicalism. He drew close to the rulers of Congo Kinshasa (Zaire) under the leadership of General Mobutu Sese Soko, who owed their position to American support. (The CIA had first intervened in 1960 to topple the radical nationalist prime minister, Patrice Lumumba, and had connived in his assassination.[5])

The alliance between the FNLA and the Kinshasa regime was cemented by the long-standing friendship between Roberto and Mobutu. Ethnic links also helped - the Bakongo people spreads across the Angolan border into Zaire. Kinshasa's patronage enabled Roberto to secure the support of the CIA, which paid him a retainer of 10,000 dollars a year for 'intelligence collection' from 1961 onwards.[6]

The CIA also penetrated the FNLA. In 1964 GRAE's foreign minister, Jonas Savimbi, resigned. According to him, Roberto's American advisers included 'Muller, American subject ... as personal counsellor'; Bernhard Manhertz, 'engaged in April 1964 to direct the Angola Liberation Army' (the UPA—GRAE military wing); and the Cuban Carlos Kessel, 'a militant anti-Castroist' with US affiliations through the American trade unions.[7]

The American investment in the FNLA paid off during the years of the colonial war. From the early 1960s the MPLA was banned from operating from Zaire, despite the long common border it shares with Angola. It was forced to base itself in Zambia, and laboriously develop a front in south-eastern Angola, where a number of rural areas were liberated from the Portuguese in the late 1960s and early 1970s. Moreover, after oil was discovered in the enclave of Cabinda in the far north of the country in 1966, an agreement between Mobutu, Roberto and Gulf Oil kept FNLA forces out of Cabinda. It was left to MPLA fighters operating from Congo Brazzaville to challenge Portuguese control of Cabinda.

The CIA took out a further insurance in 1966 when Jonas Savimbi formed the National Union for the Total Independence of Angola (Unita) in the south and centre of the country. According to one CIA source, it consisted of 'twelve guys with knives' before US backing turned it into 'a well-financed, heavily armed guerilla force'.[8] In 1972 Savimbi was corresding with the Portuguese military authorities to discuss joint action against their common enemy - the MPLA.[9]

At the time of the coup in April 1974 the military situation in Angola favoured the Portuguese far more than in the other two colonies. The MPLA, which the Portuguese saw as their main enemy because of its record of struggle, its mass support among the workers of Luanda, its commitment, affirmed in February 1974, to nationalise the oil companies, and its links with the Russian-backed ANC alliance, was in bad shape, retreating, on Agostinho Neto's own admission, towards the Zambian border under pressure from the colonial forces. The Portuguese could count on a large settler population - about 500,000 strong - and on the collaboration of the other movements. Savimbi, in particular, set out to woo the settlers, declaring that 'the people of Angola are not ready for independence'[10] and signing a separate ceasefire with the Portuguese in June 1974.

The fall of the dictatorship released a flood of strikes in Luanda, involving, for example, bank workers and public transport and sugar refinery workers, which created an atmosphere of racist hysteria among Luanda whites. Egged on by Unita, they launched a series of bloody attacks on MPLA supporters in Luanda. The workers responded with *Commissoes Populaires de Bairro* (People's Neighbourhood Committees) - mass self-defence organisations that formed the basis of what came to be known as the *poder pover* (popular power) movement of workers' militias. The MPLA took over the *poder pover* movement and used it to mobilise and arm its mass base in Luanda against the FNLA and Unita.

There were internal divisions within MPLA that helped Spinola. Daniel Chipenda, a leading commander in the war against the Portuguese, headed what was called the 'Eastern Revolt' of the guerillas in the eastern liberated zones, against Agostinho Neto's leadership. He demanded the dissolution of the MPLA and the formation of a common front with FNLA after independence. These divisions within MPLA formed the background to a secret meeting between Mobutu and Spinola that took place on Sal in the Cape Verde islands in September 1974, at which they seem to have agreed on a coalition government in Angola headed by Roberto, Savimbi and Chipenda, and excluding Neto, who appeared to have been abandoned even by his staunchest supporters, Nyerere and Kaunda.

Events in Portugal prevented Spinola from following this strategy. The MFA's opposition to his plans for the colonies led to the fall of the first provisional government in July 1974. The new government, headed by Vasco Goncalves, a sympathiser of the Portuguese Communist Party, was dominated by the MFA. At their insistence, Spinola announced that the Portuguese government would support independence for all the colonies. Rosa Continho, a pro-MPLA member of the MFA, was appointed High Commissioner for Angola.

Spinola launched a counter-offensive after the Sal meeting with Mobutu. On 10 September he appealed to the 'silent majority' to support him against the Portuguese left. He warned against 'abandoning the African populations [of the colonies] to the domination of new dictatorships',[11] and assumed personal control of the negotiations over Angolan independence. But events turned against him. He was forced from power at the end of September 1974 when the 'silent majority' demonstration he had called was blocked by the mass action of Portuguese workers.

Foreign Intervention and War

Spinola's fall began a strong shift in the situation towards the MPLA. The most important indication of this shift was in Cabinda, the enclave separated from the rest of Angola by the Congo river and hedged in by Zaire and Congo-Brazzaville. The rulers of both these countries, right-wing Zaire and 'Marxist-Leninist' Congo-Brazzaville, aspired to control Cabinda's vast oil reserves, despite the fact that each supported an Angolan nationalist movement committed to the unity of the country, the FNLA and the MPLA respectively. Each regime was backed by a rival oil company, Gulf Oil in the case of Zaire and Elf-France in the case of Congo-Brazzaville.

Zaire and Congo-Brazzaville each recognised the right of self-determination of Cabinda, and each backed a wing of the flourishing secessionist movement, the Front for the Liberation of the Enclave of Cabinda, or Flec. The Mobutu-backed group, headed by Lui Ranque-Franque and enjoying excellent relations with Gulf Oil, operated from Kinshasa; and the Congolese wing, headed first by Auguste Tchioufiou, deputy general president of Elf-Congo, and then by Alfred Raoul, a former prime minister of Congo-Brazzaville, operated from there.

In November 1974 MPLA troops moved into Cabinda, rapidly seizing control of the enclave. On Rosa Continho's orders, the Portuguese troops did not interfere with the take-over. The only resistance came from black mercenaries who had served in the Portuguese anti-guerilla special forces under the command of a French right-wing fanatic called Jean Kay. They were easily defeated, although Kay was later released by the authorities of Congo-Brazzaville into whose hands he had fallen, and returned to France to play a prominent part in the Dassault scandal in 1976.

Continho's overall strategy for the Portuguese withdrawal from Angola was based on the formation of a coalition government of the three nationalist parties. Despite the MFA's support for the MPLA, they believed that excluding the FNLA from an independent Angola's government would lead to the breakup of the country, with Roberto, who was the heir to the Bakongo throne, reviving the old Kongo Kingdom under Zairean auspices in northern Angola. Moreover, some of them saw Savimbi as an arbiter between the FNLA and MPLA, and as a guarantee that Portuguese interests would not be harmed after independence.

The result was the Alvor agreement of January 1975 to form a transitional government embracing the MPLA, FNLA and Unita, and Portuguese representatives. This government was to run the country until independence on 11 November 1975, when elections were to be held to a constituent assembly. The withdrawal of Portuguese troops would not be completed until 29 February 1976, *after* independence. An elaborate structure of joint bodies embracing the Portuguese and the three parties was set up.

The negotiations leading up to this agreement took place against a background of bitter fighting between the rival movements in Luanda. The FNLA and Unita signed a formal political and military alliance in November 1975. This was followed by Daniel Chipenda's expulsion from the MPLA. He threw in his lot with Roberto and was appointed secretary-general of the FNLA. The battle lines were crystallising.

The FNLA's strategy was to destroy the MPLA before independence was proclaimed in November. To do so Roberto could count on Western assistance, which was stepped up once it became clear that Angola's independence was inevitable. According to the *New York Times*,

> The Ford administration's initial authorisation for a substantial CIA operation inside Angola came last January [1975], more than two months before the first significant Soviet build-up, well informed officials report.
>
> The administration's high-level intelligence review panel, the 40 Committee, at its January meeting agreed to permit the CIA to provide 300,000 dollars clandestinely to Holden Roberto.[12]

With the money,

> The FNLA bought up the country's major means of communications, acquiring a TV station and the leading daily

newspaper, *A Provincia de Angola*, reinstalling as its editor Rui Correira de Freitas, who had previously been exiled after being accused of complicity with the 28th September 1974 right-wing coup attempt in Portugal.[13]

The Alvor agreement rapidly collapsed under the strains caused by the FNLA's military offensive against the MPLA. At the end of March 1975, one hundred young MPLA recruits were massacred by the FNLA in Luanda, leading to fighting in which 1,000 people died. The offices of UNTA, the pro-MPLA trade-union organisation, were sacked on 30 April; FNLA soldiers seized the union's records and office equipment and killed at least 28 people. Another attack by the FNLA on the MPLA's strongholds in the Luanda *muceques* (shantytowns) led to another 700 deaths in May.

The MPLA appears initially to have tried to work within the Alvor agreement. Indeed, Agostinho Neto advocated continuing the nationalist united front even after independence, with a joint slate in the constituent assembly elections. In February 1975 the coalition government unanimously agreed on an appeal to the 'worker and trade union organisations to suspend all their strikes until the necessary regulations and measures safeguarding the rights of the working class are passed and adopted by the Transitional Government'. What was meant by 'safeguarding the rights of the working class' became clear later in the month, when the government unanimously passed a *Lei de mobilizacao* which gave them the power to 'mobilise workers and place them under military control, discipline and jurisdiction'.[14]

But, faced with the right-wing offensive, the MPLA found itself forced to mobilise its working-class supporters in Luanda. A general strike called by the MPLA and UNTA paralysed the city on 22 May. One of the strikers' demands was the dismissal of Silva Cardoso, the pro-FNLA High Commissioner who had replaced Coutinho, who had been permitting the FNLA to bring men and material across the border from Zaire and allowing Roberto's troops to take over military installations in the north, while the MPLA was banned from bringing supplies into Luanda. The MPLA's only recourse was to arm the Luanda workers. The *poder pover* self-defence committees were revived and expanded in order to provide the framework for a people's militia.

In May and June the MPLA took the offensive. Its forces gained control of the two main approach roads to Luanda from the north, which enabled them to cut off the FNLA forces from their bases. In mid-July the MPLA launched an all-out attack on the FNLA in Luanda and drove its troops out of the city. Fighting also broke out between the MPLA and Unita. Here too FAPLA (the MPLA armed wing) scored major victories, driving Unita out of the southern ports of Benguela, Mocamedes and Lobito. It looked as if the MPLA would be in control of most of the country by 11 November.

That was the cue for foreign intervention. Massive arms shipments were provided for the FNLA and Unita by the US: US Air Force Skymaster cargo planes flew in arms direct from their bases in West Germany to the FNLA airfield at Negage.[15] British mercenaries were permitted to go through passport control at Heathrow airport, even without passports. By December 1975 it was reported that about 500 American ex-servicemen had been recruited for the FNLA/Unita forces.[16] One of the recruiters, Bart Bonner, founder of Veterans for Vietnam, was quoted as saying:

> We don't know who is bankrolling this thing... There are lots of potential sources - South Africa, Zaire and Portuguese businessmen ... and somewhere along the line there may even be some American money.[17]

In January 1976 the *Christian Science Monitor* revealed that the CIA had recruited, trained and shipped to South Africa 300 mercenaries, and was waiting for the funds to send out a second group including 15 officers in the former South Vietnamese army and men on 'indefinite' leave from the US Special Forces (the 'Green Berets').[18]

In July 1975 the 40 Committee decided to send 60 million

dollars worth of aid to the FNLA and Unita, and the Administration lobbied Congress for approval for 81 million dollars worth of aid for Zaire, much of which would also go straight to the FNLA and Unita.[19]

There were other sources of support. Zairean regular troops invaded northern Angola to back up the FNLA. There were other, more surprising, backers for the FNLA. In May 1974, 200 Chinese instructors arrived in Zaire to train its troops.[20] They remained there until November 1975. According to some sources, Nyerere played some part in the supply of the Chinese instructors, since he was disengaging himself from his previous position of complete support for the MPLA at the time.[21] It was also reported that North Korean instructors attached to the Zairean army were supplied by Mobutu to the FNLA.

A Cabindan government-in-exile was set up in Paris in July 1975, followed in August by the formation of *another* government-in-exile, this time in Kinshasa with the backing of Mobutu and Gulf Oil. The SDECE - the French secret service - also actively supported the FNLA, a fact attested to by President Giscard d'Estaing when he visited Zaire in August 1975.

Then in October 1975 a South African armoured column between 2,000 and 3,000 in number invaded Angola. Preliminary discussions concerning the invasion had taken place in July when General van der Bergh of BOSS met Daniel Chipenda at Windhoek in Namibia. (By this time Chipenda had been expelled from the MPLA and had joined the FNLA as secretary-general.) And in August South Africa took control of the Cunene dam project in the far south of the country on the Namibian border. However, the decision to invade was taken in October when the hard-pressed Savimbi used Kaunda, Mobutu and Houphouet-Boigny of the Ivory Coast as intermediaries with Vorster.[22] Savimbi, despite his later disclaimers, was a supporter of detente:

In March 1975, he had praised Vorster's 'responsible role' in seeking to promote detente, and had said: 'Economic co-operation with South Africa is only realism, however much we may be opposed to the inhumanity and injustice of apartheid.'[23]

The South African intervention reflected the Vorster regime's fears about the effects of an MPLA victory on detente. Between them, Zambia and Zaire were the lynchpin of the detente policy. Mobutu was one of the FNLA's most committed backers; Kaunda had switched his support from the MPLA to Unita during the 1972-74 period. Both were threatened by the closure of the Benguela railway, which hit at the main trade outlet of their shaky economies. Moreover, an MPLA victory would provide SWAPO with a secure base out of Kaunda's reach (SWAPO had previously operated from Zambia), give heart to the opponents of detente among the Zimbabwean nationalists, and strengthen the isolated Frelimo regime, which was MPLA's staunchest supporter in black Africa.

The invasion of Angola was seen by the South Africans as part and parcel of detente. The *Star* commented:

> Our involvement will be utterly defensible in the Western world. We will be fighting alongside Africa, for Africa. We will be paying in blood our membership dues to join the community of African nations.
>
> In this sense, there is no easy validity in some overseas comment that our role in Angola, present or future, will prejudice detente. If anything it should strengthen the new and fragile links that hold the detente policy together.[24]

A later issue of the *Star* summed up what the MPLA's defeat would mean for detente: 'If the West wins, victory could usher in - in the way already paved by detente - an unprecedented degree of economic and political cooperation between South Africa and black Africa.'[25]

The invasion column was not made up of South African troops alone, but included white mercenaries, members of the fascist Portuguese Liberation Army (ELP) and the troops of Chipenda's personal command, *Esquadrao Chipenda*. The column drove straight for the ports of Benguela, Lobito and Mocamedes, which rapidly fell, and then headed northwards for Luanda. They were joined by a further 2,000 to 3,000 mechanised South African cavalry early in December, and two wings of South African fighter bombers which operated from southern Zaire.[26]

The invaders were banking on a quick kill. They hoped to cut Luanda off from its food and water supplies, calculating that the city, its population swollen to a million by refugees, could not hold out for long.

The strategy failed. A major reason was the military aid the MPLA received from the Soviet Union. In January 1976 Henry Kissinger claimed that Russia had supplied 200 million dollars' worth of military assistance. According to Neto, the MPLA received from the Russians MiG 21s, T34 and T54 tanks, armoured personnel carriers, anti-tank and Sam-7 missiles, rocket launchers and Ak-47 rifles.[27] An expeditionary force of Cuban troops was also sent to back up FAPLA; by January 1976 they were estimated to have numbered 9,000.[28]

Neither the Russians nor the Cubans supported the MPLA out of pure altruism. The Moscow bureaucracy had a great deal to gain from the collapse of the existing regimes in the region, if only because of the blow that this would represent to Western economic and strategic interests. As for the Cubans, the American blockade had made the Castro regime heavily dependent on Russia, and led to Castro's emergence as one of the most loyal supporters of the Moscow foreign policy line in the Third World. He defended the Russian invasion of Czechoslovakia and backed the Chilean Communist Party in its search for an alliance with the Christian Democratic Party, one of the main instigators of the 1973 coup. Given the prestige deriving from their 1958 revolution, the Cubans were a much more acceptable form of military assistance to the MPLA than Russian troops would have been.

Another factor in the Russian intervention was undoubtedly the rivalry with China. Russia's prestige in the semi-colonial countries had taken a number of bad knocks, particularly in the

Arab East, as a result of the expulsion of Russian advisers from Egypt in 1972 and the US's diplomatic successes after the October 1973 war. Meanwhile, Chinese influence in Africa had been growing, particularly as a result of the Russian invasion of Czechoslovakia and the Chinese role in building the Tanzam railway.

China, meanwhile, played a major part in orchestrating the international propaganda campaign against the MPLA. A statement issued in Peking when Angola became independent in November 1975 called for 'a government of national unity' in the country. The war, it continued, was

> entirely the result of the rivalry between the two Super-Powers, and particularly the undisguised expansion and crude interference of the Soviet Union... They [the Russian leadership] deliberately created a split among the liberation organisations, sent in large quantities of arms, supported one organisation alone and wantonly slandered and attacked the other two organisations, and thus single-handedly provoked the civil war in Angola. The Soviet Union had also tried constantly to sow discord and create disharmony among African states. These actions of the Soviet leadership have fully revealed its true features as social-imperialism.[29]

This statement is a good example of the pro-Western character of Chinese foreign policy. It starts off by denouncing *both* Superpowers, and then rapidly switches to an attack on one of them: the Russians. The Chinese rhetoric of 'Superpower hegemonism' and 'Soviet social imperialism' became a regular feature of the litany by which the leaders of the anti-MPLA alliance - Kaunda and Mobutu, Roberto and Savimbi - justified their position: thus Kaunda's speech at the OAU conference in January 1976 extravagantly praised China's role at the same time as it laid the blame for the war at the door of the 'Superpowers' (although he refused to condemn American or South African intervention).[30] The Chinese rhetoric crept even into the South African leaders' speeches: thus Hilgard Muller accused Russia and Cuba of 'Red neo-colonialism in its most aggressive form'.[31]

No rhetoric could conceal the fact that the South African quick kill strategy had failed. The expeditionary force had been halted before it could reach Luanda and the MPLA was exploiting the stalemate in the south to attack FNLA strongholds in the north. It rapidly became clear that FNLA and Unita could not survive militarily on their own and that in order to win South Africa would have to commit far more men and material over a much longer period than had been anticipated.

At the same time, a backlash of support for the MPLA was building up within Africa. Even the pro-Western and conservative Nigerian military regime could not stomach the idea of an Angolan government being placed in power by South African bayonets. At the OAU conference Nigeria switched from opposing to supporting the Russian and Cuban presence. Nyerere then came down on the MPLA's side. It was clearly one thing to trade and negotiate with South Africa and quite another to permit Pretoria to become the arbiter of who ruled individual African states.

An additional factor assisting the MPLA was the vacillating policy pursued by the US. Intervention in Angola was the personal policy of Ford and Kissinger. It was opposed by the African specialists in the State Department, who favoured a diplomatic offensive to isolate the MPLA in Africa and build up support for an all-party coalition government. Kissinger sacked two successive Assistant Secretaries of State for African Affairs, Donald Easum and Nathaniel Davis, who wished to press ahead with the 'African' option. Support for this option was also provided by the CIA, the Department of Defence and the Joint Chiefs of Staff. However, Kissinger, preoccupied with the need for a show of strength to rebuild American credibility after Vietnam, overruled them at the July 1975 National Security Council meeting. With Ford's backing he went ahead and ordered direct US intervention in Angola.[32]

However, the American ruling class as a whole was not prepared to risk a repetition of the Vietnam debacle. Congress was opposed to direct involvement, and in December 1975 the Senate voted to block the funds necessary for further intervention in Angola.

The way was now clear for the 'African' solution advocated by Amin, Kaunda and other OAU leaders, as well as by European governments like the British: an attempt to persuade the MPLA to return to the pre-July situation of participating in a coalition government with the FNLA and Unita. The way would then be open for the right-wing movements, with backing from Zaire, Zambia, the US and South Africa, to mount another, possibly more successful, attack on the MPLA, similar to that attempted during the first half of 1975 under the Alvor agreement.

This strategy required time to work. The economy was deteriorating by the beginning of 1976, industrial production was down to 20 per cent of capacity and many crops had not been picked or sown because of the war.[33] Moreover, in December 1975 Gulf Oil suspended operations in Cabinda, under pressure from the US Administration. According to one source, nearly all MPLA's foreign exchange came from Gulf's royalties.[34] Lopo de Nascimento, prime minister in the MPLA government, estimated that 75 per cent of their fuel had been supplied by Gulf. However, he ruled out the nationalisation of Gulf's interests or those of other foreign companies in the country.[35] It looked as if economic pressure alone would force the MPLA to settle.

However, events moved more quickly than the supporters of the 'African' solution had bargained for. After driving off the South African attack on Luanda, the MPLA took to the offensive. Pushing north, FAPLA smashed through FNLA's defences. This was followed by an offensive in the south at the end of January. By mid-February FNLA and Unita had been defeated.

These victories swung the diplomatic battle in the MPLA's favour. By early February a majority of the OAU had recognised Neto's government; the EEC followed suit on 17-18 February.

The South Africans decided to cut their losses. Vorster had been subjected to very heavy pressure to withdraw, especially from big business. By the end of January 1976, the Johannesburg *Financial Mail* could write: 'Our involvement has been a military miscalculation and a diplomatic disaster for which the country may have to pay a very high price indeed.'[36] By early February, South African troops had been withdrawn to a *cordon sanitaire* 50 kilometres deep on the Angolan side of the Namibian border.[37] The victorious MPLA forces avoided a military confrontation with them, and eventually an agreement was reached under which the South Africans would withdraw in exchange for the MPLA guaranteeing the security of the Cunene dam.

8. Soweto:
the Black Townships Explode

In June 1976 a youth rebellion exploded in the black townships of South Africa.

There was a direct relation between the Angolan war and the black revolt. The South African intervention had led to the largest military mobilisation since the second world war; the length of service for national servicemen in the 'operational area' had been extended from three to twelve weeks. A war fever had gripped white South Africa in the first few months of 1976, as the scale of the country's involvement filtered through the censorship.

At the end of it all there was nothing but humiliation. White South African prisoners of war were displayed at press conferences in various black African capitals. The invading troops had to pull out: the most powerful military machine in Africa south of the Sahara had been bested by black fighters. No amount of talk about Russians or Cubans could mask this fact.

The message of the South African defeat spread among black people like wildfire. An eye-witness described to us how in Cape Town huge black audiences would watch the television news in Coloured hotels and cheer every report of South African casualties in 'the operational zone'.

The MPLA's victory in Angola, along with Frelimo's victory in Mozambique (remember the flow of Mozambicans going to the gold mines every year), helped to instil in black South Africans the confidence that their white rulers could be taken on and beaten.

The Background to the Uprising

While the Angolan debacle provided the catalyst to the revolt, other factors combined to create in South Africa the severest crisis it had faced since Sharpeville.

The boom had run to a halt. The real rate of growth in 1975 was 2.5 per cent.[1] In 1976 industrial activity fell sharply. In the crucial metal and engineering industries investment spending was expected to fall by 20 per cent in real terms in 1976.[2] The motor industry was particularly badly hit, with sales falling, prices slashed, dealers going out of business, workers being laid off or put onto short time working.

The economic crisis was partly a delayed product of the international recession, partly a result of the fall in the price of gold, which played havoc with the balance of payments. Added to this was a very high level of government spending. Government real consumption rose by 15.5 per cent that year, reflecting the investment in huge state and parastatal projects started during the heady period when the gold price was high; capital spending by the public sector grew by 38 per cent.[3]

A more serious long-term worry for South African capitalists was the rise in defence spending. The 1975 defence budget had gone up by 50 per cent; this was followed by another 42 per cent increase in 1976, lifting the defence outlay to R1,350 million in 1976/77, 300 per cent more than its level in 1973/74, and 17.2 per cent of the total budget.[4] The result of all these factors is that South African capitalists are finding it increasingly difficult to finance new investments from their own internal resources: in 1973 own funds covered 74 per cent of new investments; in 1974 47 per cent; in 1975 30 per cent.[5] Forced to borrow, they find themselves competing with the government for funds and paying the high interest rates that result from the government's need to pay for the military machine and to attract back frightened foreign capital. Fixed investment rose only 4 per cent in 1975.[6] No wonder big business demanded that public spending be cut, and that the government withdraw from Angola.

The effect of the crisis on black workers was devastating. Unemployment was expected to reach 2 million by the end of 1976 (out of a total population less than half the size of Britain or West Germany). The government and the employers exploited the situation to strike hard at trade-union activists. Strikes by black workers fell off markedly: according to the Minister of Labour they caused 1.3 million man-hours lost in 1973, 653,000 in 1974 and only 86,000 in the eight months to September 1975.[7]

At the same time, inflation bit into black wages. Price rises ran at about 14 per cent in 1975. Food prices rose much more rapidly - about 30 per cent. In May 1976, the poverty datum line (PDL), the lowest subsistence level for an African family of five in Soweto, was estimated at R129.05 a month, 75 per cent above what it had been in November 1970. In the six months between November 1975 and May 1976, fuel and transport costs rose 18 per cent, clothing 9 per cent, food 7 per cent.[8] Meanwhile, the average African family was estimated to have a monthly income of R73 a month.[9] Even a black representative on the government's own regional labour committee for the East Rand protested against increased bus fares and school fees, saying: 'The black man can no longer live... You are killing the future of our children.'[10]

The black people of South Africa faced a deteriorating economic situation while they watched their rulers retreat before black resistance in Mozambique and Angola.

The situation was compounded by the fact that the regime had been pledged, by its ambassador at the UN, Pik Botha, in a speech in September 1974, to move away from discrimination based on race and colour, and by the deep divisions within the Nationalist Party between the *verligtes* (the so-called liberals committed to the new policy) and the *verkramptes* (the hardliners opposed to it) two of whose leading spokesmen are M.C. Botha, Minister of Bantu Administration and Development, and his deputy, appointed in January 1976, Andries Treurnicht.

This promised 'domestic detente' was not, as it might seem,

a renunciation of Catholicism by the Pope. It was seen to fit in with separate development. It involved an extension of the moves already taken in some places to eliminate what is called 'petty apartheid' - separate white and black benches in public places, etc, and to integrate black workers in the negotiating machinery - hence the promised, although not implemented, introduction of industrial committees.

It involved some improvement in the status of black workers. At the time of the rand devaluation in 1975, the government announced in a joint statement with employers and white union leaders that:

> In cases where trade unions and employers are unwilling to take steps with regard to the reclassification of work ... government undertakes to motivate continuously, in a positive manner, employees and employers to reach agreement.

In other words, the regime pledged itself to push the colour bar upwards and bring cheaper black workers into more skilled jobs. This did not stop the wage gap between white skilled workers and black semi-skilled workers widening from R158 a month in 1975 to R182 a month in 1976.[11]

The regime pressed ahead with the granting of independence to the Homelands, with the Transkei as the first (in October 1976). Vorster insisted that the 1.3 million Xhosas living outside the Transkei should be forced to become citizens of the new statelet, and should be deprived of South African citizenship. Concessions to urban blacks were tied to the Bantustan policy: when the government announced that blacks would once again be permitted to take 30-year urban leaseholds, it was made conditional on citizenship of a Homeland; similarly, relaxations in restrictions on African traders were made conditional on citizenship of a Homeland.

Domestic detente involved no relaxation of the aim of separate development - the denial of political rights to blacks in the town. Soon after Pik Botha's speech in the UN, Vorster underlined this fact: outside the Bantustans 'the Whites will rule and let there be no mistake about it'. As the *Financial Mail* summed it up:

> Government's ultimate aim is to force each and every African in the Republic ostensibly to become a citizen of one or other Bantustan, so that it can legitimate its refusal to grant them political rights in 'White' South Africa. They will then be 'foreigners' present temporarily in the 'White' areas as guest workers. The Transkei is the first step in this direction. Discrimination will no longer be based on race or colour, so the government will claim, but on nationality.[12]

At the same time the regime took steps to tighten the migratory labour system. It enforced the Physical Planning Act which makes it an offence for industrialists in most areas to employ more than 2 or 2.5 blacks to every 1 white. 100,000 black workers could lose their jobs if the law were applied rigorously.[13]

The effect of domestic detente on the lives of black South Africans was so small as to be non-existent. A review of the policy by the *Financial Mail* about a year after it was introduced hammered the grim facts home: the *increase* in defence spending in 1975-76 was more than the *total* allocated to African education; the daily prison population was 99,000, of whom one third had been gaoled under the pass laws; one in every four blacks was arrested every year for technical infringements of laws applicable to blacks only.[14]

When the explosion came it was over the enforced teaching of Afrikaans in African schools in Soweto, an illustration of the way in which African education was subordinated to the priorities of the apartheid system. Verwoerd had long since explained:

> There is no place for [the African] in the European community above the level of certain forms of labour... For that reason it is of no avail for him to receive a training which has as its aim absorption in the European community. What is the use of teaching a Bantu child mathematics when it cannot use it in practice?[15]

Thus, in 1973-74, 483 rand were spent by the government on the education of every white child and 28 rand on the education of every African child.[16]

There were other issues in the uprising. Soweto is a vast black city of between 1 and 1½ million inhabitants, lacking in most facilities (86 per cent of homes are without electricity, 93 per cent without a shower or bath, 97 per cent without hot water). It has an unemployment rate of 54 per cent.[17] School-children with a prospect of little but unemployment and starvation wages ahead of them and the young unemployed led the rebellion.

Organisations willing to lead the rebellion were not lacking. The black consciousness movement had emerged in the early 1970s among African students. It took shape in the South African Students Organisation (SASO) and then the Black People's Convention (BPC), whose distinctive note, apart from opposition to any form of collaboration with the regime through the Bantustans, Urban Bantu Councils etc, was a stress upon the liberation struggle as a struggle of blacks. Only as a movement of blacks, led by blacks, could it succeed. Whites could only play a supernumerary role.

Their approach cut across the SACP's strategy of an alliance between blacks and white 'democrats' and recalled the Africanism of the PAC. Indeed, the PAC has, at the level of ideas at least, had an influence upon BPC and SASO, as have various Churches and other bodies on the ANC itself. In its essentials, however, the black consciousness movement was a new movement. It reflected the militancy of a generation of young blacks who had been born and raised under Nationalist rule, and whose ideas were far closer to those of the US Black Power groups of the 1960s than to those of either ANC or PAC. It is worth noting, in the light of ANC's claims to have led the black youth movement, what Tsietsi Mashinini, exiled president of the Soweto Student Representative Council which led the rebellion in the township, has to say:

As far as the students in South Africa are concerned, the

ANC and PAC are extinct internally. Externally we are aware they exist. Internally they are doing no work, there may be some underground work they are doing which we are not aware of, but as far as the struggle is concerned they are not doing anything.[18]

After the April coup in Portugal, SASO and BPC organised a demonstration in solidarity with Frelimo. They declared their support for the MPLA while South African troops were still in Angola. Their school-student wing, the South African Student Movement (SASM) was active in the Soweto schools in the lead-up to the June 1976 uprising.

There were other indicators of the explosion to come. A militant bus boycott against fare increases had won massive support from the workers of Kwa Thema township near Johannesburg in March 1976. A small 500-strong demonstration outside the Rand Supreme Court in Johannesburg, also in March, was joined by black workers on the way to catch trains home from Johannesburg Central Station nearby. The demonstration rapidly swelled to 2,000 or more, chanting black power slogans and throwing stones and bottles at the police and passing cars. The police had to draw their guns to disperse them. The ANC was also more active underground than it had been for many years. However, in the period immediately before the uprising, a number of its leading activists were picked up by the police.

The Uprising and the Regime's Response

The time has not yet come to make a final judgement about the uprising in Soweto and the other black townships, although a number of points can be made.

First, the Soweto events have been compared with the Sharpeville massacre sixteen years before. This is fine as far as it goes: the regime responded to the rebellion with its customary brutality - with guns, nightsticks, armoured cars, helicopters, tear gas, alsatians, detention orders. But there is a fundamental difference between the two events. Sharpeville was simply the most prominent in a series of events in which a mass movement that had fought throughout the 1950s was crushed. Soweto, by contrast, is the highest point reached so far in a *rising* wave of struggles. There are a number of other struggles one can point to - the Natal strikes, the turmoil in the mines, the emergence of the black consciousness movement among African students, there are the struggles reflecting the *general* crisis in Southern Africa - the liberation wars in Angola, Mozambique, Namibia and Zimbabwe, the evolution of the Kaunda regime, and so on. South Africa is clearly entering a period of massive confrontations between the regime and the oppressed black population.

Second, the rebellion was the work of the black youth in the townships. It is they who seized and maintained the offensive in both Soweto and Cape Town. Not only did they organise and lead the movement *within* the townships, they took it beyond to the streets of central Johannesburg and Cape Town. It was also they who called for and organised two massive solidarity strikes in late August and mid-September in the areas where the youth movement was strongest.

In the Cape it was the Coloured youth who swept into the leadership. By proclaiming their unity with their African brothers, they nullified the regime's efforts to buy them off with a status slightly higher than Africans or Indians, a status that was simultaneously being undermined by measures such as the reintroduction of influx controls for Coloureds, for the first time since 1828, the imposition of forced labour for Coloured youths under the Coloured Cadet Centres scheme, and massive removals of Coloureds in the Western Cape.

Third, the movement rejected the leadership of the African petty bourgeoisie. We have already noted how T.J. Makyaya and Richard Maponya, leaders of Soweto's petty bourgeoisie, were forced to flee to white areas to save themselves from the anger of the young blacks. This anger was aimed not only at the property of the Bantu administration - offices, schools, bottlestores - but also at the organs of black collaboration: the puppet parliament of the Bophuthatswana Homeland was burned down by young blacks in Mafeking.

The response to the rebellion was complex. In March Gatsha Buthelezi, the most politically astute of the Bantustan leaders, addressed a rally of 10,000 blacks in Soweto to launch his Zulu movement, *Inkatha Ye Sizwe*. Wearing a guerilla-style uniform he told white South Africans that it was up to them to choose between majority rule and bloodshed.

A few months later Buthelezi was playing a different, more sinister role. The mass of his support in the township came from Zulu migrant workers crowded together in all-male barracks like the huge Mzimhlope hostel with 10,000 inmates segregated on tribal lines. During the stay-at-home of 23-25 August, Zulu workers from Mzimhlope went on the rampage. Armed with butcher's knives, *pangas* (canecutters), tomahawks, *insthumentsu* (sharpened spikes), knobkerries and stones, they attacked and killed a number of black youths while armed police stood by.

The attack was undoubtedly encouraged by the police to break the strike. A journalist from the *Rand Daily Mail* overheard an officer telling off a meeting in Mzimhlope hostel for burning down houses: 'We didn't order you to destroy property. You were asked to fight people only, so you are asked to withdraw immediately.'[19] More Zulus serve in the police than any other African tribal group. Buthelezi was forced to backtrack: he denied that there was an alliance between the police and *Inkatha*, although he did admit that '*Inkatha* had been a force for peace in Natal'.[20]

Inkatha's activities in Soweto fitted in with the regime's tactic of forming black vigilante squads. A few weeks before the August stay-at-home, M.P. Botha, the Minister of Defence, told the Natal Nationalist Congress that blacks would be allowed to form units connected with the Defence Force commandos. He explained that the security of South Africa could be ensured only if 'we can succeed in establishing a strong middle class among the Black and Brown people as well.'[21]

Soweto forced the South African ruling class to take account of the urban blacks. There were a number of calls for reform. *Volkshandel*, organ of the *Afrikaanse Handelsinstitut*, the Afrikaner Chamber of Commerce and Industry, called for a new deal for blacks in 'white' urban areas - the right to a healthy family life and to own their own homes, improved education and training, better job opportunities - based on the heretical recognition that black urbanisation was inevitable and desirable.[22]

The editor of the influential Nationalist paper, *Die Transvaler*, Wilhelm de Klerk, wrote: 'If we want to avert the revolution now is the time for the White rulers to judge and give effect to the justice of Black claims.'[23] De Klerk, along with Louis Nel, a rising Nationalist back-bencher, called for home ownership and local government rights for urban blacks; improved facilities in the townships; higher wages and better job opportunities for blacks; and political bargaining rights via the Homeland governments.[24]

The Transvaal Chamber of Industry, representing the major concentration of industrial capital in South Africa, submitted a memorandum to the government in which it argued: 'We regard it essential to recognise the permanence of the urban black in contrast to viewing him as a temporary sojourner... The Blacks' desire for a form of civil self-government in the townships must be recognised.'[25] However, the memorandum went on to argue that 'influx control is in the interest of both Black and White' and it did not mention Africans' political or trade-union rights.[26]

The regime has already gone some way towards implementing these reforms. 30-year leasehold rights for urban blacks have finally been conceded, without the requirement that leaseholders be Homeland citizens. Statements by ministers like M.C. Botha (Bantu Administration) and Jimmy Kruger (Police) suggest that Africans will be given self-government within the townships. There is a move towards what might be called the Bantustanisation of the townships, in which the black petty bourgeoisie will be given a few political spoils and some economic incentives in exchange for running the townships and maintaining the structure of apartheid.

There are undoubtedly blacks who will be prepared to play this role. An example is Sam Motsuenyana, president of the National African Federated Chamber of Commerce and chairman of the African Bank of South Africa, who told the *Financial Mail* that he feared the young blacks were taking 'the path of destruction' and put his faith 'in the business community'.[27]

There have been conflicts within the anti-apartheid movement in the townships. Two main currents have emerged. The first is that of the young black militants influenced by BPC and SASO, who organised and led the marches on Johannesburg and the stay-at-homes. Their strategy seems to be a simple one - black power now.

The second current is centred around the Black Parents' Association (BPA) in Soweto. Formed in June as an umbrella organisation it embraces SASO and BPC, as well as more 'moderate' organisations. The support of ANC is suggested by the presence on its Executive of Winnie Mandela, the wife of Nelson Mandela. BPA has been careful to keep the lines open both to the quisling Urban Bantu Council and the minority of South African capitalists like Anton Rupert and Harry Oppenheimer who might not oppose black involvement in the national government. BPA leaders have been careful to stress their respectability. Thus Winnie Mandela said: 'There is nothing subversive about our aims. We will speak for the black parent and child just as the Whites speak for their child...'[28]

There have already been clashes between the BPA and the young militants. Before the second march on the police headquarters in John Vorster Square, Johannesburg, to protest against the many arrests after the June uprising, a mass meeting was held to discuss the demonstration. A plea to delay the march until Kruger had replied to a BPA memorandum was rejected, and the march went ahead.[29]

In the event, the BPA's approaches were spurned. All of its executive, except for Manas Buthelezi, the chairman, have been detained. A minority of capitalists like Oppenheimer might well be prepared to see trade-union and even limited political rights conceded to blacks. But they are a minority. Most capitalists in South Africa need apartheid, and with it repression.

The Youth Rebellion and Workers' Struggles

South Africa's young blacks have put the destruction of apartheid on the agenda again. Their rebellion has been carried out with tremendous courage and militancy. They have shaken the regime to its foundations and braved one of the strongest and most ruthless repressive machines in the world. However, their rebellion has its limits. Young unemployed blacks and schoolchildren do not have the power to topple apartheid. That power lies only in the hands of the black working class, which did not take the lead in the Soweto events. Workers acted, massively, but only in response to, in solidarity with, the initiatives of the black youth.

The black youth rebellion bears similarities with the student revolts in the advanced capitalist countries in the 1960s. Both movements developed with fantastic militancy, verve, imagination, spontaneously and rapidly generalising from their own specific oppression to the overall political battle, leaving the workers' movement way behind. At the same time, both movements lacked the power to break the system.[30]

The gap between the black youth movement and the mass of workers is indicated in two ways. The first, of course, was the strike breaking part played by the Zulu workers in Soweto at the end of August 1976, reflecting their position halfway between the stable urban working class and the mass of impoverished dependents in the Homelands; atomised, unsettled, still open to the tribalist appeals of quislings like Buthelezi. However, it is worth noting that those same Zulu workers, stung by the hostility they met in August, played an active role in winning support for the mid-September strike.[31]

More significant was the comparative calm that ruled at the centre of the 1973 strikes, the Durban area, where black workers are comparatively well-organised and have a record of militancy. There the movement adopted a cautious, defensive posture, and were clearly reluctant to risk jobs and wages at a time of high unemployment, recession and inflation. The leadership of the Durban workers' movement has also been a factor. Buthelezi and the KwaZulu tribal leadership have some influence over workers in Natal, many of whom are Zulu. Moreover, as we have seen, the leadership of the black trade unions either has identified itself with the white trade-union bureaucracy, as in the case of Lucy Mvubelo of the National Union of Garment Workers, or has ducked political questions, like TUACC, which is the most influential black trade-union grouping in Natal.

Nonetheless the attitudes of both government and employers towards the black trade unions hardened in the wake of the township rebellions. One indication of this was the treatment meted out at a strike by black workers at Armourplate Safety Glass, owned by Pilkingtons in Britain, against the dismissal of three workers. The strike began in late August 1976 and dragged on until early November, the longest African strike in the country's history, an impressive feat by miserably underpaid workers organised in a union, the black Glass and Allied Workers Union, too poor to provide strike pay. The employers went all out to break the strike. When the chairman of the African works committee went to meet the manager, the latter and his three companions were ostentatiously brandishing revolvers (there has been a tremendous boom in gun sales to white South Africans since Soweto). The police were there to back up the management. 27 strike pickets were arrested and fined under the Riotous Assemblies Act. Groups of workers were hauled in for questioning by the security police.

Shortly after the collapse of the Armourplate strike, the government moved against the black trade unions. A number of leading union activists were served with banning orders effectively excluding them from all political, trade-union and social activities and forbidding them to leave their town of residence. The TUACC group of unions was particularly badly hit. Alpheus Mthethwa, general secretary of the Metal and

Allied Workers Union, which had led bitter recognition disputes in Leyland and Heinemann Electric, was among those banned, along with two other union officials; an organiser in the National Union of Textile Workers was also banned. White trade union activists did not escape the banning orders either: Loet Doewes Dekker of the Urban Training Project was banned, along with five young whites connected with the Institute for Industrial Education. The scrupulous avoidance of political involvement by these groups had not saved them from government repression.

The problem of relating the black youth movement to the mass of African workers has been compounded by the traditions of black resistance in South Africa. The main weapon used to draw in black workers has been the stay-at-home, a form of political general strike.

However, as a tactic, the stay-at-home has definite limitations. These were summed up by South African revolutionary socialists at the time of Sharpeville:

> Firstly, the people of the townships cannot stay at home indefinitely. To do so is to starve. Even if food is stored in advance the families cannot hold out for long because of the presence of the children, the sick and the aged. The townships can be sealed off and starved out only too effectively by small detachments of the army and the police...
>
> Secondly, by staying in the townships, the worker surrenders all initiative. He cuts himself off from his fellow-workers in other townships. He divides himself from his allies in the rural areas, and he surrenders the entire economic centre to his enemies.[32]

A political general strike is the most direct challenge to the ruling class short of armed insurrection. But it does not resolve the question of power. That can only be done by a seizure of power on the part of a revolutionary party. However, if the conditions for such a seizure of power do not exist - and they certainly do not exist in South Africa today - resort to continual general strikes will either exhaust and demoralise the mass of workers or turn such actions into the sort of gestures that they have become in the hands of the Italian and French Communist Parties. In the South African situation, where bourgeois democracy does not exist for black workers, exhaustion, demoralisation and repression is the greater danger. It is no surprise that the threatened three-week stay-at-home in Soweto that was being discussed in September 1976 did not materialise.[33]

A call by the Soweto Student Representative Council for a further stay-at-home in November 1976 also met with little response. The workers were not prepared to lose money for a purely demonstrative action. In other respects the SRC continued to exercise enormous influence, closing down the township's *shebeens*, or illegal bars, and successfully banning sports events - football in particular is immensely popular - for a number of weeks. The danger is that a growing alienation between the youth and the mass of workers in the township will, combined with the ferocious repression of school students with which the police responded to the successful boycott of exams in Soweto, encourage the young militants to take up arms against the regime. The prospect would then be a repetition of the early 1960s, with the mass of black workers looking on passively while isolated young fighters take on the massive military power of the regime and are crushed.

The stay-at-home tactic has sharply diminishing returns. Unfortunately, it is deeply embedded in the traditions of the black resistance in South Africa. For example, in 1963, at the height of the post-Sharpeville repression, the South African Communist Party argued that: 'In the present period the advanced section of the workers ... should strive to broaden out every militant struggle for higher wages with a view to including every category of workers in regional and national general strikes.'[34]

Of course revolutionary socialists should always be looking for ways to raise the level of workers' struggles and to generalise them into the struggle for political power. However, the workers' movement is too valuable to be squandered in battles that are lost before they are joined. If the mass of workers do not have the confidence in their ability to confront the state - as was true in South Africa in 1963, and as is true today - it is criminal to demoralise and exhaust them in strikes that can be fought through to the finish only by armed insurrection. But if workers are not prepared to fight for power, they may well be prepared to engage in 'the traditional trade union pattern of each section fighting piecemeal for its particular demands'.[35] Such partial economic struggles - especially if they are won, and the Natal strikes show that black workers *can* win in South Africa - may instil in workers the confidence and the organisation to take on the wider battles.

The importance of economic struggles in developing workers' confidence arises from their position in capitalist society. The exploitation of workers is a product of their place in the process of capitalist production. They are exploited because the capitalist sets them to work in his factory for a longer time than that necessary to replace the value of their labour power. This differentiates workers from peasants, who are exploited through the political apparatus - taxation or the landlord's monopoly of violence - or through the market - the moneylender and the middleman. We have seen that the exploitation of workers in South Africa is fundamentally the same as that of workers everywhere. It is his position in the productive process that sets the worker at odds with the capitalist and forces him to combine with his fellow workers to fight the boss. It is through the struggle for power where they are exploited - in the factory - over wages, conditions, speed-up, etc, that workers acquire the confidence and organisation to move beyond the factory to take on the capitalist state.

Rosa Luxemburg, summing up the experience of the Russian revolution of 1905, where, as in South Africa, anti-capitalist and democratic struggles merged, analysed the way in which political and economic struggles interact:

The movement on the whole does not proceed from the economic struggle to the political struggle, not even the reverse. Every great political mass action, after it has attained its political highest point, breaks up into a mass of economic strikes. And that applies not merely to each of the great mass strikes, but also to the revolution as a whole. With the spreading, clarifying and involution of the political struggle the economic struggle not merely does not recede, but extends, organises and becomes involved in equal measure. Between the two there is the most complete reciprocal action.

Every new onset and every fresh victory of the political struggle is transformed into a powerful impetus for the economic struggle extending at the same time its external possibilities and intensifying the inner urge of the workers to better their position, and their desire to struggle. After every foaming wave of political action a fructifying deposit remains behind from which a thousand stalks of economic struggle shoot forth. And conversely. The workers' condition of ceaseless economic struggle with the capitalists keeps their fighting energy alive in every political interval, it forms, so to speak, the permanent fresh reservoir of the strength of the proletarian classes, from which the political fight ever renews its strength and at the same time leads the indefatigable economic sappers of the proletariat at all times now here and now there, to isolated sharp conflicts, out of which political conflicts on a large scale unexpectedly explode.[36]

The problem in South Africa today is to translate the political militancy of the black youth into a revolutionary leadership in the factories. The ruling class is well aware of the danger such a prospect presents. The *Financial Mail* wrote: 'Today's Black youth are clearly far more militant than the youth of yesterday. What may happen when they themselves enter the labour force and start taking jobs in factories, mines and offices is a chastening throught.'[37] We shall pursue this question in the final chapter.

9. Detente Phase Two: the Kissinger Deal

The MPLA victory was a devastating defeat for detente in Southern Africa. South African intervention led to a backlash in MPLA's favour in black Africa and once its victory was assured, even Mobutu moved quickly to recognise the Neto government.

More important, the Angolan debacle made impossible the overt alliance between Vorster and Kaunda that had been the main result of detente. Kaunda hastily shifted his ground, announced that a settlement in Zimbabwe was out of the question, and that only a bloodbath would free the country. With the collapse of the settlement talks between Smith and Nkomo (announced in March 1976 but already a foregone conclusion), Kaunda had in any case nothing concrete to show for his highly compromising dealings with Vorster. The situation was compounded when South African troops entered Zambia on 11 July and killed a number of villagers at Sialola. By August 1976 Kaunda was making emotional speeches, dismissing any possibility of negotiation and declaring: 'Now we fight'.

It looked now as if the five black frontline presidents - Kaunda of Zambia, Nyerere of Tanzania, Khama of Botswana, Machel of Mozambique and Neto of Angola - were presenting a solid front in support of armed struggle in Zimbabwe and Namibia and in opposition to any further talks with Vorster and Smith.

The reality was a bit more complex, marked by a major shift in the policy of the Western imperialist governments towards Southern Africa.

First, the United States thrust aside the traditional colonial power, Britain, and intervened directly in the region in order to end the confrontation between the black and white states. Henry Kissinger visited the major black African states in April 1976, followed this up with a meeting with Vorster in June, and then, apparently, won a settlement in Rhodesia after meeting Vorster and Smith in Pretoria at the end of September 1976.

The US diplomatic offensive was motivated by the realisation after the Angolan war that the crisis in Southern Africa seriously threatened the interests of Western capital and offered the Russian bureaucracy major opportunities.

The US administration set out to stabilise the situation by building up those states crucial to its interests in Africa. This policy operated well beyond the limits of Southern Africa. Kenya, one of the most pro-Western states in the continent, was surrounded by hostile regimes armed by Russia and China - Tanzania, Uganda and Somalia. The crisis in the East African community and the raid on Entebbe by Israeli troops, although largely the product of the vagaries of the brutal and incompetent Amin regime in Uganda, indicated some of the tensions in the area. Added to this was the crisis in Ethiopia, where the pro-Western *Derg* faced a rebellious working class and peasantry, the Eritrean independence movement and the possibility of war with the Russian-backed Somalian regime. And of course, within Southern Africa itself, the shaky Mobutu regime in Zaire was faced with a hostile and pro-Russian state across the border in Angola.

In June 1976 the US Secretary of Defence, Donald Rumsfeld, paid a visit to Africa which, although much less publicised than Kissinger's, was equally significant. He drew up with Kenyatta and Mobutu the outlines of major arms deals. As the *New York Times* put it: 'If Congress approves these programmes, the United States could be on its way to becoming the major source of arms to these countries and Ethiopia.'[1]

But guns would not solve the problems of the state crucial to Western interests below the Sahara, South Africa. There the outstanding problem was to find a means of renewing the movement towards detente between Vorster and the black governments.

Its solution involved three elements. First, the Western governments needed to take a much clearer line than hitherto in favour of majority rule. So, while he was in Africa in April, Kissinger declared the US government's support for majority rule, and its opposition to apartheid. He followed this up in September with another very strong condemnation of apartheid.

Kissinger's object was to make the second element of the Western strategy possible, namely that he operate as an intermediary between the black governments and Vorster.

The third element in the strategy involved bringing the white settlers in Rhodesia to the conference table. Two factors could play a part here: intensification of the guerilla war could make life so difficult for the settlers that they might consider a deal, and second, Vorster could bring economic and military pressure to bear on the regime.

The Kissinger strategy dovetailed perfectly with the objectives of the black governments. Nyerere had been arguing for some time that the first round of detente had failed and what was necessary was a further round of fighting in order to concentrate the minds of the settlers. He made the point publicly on a number of occasions, and in March 1976 told *The Observer*: 'We are building up the pressure that will deliver Smith to London'.[2]

It was in March that the talks between Smith and Nkomo collapsed and that Mozambique closed its border with Rhodesia (about 30 per cent of Rhodesia's trade had previously been routed via the ports of Beira and Maputo, formerly Lourenco Marques). These moves were undoubtedly co-ordinated with the Western governments: the Zambian Foreign Minister happened to be in London the day the border was closed. Britain and the US both offered Frelimo economic aid to offset the effects of the closure. Mark Chona, Kaunda's key foreign affairs adviser, flew in to London after the breakdown of the Smith-Nkomo talks. James Callaghan then outlined in the House of Commons on 22 March the basis for a settlement in Rhodesia - acceptance by the regime of majority rule within two years. He added: 'We may have to appeal to a wider constituency also including forces which some MPs may not care for. I refer to the guerillas.'

The Rise of ZIPA

The front-line presidents were in some difficulty in that during the first phase of detente in 1975, they had, individually and collectively, done all they could to smash the main guerilla force, ZANU. Moreover, the old political leadership of the nationalist movement was more bitterly split than ever after the collapse of the ANC united front. Yet a united leadership would be necessary in order to negotiate a settlement with the regime should the guerilla offensive succeed.

They hit upon the strategy of the 'Third Force', which appears to have originated with Machel and Nyerere, both traditionally closer to ZANU than Kaunda. The idea was to by-pass the existing Nkomo and Muzorewa-Sithole leaderships by forming a reconstructed and united guerilla army out of the rank-and-file of both movements, although ZANU's military predominance would mean that its members would be numerically in the majority. Hopefully from the ranks of the new Zimbabwe People's Army (ZIPA) a new united leadership would emerge to negotiate with the defeated settlers.

Ironically, the strategy rested on an alliance between the frontline presidents and the ZANU radicals whom they had crushed as obstacles in the way of detente. In December 1975 Kaunda released, at the insistence of Nyerere and Machel, the bulk of the ZANU guerillas gaoled in Zambia. They were transferred to camps in Mozambique and Tanzania, where they were joined by young Zimbabweans who had fled into exile to take part in the armed struggle.

The new strategy was aided by new divisions within the ranks of the Zimbabwean nationalists. The mass of the ZANU guerillas broke with Muzorewa and Sithole, for reasons explained in a memorandum written in December 1975 by guerillas at Mgagao camp in Tanzania. The document condemns Kaunda and Nkomo for collaborating in 'various schemes worked out in the political laboratories of Salisbury and Pretoria'.[3] It goes on to denounce the Muzorewa-Sithole leadership:

> These men have proved to be completely hopeless and ineffective as leaders of the Zimbabwe revolution. Ever since the Unity Accord was signed on 7.12.75 [sic - the agreement was in fact signed in December 1974 - AC and JR], these men have done nothing to promote the struggle for liberation of Zimbabwe, but, on the other hand, they have done everything to hamper the struggle through their power struggle. They have no interest in the revolution or the people at heart, but only their personal interests. They cherish an insatiable lust for power.[4]

The memorandum is particularly critical of Sithole for taking the Zambian government's side in the Chitepo affair and co-opting Noel Mukono and Simpson Mutambanengwe onto the Zimbabwe Liberation Council that he and Muzorewa formed after the Victoria Falls talks. As we saw, Mukono and Mutambanengwe have been accused of leading the Nhari revolt against the ZANU military command in December 1974. For Sithole to have taken the side of Kaunda and the Mukono-Mutambanengwe group infuriated the guerillas who had been thrown into gaol after Chitepo's death. The document concludes by appealing to the Mozambican and Tanzanian governments and the OAU Liberation Committee to evacuate the guerillas from Zambia and 'to make the necessary arrangements for the prosecution and intensification of armed struggle inside Zimbabwe'.[5]

ZIPA was not formed of ZANU members alone. A number of ZAPU guerillas were included in the new army, and ZAPU leaders were involved in the formation of its Joint Military Command (JMC), consisting of 9 ZAPU members and 9 ZANU members. However, the JMC did not last long as an effective body; the ZAPU guerillas in Mozambique were far outnumbered by ZANU members, and armed clashes took place between the two groups. The ZAPU guerillas were transferred to Zambia to join a force, estimated by some to be as large as 5,000 men, drawn up on the northern bank of the Zambesi, and controlled by the Zambian army. This force was clearly meant to serve as a counterweight to the ZANU guerillas in Mozambique.

Muzorewa and Sithole protested in a memorandum to Nyerere that the frontline presidents and Colonel Mbita of the Tanzanian army, Executive Secretary of the OAU Liberation Committee,

> have taken it upon themselves to be decision-makers, the planners, the organisers and the spokesmen of the Zimbabwean liberation struggle. They have taken it upon themselves to decide when, where, how and what for talks or armed struggle should be organised, launched and prosecuted. In this game we have at every turn been presented with a fait accompli.[6]

Their memorandum claims that the Mozambican government had prevented the ANC leadership from visiting the guerilla camps by force, while Nkomo had been specially flown in to Mozambique 'with a view to imposing him as a leader'.[7] It complains that the JMC had been formed without consulting them and that it consisted of 'dissidents' and 'criminals' responsible for Chitepo's murder.[8]

The frontline presidents responded in kind. Machel accused Muzorewa and Sithole of 'siding with the enemy'.[9] An editorial in the government-owned Tanzania *Daily News* dismissed Muzorewa as 'factionalist' and 'irrelevant'.[10]

The political leadership of ZIPA remains rather mysterious. Robert Mugabe, secretary-general of ZANU and a Catholic socialist, is identified with the ZIPA guerillas. The military leadership appears to be dominated by Rex Nhongo, who is one of those accused by the Zambian government of murdering Herbert Chitepo. The politics of ZIPA are those of ZANU - radical nationalism, sympathy with the Chinese bureaucracy, opposition to detente, stress on protracted armed struggle as the road to majority rule. The real leader of ZIPA was, however, said to be Josiah Tongogara, the former chief of ZANU defence, languishing in a Zambian prison for the murder of Herbert Chitepo.

However radical its leaders' politics, ZIPA was not a free force. It was constructed and controlled by the frontline states in order to force Smith to the negotiating table. Although there were differences between the different regimes - Nyerere and Machel traditionally having supported ZANU, Kaunda backing Nkomo - the black rulers drew significantly closer after the Angolan war. A correspondent in Zambia wrote in August 1976:

> Only a year ago Samora Machel ... refused even to speak to Kaunda. Nyerere was reported as having to scuttle back and forth carrying messages when they met.
>
> Now the situation is very different, with state visits every few weeks, smiling posed photographs, and even an amazing statement by Kaunda that he would be willing to step down to allow Machel to become joint head ot state of Mozambique and Zambia (not suprisingly no more was heard of this).

Machel, meanwhile, called Kaunda 'a hero of the liberation struggle'.[11] The sweetness and light even extended to Angola. It was ironic in the light of events only nine months previously to watch a television film of Kaunda and Agostinho Neto embracing at Lusaka airport in September 1976.

The armed struggle in Zimbabwe was resumed in January 1976. By July the settler forces found themselves fighting on three fronts - the old north-eastern zone, as well as two new ones, one in the south-east threatening the direct rail and road link with South Africa, and another in the south-west bordering on Botswana. Moreover, guerillas operating from Zambia began harassing attacks in the north-west.

The new offensive threatened the regime's vital links with the outside world. With the Mozambique border closed since March, the settlers' access to the sea was limited to two rail and road links to South Africa, one direct via Beit Bridge, the other through Botswana, which the Khama government allowed to remain open.

The regime was thus thrown into even greater dependence on South Africa. Although Pretoria continued to provide the helicopters and pilots vital for counter-insurgency operations, and there were reports of war material and 'advisors' being supplied to the Rhodesian forces, Rhodesian exporters began to complain about delays in routing their goods through the South African rail system. This began to be taken as an indicator of the pressure being put on the regime to settle by Vorster.

The war continued with increased bitterness into the dry winter season, which coincides with spring and summer in Europe. Despite the fact that winter conditions are the least favourable for guerillas, the ZIPA fighters pressed the regime's forces hard. On the estimate of P.K. van der Byl, the Rhodesian Minister of Defence, there were 1,300 guerillas operating inside the country in June 1976, and another 5,000-6,000 in Mozambique.[12] The Rhodesian army consists of 4,500 regulars and 10,000 territorials.[13] Even taking into account the paramilitary police force and its reserves, the line-up was not one that favoured the regime given the need in counter-insurgency warfare to outnumber guerilla infiltrators heavily.

There were many signs of growing mass support for the guerillas and of increasingly indiscriminate retaliation by the regime. One small example will give an idea of the situation: in July 1976, 56 black farmworkers were sentenced by a Bindura court to ten years' gaol apiece for failing to report the presence of 'terrorists'.[14] In areas where the African peasants had been driven from their homes, and herded into 'protected villages', curfews were imposed. In the casualty figures published by the regime, an increasing number of the dead were black 'curfew-breakers'. 500,000 Africans were estimated to have been affected by the introduction of protected villages.

In addition, more and more Africans were killed while 'running with terrorists' or 'mingling with terrorists'. A report by the Rhodesian Catholic Commission for Justice and Peace explained:

'Mingling with terrorists' does not necessarily mean being found in the company of insurgents. There is a widespread belief in the Mtoko area that the Security Forces are liable to open fire on people found near the place where a land-mine has just exploded. Often such a person would be sus-pected of complicity in the laying of the landmine. Also people coming from the direction where insurgents have sought refuge or have fled are regarded as 'mingling with terrorists'. The phrase can also include people suspected of being present at meetings called by insurgents.[15]

In August 1976 van der Byl admitted that since the ZANU offensive began in December 1972, 106 Africans had been shot for breaking curfew and 326 while 'running with terrorists'.[16]

Sagging white morale - expressed in an outflow of emigrants and increased draft-dodging by young whites - reflected the deteriorating military situation. In August 1976 Smith made a desperate attempt to internationalise the war. Rhodesian troops wearing Frelimo uniforms crossed into Mozambique and attacked a Zimbabwean refugee camp at Nhazonia: over 600 people were shot and buried in hastily dug mass graves.

The Machel government had been extremely active in supporting the ZIPA offensive. Frelimo border guards often swapped fire with the Rhodesians. By ordering the raid, Smith hoped to provoke a full-scale confrontation with Mozambique, which, he believed would force the Western powers and South Africa to intervene. The attempt failed, although it may have added urgency to the Kissinger mission. Hilgard Muller delivered an oblique rebuke, when, in a speech endorsing the Kissinger initiative a week after the raid, he told the Natal Nationalist Congress that the direction the Rhodesian war was developing 'is precisely what the Russians and Cubans are waiting for - the excuse'.[17]

The Kissinger Mission

Thus when Kissinger flew to Southern Africa in September 1976, it was to a subcontinent dominated by the rising guerilla tide in Zimbabwe and the black rebellion in South Africa. The Johannesburg *Star* outlined his strategy. First, Kissinger adopted the Callaghan target of majority rule in Zimbabwe within two years. Continuance of the armed struggle would only favour the radicals in ZIPA: 'the choice is Mr Joshua Nkomo, or Mr Robert Mugabe and the marxists behind him'. Second, an independence settlement for Namibia based on an agreement between the white and tribal leaders represented at the Turnhalle conference on the one hand, and SWAPO on the other. The SWAPO leadership had already been subjected to tremendous pressure by the Western governments to take part in negotiations. Third, 'to make these compromises possible, Zambia, Mozambique and perhaps Angola, must be persuaded, probably with offers of very substantial aid and technical assistance, to shut their borders to the guerillas, so that the transitions can take place in peace, under moderate black leaders'. Fourth, there would have to be 'dramatic *gestures*' (our italics) by South Africa aimed at eliminating racial discrimination. Fifth, 'within the context of these moves, the major Western powers would, Dr Kissinger hopes, be prepared to make a major investment with the goal of keeping Southern Africa out of the hands of the communists'.[18] Kissinger had taken over Vorster's detente policy lock, stock and barrel.

Although he had already prepared the way with two meetings with Vorster, the critical factor in Kissinger's strategy remained the South African regime. Only Vorster could deliver the military and economic power necessary to force the Rhodesian settlers into line; similarly, it was Vorster who needed to be persuaded to negotiate with SWAPO, which he remained reluctant to do.

Kissinger was careful to clear his initiative also with the black leaders. He visited Zambia and Tanzania before flying on to Pretoria. The new and public commitment of the US to majority rule made it possible for Nyerere and Kaunda to back the Kissinger mission without facing criticism in black Africa.

However, the decisive point was the meeting between Smith, Vorster and Kissinger in Pretoria. Kissinger had two strong cards in hand. First, there was the knowledge common to all present that a massive guerilla offensive was to be expected with the coming of the rains in November and December, an offensive which the regime would find very difficult to withstand on its own (Smith was accompanied by members of the Rhodesian military, who were known to have given him much the same advice). Second, there was the power of the South African regime, on which the Rhodesian settlers were completely dependent. Vorster had been constrained in the past from threatening to withdraw all support to the settlers by a threat of a backlash among his own supporters. Now, with Kissinger at his elbow, Vorster had the opportunity to hide his part in the Rhodesian surrender beneath the mantle of American power.

The regime was offered incentives to give way. There was talk of a massive (2 billion dollars) fund to be provided by the Western powers for Rhodesian development. Originally, Nyerere had proposed the fund as a means of compensating whites who wanted to leave a black-ruled Zimbabwe. Now, however, it was seen more as a method of bribing the settlers to stay. Moreover, the fund could be used to finance investments that would create the economic climate favourable to 'moderate' nationalists like Nkomo.

Rhodesian capitalists had already been shifting towards the idea of a black-ruled Zimbabwe. Josiah Chinamano, a Nkomo supporter, speaking after the Mozambique border closure,

> said that one major change which had taken place was that members of the European business community, the professions, and other groups were seeking meetings with Mr Nkomo and other members of the ANC team. They were saying that they would not object to majority rule provided that the change could be brought about in such a way that it did not threaten the economy.[19]

Moreover, the terms which Kissinger and Smith agreed did not amount to a complete surrender by the settlers. The text of the agreement, which Kissinger gave to Nkomo (the only nationalist leader he met) stated:

1. Friday, September 24, 1976, Ian Smith will make a statement accepting majority rule within two years, as demanded by the British and the Americans. Before Friday, Smith is informing his Cabinet, and his party caucus.

2. In his statement, Smith will invite black leaders (whoever they are) to come forward in order to form an interim or transitional government.

3. The structure of the transitional government will be as follows:

(A) Council of State consisting of an equal number of black and white representatives. The chairman of the Council of State should be white. The size of the Council of State can be as small as four (two nationalists and two whites) or it can be eight (four nationalists and four whites). The function of the Council will be like a governor-general or a high-commissioner, as in the case of Mozambique. The Council of State will supervise the drawing up of a constitution.

(B) A Council of Ministers consisting of a black Prime Minister and a majority of black Ministers. The Rhodesians specifically requested that they control the Ministries of Defence and Law and Order. The reason for this is the fear of a possible collapse of the administration during the period of transition. They refer to Angola, where arrests and counter-arrests finally led to the breakdown of government machinery.

4. Decisions will be by two-thirds majority of the Council of Ministers.

5. The rebel constitution will be suspended.

6. Britain will pass enabling legislation.

7. Once the transitional government is formed, the sanctions will have to be lifted and normality restored.

Members of the Council of State will be chosen by each side, namely, the nationalists on the one side and the whites on the other. This will apply to the members of the Council of Ministers.

8. The transitional government can be established as early as next month and independence within 24 months.[20]

The structure of settler power was untouched. The agreement made no provision for ending the state of emergency, freeing political prisoners, ending political trials, or permitting open political activity. White control of the economy, the racialist legislation passed over the years, the Land Tenure Act (which even a Rhodesian government commission had just agreed should be scrapped) were ignored. In his speech on 24 September announcing the settlement Smith exploited the ambiguities in the agreement for all they were worth: he made 'the cessation of terrorism' a condition for implementing the agreement; he said that the Council of State, which would have a white majority, would be the 'supreme body' during the transitional period; he turned the Rhodesian claim to control the Ministries of Defence and Law and Order into part of the agreement. He added: 'I hope to share the privilege of continuing to play an active role in helping to guide the destiny of Rhodesia'. For Smith the battle was far from over - he clearly intended to use all his negotiating skills to preserve effective settler control of the state and the economy.

An interesting indication of the tight squeeze in which the Rhodesian regime found itself in September 1976, and how it hoped to exploit the Kissinger deal, was provided by the purported report of a speech by Ted Sutton-Pryce, Deputy Minister in Smith's office, to a closed Rhodesian Front meeting:

The Rhodesian Front do not agree that Dr Kissinger's solution to Rhodesia's problems is the best.

The communist influence in Africa is growing and America is worried about the saddle formed across Africa. America must react or lose by default. South Africa and Rhodesia are the plums of Africa ... raw materials, Cape sea route, development.

America cannot support Rhodesia with a white minority government because of world opinion. If there were an acceptable government in Rhodesia, America would support this country with everything to combat communism except troops.

Vorster is the bad guy. The reason for the RF failure was because of pressure put on Rhodesia.

US dollars 60 million exports are in the pipeline rising to 100 million dollars by December. Without these exports moving, the government could not support an agricultural crop next year [settler agriculture is heavily subsidised by the state - AC and JR].

Fifty per cent of the Rhodesia defence bill was paid by South Africa up until June. A reply has not been given since then as to whether they would support it for a further year. There has been a delay on war items for as long as 2½ years.

The railway system is moving very few goods - reported congestion. The border [with South Africa - AC and JR] was closed over the period of the Kissinger talks 1-4 days. Fuel supply down to 19.6 days. It is difficult to prove these facts as we cannot afford to antagonise South Africa by exposing her.

The Prime Minister has considered appealing to the South African public over Vorster's head, but did not have enough time.

Against this background they had no alternative but to accept the Kissinger package deal.

Saying no would have meant fighting a rearguard action to Beit Bridge [on the border with South Africa - AC and JR]. They have done the responsible thing in accepting the deal.

Kissinger deal: set up an interim government and would have two years to sort out the constitution, after which majority rule. Not seen as one man one vote. America understands the problem better than the UK.

Parliament would go into recess and would not be

dissolved. If the agreed constitution was not liked after two years, parliament could reject it.

At worst we would be in a better position to fight the war than at present. We would have ... two years' trading on an open market. Revive the economy with the two billion development fund. Two years to build up arms and war materials and the armed forces. The market for recruiting into the forces would be widened.

RF stands for equal opportunity for all races [sic], civilised standards, stable government, permanent homes and maintenance of law and order.

Two billion development fund set up to try to keep the whites here, on a sliding scale [i.e. the longer you stay the more compensation you get if you finally leave - AC and JR].[21]

The frontline presidents rejected the agreement on the terms announced by Smith. However, they continued to press for a constitutional conference convened by Britain to set up a transitional government. It appeared that the black leaders were quite ready to use Smith's public commitment to majority rule within two years as a basis for negotiations. There were even suggestions that Nyerere knew of the objectionable features of the Smith-Kissinger deal before they were announced and that their public rejection by him was a bargaining ploy to extract concessions during the negotiations. Nyerere's whole strategy after the collapse of the Vorster-Kaunda alliance was aimed, not at the destruction of settler power, but at placing the nationalist leaders in a better position to bargain with Smith.

The British government convened the conference in Geneva on 28 October 1976.

Four nationalist delegations attended, headed by Nkomo, Mugabe, Muzorewa and Sithole (in September the latter had resigned from ANC and resumed the presidency of ZANU, only to be spurned by his former followers). However, the running among the nationalists was made by the 'Patriotic Front' formed by Nkomo and Mugabe on 9 October, which froze out

Muzorewa; enabled Nkomo to claim to speak for the guerillas; confirmed Mugabe's claim to be a force to be reckoned with, and, as part of the pay-off, secured the release of Josiah Tongogara and a number of his companions from gaol in Zambia shortly before the opening of the conference. Tongogara joined Mugabe's delegation at Geneva.

Muzorewa remained a force to be reckoned with. 100,000 people turned out to meet him in Salisbury when he returned to Rhodesia at the beginning of October 1976. In Geneva, however, once it became clear that the Nkomo-Mugabe axis was going to dominate the proceedings, there were reports that numbers of Muzorewa's followers were rejoining their old ZANU comrades in Mugabe's delegation. The Mugabe bandwagon also attracted members of Sithole's delegation - by far the weakest of the four groups.

In the conference discussions, Nkomo and Mugabe put heavy pressure on the British government, through the Whitehall-appointed chairman, Ivor Richard, to take responsibility for the transitional government. A British Governor-General, British Ministers of Defence and Law and Order and perhaps British army officers to replace Smith's commanders during the interim period would be acceptable to both sides, while favouring the forces driving towards a black neo-colonial government in Zimbabwe. The Labour government, with heavy military commitments in Germany and Northern Ireland and in the midst of an economic crisis, resisted the nationalist pressures. However, the same solution was canvassed by the frontline presidents, especially Nyerere, and found support in Washington. With an IMF team inspecting Whitehall's books and the US Treasury exercising the decisive say about the terms of the international loans needed to prop up British capitalism, Callaghan and Crosland's ability to resist such a solution was limited.

Smith resorted to the delaying tactics that were the hallmark of his diplomacy. He left Geneva shortly after the conference began, confiding leadership of the white delegation in the hands of P.K. van der Byl, Foreign Minister, and a racialist dandy well known as a representative of the RF hardliners. Back in Salisbury Smith hinted that he would implement the deal with the aid of 'moderate' blacks if and when the conference collapsed. (This may have been an unrealistic attempt to exploit Muzorewa's chagrin at the Patriotic Front's success in steamrollering its line through the conference.)

The war continued. Early in November, shortly after the conference began, the white security forces launched a series of attacks against the guerilla bases in Mozambique, in what appears to have been an attempt to forestall the guerilla offensive expected within the beginning of the rainy season in November. If so, it failed. Without ten days of the attacks a security forces spokesman announced that there were at least 2,000 guerillas in the country.

Nonetheless, the ZANU radicals who control ZIPA may have to pay the price of their pact with the devil. They are completely dependent on the Mozambique government. Should Frelimo decide to back the settlement - and it would be very difficult for it to stand out against the other black states - ZIPA would be forced into line willy-nilly.

The problem is larger than one of the national leaders cynically scrabbling for office or their dependence on the different black governments. African nationalism in Zimbabwe has ignored one very simple fact, that Rhodesia is a country with a large black working class. The peasant economy, as in South Africa, has been shattered, forcing more and more of the rural population into dependence on urban wage-earners. Because the Rhodesian economy is not growing fast enough to absorb black school-leavers and peasants drifting into the towns for jobs (one estimate is that 54,000 new jobs would have to be created annually between 1976 and 1985 to do this![22]) the mass of black unemployed is growing fast.

These black workers and unemployed in the towns could be the driving force of a revolution that would smash the whole structure of settler power in Rhodesia, if they were supported by peasant and guerilla struggles in the countryside. Yet for Zimbabwean nationalists they are either a source of passive support in a power struggle with the regime or (more usually) one another, or a supply of recruits for their guerilla armies. The failure of the nationalists to base themselves upon the urban masses explains the dependence of even the radicals amongst them on black governments who will toss them aside the moment their interests command it.

The orientation of even the radical wing of the nationalist movement on peasant guerilla warfare in an increasingly urbanised and proletarianised country creates other dangers. ZIPA is a hierarchical military structure cut off from the mass of the population and operating from another country. While it may receive mass support, it is not based on the masses, not even on the mass of the peasantry, many of whom are now corralled into protected villages under government control. In the period of shifting, opportunist combinations that the nationalist movement appears to be entering, ZIPA could well become the praetorian guard of one set of leaders against another, to be used to choke off a developing mass movement in the towns. The only guarantee that ZIPA will not play such a role lies in the political commitment of its leaders. Unfortunately, good intentions, as history has so often shown, are never enough.

To smash settler power and establish a popular government that would take the country out of the hands of the British and South African companies that control it will involve more than trust in one nationalist leadership against another. It will require the arming of the Zimbabwean workers and peasants and the formation of a revolutionary government based on directly elected workers' and peasants' councils.

The alternative is an independence in which the multi-nationals remain in the saddle and a majority rule which replaces whites with blacks in the cabinet and the civil service and on the boards of the multinationals' local subsidiaries; in which the mass of workers and peasants would remain where they are; and in which many of the settlers would remain to enjoy one of the highest standards of living in the world, just as they have in Zambia and Kenya.

Ultimately, the outcome of the struggle for Zimbabwe will

depend on what happens beyond its borders. Like Zambia, Zimbabwe is locked into an economic system dominated by South Africa. Its fate is tied up with the fate of South Africa. It is to the interlocking destinies of the different Southern African states and their common dependence on the apartheid regime in South Africa that we turn in the final chapter.

10. Results and Prospects

The crisis in Southern Africa is not only a crisis for the minority regimes and for the imperialist West. It is also a crisis for African nationalism. We have seen how black governments like those of Kaunda and Nyerere have collaborated with the imperialist countries and the Vorster regime in order to reach a neo-colonial settlement in the area, and how many black nationalists have thrown in their lot with the detente policies. Moreover, black nationalists have fought a bloody civil war in Angola.

The struggle for national liberation in Southern Africa requires the critical examination and, indeed, we would argue, the rejection of, the ideology that has given expression to that struggle - African nationalism. In saying this, we would be the last to deny that the nationalists have led the most heroic struggles against apartheid, colonialism and imperialism, with many thousands of men and women laying down their lives, tens of thousands facing gaol and torture, in order to free their countries. Unfortunately, heroism is not enough.

The Politics of African Nationalism

We shall concentrate our analysis on the radical nationalist wing in Southern Africa - those movements like ANC in South Africa, ZANU in Zimbabwe, MPLA, Frelimo and PAIGC in the former Portuguese colonies which seek to link their struggles to the broader, world-wide struggle for socialism.

There are three interlinked components to their theory, which they hold in common with many national liberation movements throughout the world and many socialists in the advanced capitalist countries. They may be called populism, the flight from the towns, and the drive for economic autarky.

Populism expresses itself in the notion of an all-class alliance against the enemy. The argument goes something like this: the struggle in Southern Africa is primarily a struggle for national independence; all classes - workers, peasants, bourgeoisie and petty bourgeoisie alike - find their development blocked by colonialism (we should remember that for the ANC and the South African Communist Party, apartheid is a form of colonialism); therefore, all classes have a common interest in the pursuit of the liberation struggle. The implication is, of course, that the working class should subordinate *its* struggle and *its* interests to the common, all-class, patriotic struggle against the colonial power.

Underlying this approach is the theory that the national struggle for independence and majority rule occupies a separate stage to the struggle for workers' power and socialism; the latter stage can be put off to some time in the future after the national struggle has been won. 'Seek ye first the political Kingdom', said Kwame Nkrumah.

The conclusion that the SACP draws is applicable to all the national liberation movements:

> *As a national liberation organisation, the ANC does not represent any single class, or any one ideology. It is representative of all the classes and strata which make up African society in this country.* [1]

It underlines the point by arguing:

> *The special character of colonialism in South Africa, the seizing by Whites of all opportunities which in other colonial countries have led to the growth of a national capitalist class, has strangled the development of a class of African capitalists... The interests of the African commercial class lie wholly in joining with the workers and rural people for the overthrow of White Supremacy.* [2]*
> [emphasis in original]

However, the class struggle does not cease even within such all-class coalitions. The SACP emphasises the leading role of the working class within ANC and argues that 'its place ... would be swamped, diluted and emasculated in the absence of its independent political instrument', the Communist Party.[4] But the argument is used more to dress up the organisational power that the SACP exercises behind the scenes within the ANC than to provide a basis for the Party's own mass work.

The leadership of the national liberation movements (including the ANC) have typically been petty-bourgeois both in social position and in ideology. As Amilcar Cabral, one of the most gifted of the leaders of the African colonial revolution, explained:

> The colonial situation, which does not permit the develop-ment of a native pseudo-bourgeoisie and in which the popular masses do not generally reach the level of political consciousness before the advent of the phenomenon of national liberation, offers the petty bourgeoisie the historical opportunity of leading the struggle against foreign domination, since by nature of its objective and subjective position (higher standard of living than that of the masses, more frequent contact with the agents of colonialism, and hence more chances of being humiliated, higher level of education and political awareness etc.) it is the stratum which most rapidly becomes aware of the need to free itself from foreign domination.[5]

We should note how Cabral emphasises another strand in

---

*The 'left' Maoist critics of the SACP share the same assumptions. The statement of principles of the South African 'Marxist-Leninist' journal *Ikwezi* includes the following passage: 'The struggle in South Africa is not a straightforward struggle between Labour and Capital, a political struggle between the working class and bourgeois [sic] as the two main opposing protagonists. The oppressed Black masses must first win their democratic rights in their own land — Equality before the Law — before it can be established as a fact by extending the struggle for national democratic rights to fight for socialism which attempts to put an end to the exploitation of man by man.'[3]

the populist ideology, whereby the petty-bourgeois nationalist party becomes the custodian of the popular will. The masses are denied a political existence outside the party, whose tutelage is imposed upon them 'because of the economic and cultural limitations of the working masses'.[6] For example, in the most advanced national struggle Africa has so far seen, that in Angola, the *poder pover* movement of factory and neighbourhood committees was placed under the firm control of the MPLA, lest the workers of Luanda get out of hand.

Populism made some sense in the Portuguese colonies, where, as we have seen, the peculiar form of colonial domination kept the population a mass of starved and illiterate peasants. That the analysis of society underlying it is nonetheless wrong will be shown when we consider the third component of nationalist ideology - the drive towards economic autarky.

At this stage, however, we shall limit ourselves to pointing out that the populist strategy is completely inapplicable to South Africa and Zimbabwe. In both these countries the capitalist mode of production is dominant, and has been for a long period: in South Africa since, roughly, the turn of the century and in Rhodesia since the collapse of the peasant economy in the 1920s. In earlier chapters we have shown how the apartheid systems established in both countries have nothing to do with a colonial-type continued control of a pre-capitalist mode of production by the capitalist sector of the economy, but rather are methods of labour control arising from the specific needs for cheap labour of the capitalist economy in each country.

Why, then, was the populist analysis adopted by the nationalists in both countries? For one thing, it justified the role of the petty-bourgeois nationalist leaderships. We should also remember that the populist strategy of an all-class alliance against imperialism and the stages theory that underlies it were developed in their classic form in the 1920s by the Russian bureaucracy under Stalin and Bukharin. A version was, as we saw, imposed upon the SACP by the Comintern in 1928.[7] The SACP remains one of the most loyal and orthodox pro-Moscow Communist Parties in the world. One is inclined to speculate that the theory of 'internal colonialism' in South Africa was developed in order to justify the SACP's strategy, rather than the other way round!

The crux of the theory is the proposition that the African petty bourgeoisie will play a progressive role in the struggle for national liberation. Yet if the struggle for national liberation in South Africa is a *class* struggle, if smashing apartheid involves the destruction of capitalism in South Africa, then, as that struggle develops, the black petty bourgeoisie can be expected to play an increasingly reactionary role. Cabral touches on this problem in relation to the struggle in the Portuguese colonies:

> This alternative - to betray the revolution or to commit suicide as a class - constitutes the dilemma of the petty bourgeoisie in the general framework of the national liberation struggle. The positive solution depends on what Fidel Castro recently correctly called *the development of revolutionary consciousness*. This dependence necessarily calls our attention to the capacity of the leader of the national liberation struggle to remain faithful to the principles and fundamental cause of this struggle. This shows us to a certain extent, that if national liberation is essentially a political problem, the conditions for its development give it certain characteristics which belong to the sphere of morals.[8]

Once again, ethics substitute for the class struggle, good intentions take the place of material interests.

The SACP, however, does not follow Cabral in putting total faith in the good will of the nationalist petty bourgeoisie. They argue that there is a material basis to the revolutionary role of this class:

> In the case of the black middle strata ... class mobility cannot proceed beyond a certain point ... this point is defined in race rather than economic terms. Objectively speaking, therefore, the immediate fate of the black middle sections is linked much more with that of the black workers

and peasants than with their equivalents across the colour line.[9]

However, the whole thrust of domestic detente in South Africa is aimed at giving the black petty bourgeoisie greater economic and political scope. As the SACP itself now concedes, there is a small but growing African commercial bourgeoisie in the townships and the Homelands, with sufficient resources to accumulate capital and even set up their own banks.[10] There is also a growing class of small capitalist farmers producing for the market in the Homelands: the other side to the coin of mass impoverishment amongst the rural population is the concentration of land and wealth in the hands of a small minority of rich peasants, so that in 1956 12.7 per cent of the families on the Reserves earned 46.3 per cent of the income.[11]

This black petty bourgeoisie aspires to the political power which its equivalents enjoy in the rest of Africa. However, to attain majority rule in South Africa would entail mobilising the black working class and would involve, as the SACP admits, 'a *complete* change in the way in which the country's wealth is appropriated'.[12] Such a development might well threaten even the limited ability to exploit labour that the black middle class enjoys at present. It is therefore likely to become more and more hostile to the liberation struggle and to become more like the black petty bourgeoisie in Soweto, which we described in Chapter 8.

This response to the national struggle is not without precedent. During the revolution of 1848 the German bourgeoisie initially participated in the struggle against the feudal rulers. However, as the working class began to play the leading role in the revolution, the bourgeoisie retreated. They were prepared to see political power remain in the hands of the feudal *Junkers* represented by Bismarck in exchange for social peace. At first, Marx and Engels advocated an alliance between the working class and the 'democratic petty bourgeoisie'. However, they came to see that:

'The democratic petty bourgeois, far from wanting to transform the whole of society in the interests of the revolutionary proletarians, only aspire to a change in social conditions which will make the existing society as tolerable and comfortable for themselves as possible.'[13]

As for the German working class:

They themselves must contribute most to their final victory, by informing themselves of their own class interests, by taking up their independent political position as soon as possible, by not allowing themselves to be misled by the hypocritical phrases of the democratic petty bourgeoisie into doubting for one minute the necessity of an independently organised party of the proletariat. Their battle-cry must be: The Permanent Revolution.[14]

In practice, populism leads to a complete lack of clarity as to how power can be won. Mass working-class action is seen simply as a way of putting pressure on the regime. In 1962, during the post-Sharpeville repression, the SACP could write: 'The Party does not dismiss all prospects of non-violent transition to the democratic revolution.'[15] Apartheid, apparently, might be destroyed without smashing the apparatus of white political power.

As we have seen, the ANC alliance used strikes and other forms of mass action as purely demonstrative acts of protest. They never sought to relate them to the seizure of power. The same was true of the Zimbabwean nationalists in the 1950s and early 1960s. When forced underground they resorted to acts of terrorism that represented no threat to the structure of white power, did not involve the masses, and provided the security forces with the opportunity to tighten the screws of repression even further.

The defenders of African nationalism will argue that the various movements went on, after these defeats, to develop strategies of armed struggle. The failure of their urban strategies led the South African and Zimbabwean nationalists, and the main movements in the Portuguese colonies, to embrace guerilla warfare based on the peasantry. This *flight from the towns*, which we see as the second component of African nationalism, did not alter the character of the movements. Where they were successful in the Portuguese colonies and, to a certain extent, in Rhodesia after 1972, they developed a peasant base and a guerilla army composed largely of peasants. But they remained under the leadership of petty-bourgeois intellectuals.

The effectiveness of this strategy varied. In the most under-developed of the countries concerned - Guinea-Bissau and Mozambique - the military battle was going the nationalists' way by the time the dictatorship fell, partly, of course, as a result. In the more developed countries, the countryside was not decisive. The MPLA's victory was won in Luanda, not in the liberated zones of rural eastern Angola. In South Africa, the regime was able to suppress the rural revolts that did take place, and to brush off the ANC offensive, which was defeated in Zimbabwe even before the fighters could reach South Africa. As for Zimbabwe, the outcome will clearly depend on what happens in the cities.

The reason is simple. In both South Africa and Rhodesia, as we have seen, the pre-capitalist rural economy has been smashed. In South Africa this process was well under way by the time the gold mines were discovered; in Rhodesia, it was the slumps in the 1920s that forced the change.[16] In both the rural population is dependent on the black working class for its survival. Under the circumstances, it is absurd to base a strategy of armed struggle on the countryside.

In the light of this reality, the ANC/SACP in South Africa have argued that their strategy of armed struggle is not confined to the countryside:

> Guerilla warfare can be, and has been, waged in every conceivable type of terrain, in deserts, swamps, in farm fields, in built-up areas, in plains, in the bush and in countries without friendly borders or in islands surrounded by the sea. This whole question is one of adjusting survival tactics to the sort of terrain in which operations have to be carried out.[17]

If meant seriously, this implies some sort of commitment to urban guerilla warfare. We hope it is not meant seriously, since leaving aside the failure of *Umkonto we Sizwe* in the early 1960s, urban guerilla warfare, wherever it has been attempted - West Bengal, Brazil, Argentina, Uruguay - has led to the most disastrous and bloody defeats for the left. Even to present the question in the way the ANC does places the technical question of how to organise armed struggle in priority over the political problem of the relation between the working class and the armed struggle, which reflects the whole orientation of nationalism - the masses are there to support the armed struggle, not to emancipate themselves by their own action.

None of this is to deny the importance of the rural struggle in both South Africa and Rhodesia, not to speak of the other, more agrarian countries. The unequal distribution of the land is at the basis of the proletarianisation and impoverishment of the African population. The high proportion of the South African working class who are migrant labourers or who work in border industries means that the urban proletariat has many residual ties to the countryside even in this highly industrialised country. We have seen how rural and urban struggles have fed each other in South Africa. There is no question but that the struggle for land by the rural African population - farm workers, unemployed migrant workers and peasants - will be one of the driving forces of the revolution.

However, it will be the struggle in the cities that will decide. The history of the South African peasantry since the conquest is that of peasants the world over - a series of bloody and heroic revolts that are always crushed.[18] Even in Pondoland the regime was able to cut off the affected areas and destroy the rebellion. This is not a result only of the destruction of the peasant economy in South Africa. It also reflects the social character of the peasantry. The horizons of the peasants' world - even when the appropriation of nature is collectively organised, as in the African communal economy - are determined by the limits of their village. They see the solution to their problems as an extension of *their* land or, if they are landless, through the seizure of adjoining land. A larger solution to the problems of society does not enter into their world-view. They can be drawn into national political struggles, but only under the leadership of an urban class.

In most of Africa, including the former Portuguese colonies, the urban leadership has come from the black petty bourgeoisie up to now. But in South Africa and Zimbabwe in particular, there is a rival contender for the leadership of the national struggle - the urban working class. For the solution to their problems involves the destruction of both apartheid and capitalism, which is also the only solution for the semi-proletarianised groups that make up the mass of rural African population.

To be successful, the national struggle requires the leadership of the black urban working class, drawing behind it the mass of the town and rural people. Any alternative perspective will lead to disaster. (Let us note once again that the 'left' critics of the ANC/SACP offer an even worse alternative to the present strategy. Thus *Ikwezi* and the South African marxist scholar Martin Legassick talking of building 'red bases' in the townships and the Bantustans. *Ikwezi* says 'the leaders of the Bantustans are bound sooner or later to move along a more radical road, as some are already doing'! Let us repeat once again: it is comparatively easy for the regime to crush township and rural revolts, as they have done often in the past; it is much more difficult to crush a sustained offensive by the black working class on whom the South African economy rests.[19])

However, a perspective of working-class leadership of the national struggle cuts across the third component of the nationalist ideology - *the drive to economic autarky.*

Nationalism assumes that the main conflict in the world is between oppressed and oppressor nations. It points to the network of economic and political relationships which holds the mass of the population of the 'Third World' countries in misery and poverty, and argues that the solution is to break out of this imperialist web; only by winning complete economic independence of the world economy can the problems of under-development and poverty in the oppressed nations be solved.

Too weak to compete with Western capital as private capitalists, the new black bourgeoisie seek to win their place in the sun by using the state as a buffer against the world economy and a means for the national accumulation of capital. This involves them in a confrontation with the mass of workers and peasants, for the resources necessary for state-directed accumulation of capital can only come from their surplus-labour. The nationalist claim that all classes have a common interest in national autarky merely justifies this offensive on working people.

The problem for the African bourgeoisie is that they are too weak to implement even this programme. Attempts at state capitalism in countries like Tanzania and Zambia remain half-hearted. The reason is simple. The entry-price to the world market is now too high for a Third World country - even for the most successful exponent of state capitalism among the poor countries, China. Because of the internationalisation of the relations of production and the development of the productivity of labour in the advanced capitalist countries, the scale of investment necessary in order to be competitive on the world market is way beyond the resources of the semi-colonial countries. The rules of the game are against them.[20]

At the same time, the poor countries must play the game. Their economies are shaped by the world economy and success or failure depends on its fluctuations. The high hopes raised by Zambia's struggle for economic independence were based on the foreign exchange reserves earned by one commodity - copper - whose world price happened to be high for much of the first decade after decolonisation. The fall in the copper price had, as we have seen, a shattering effect on Zambian politics and economics, forcing Kaunda into collaboration with Vorster.

The solution lies not in opting out of the world economy, but in smashing it. This means looking beyond the borders of individual nation states. It means linking together national struggles in an *international* struggle. Here the argument against populism links in with the argument against economic autarky. The situation of the semi-colonial countries can only be resolved through the transformation of the world economy - the replacement of capitalist competition and waste by an economy that is collectively and democratically planned on an international scale. Such a transformation can only be achieved by an alliance of the workers and peasants of the semi-colonial countries with the workers of the imperialist countries.

Such an alliance could only be led by the working class. Only the working class is an *international* class. The nationalist petty bourgeoisie is defined by its aspiration to national political power. The peasantry is too fragmented to lead a national struggle, let alone an international struggle. However, the exploitation which is the basis of workers' collective action, is dictated by the needs of the international economy. The same companies that exploit British or West German workers exploit South African workers. The argument for working-class leadership of the national struggle is also an argument for transforming the national struggle into an international struggle for socialism.

Angola and Mozambique since Independence

The argument against nationalism can be confirmed from the record of the two radical nationalist regimes that came to power in Southern Africa after the fall of Portuguese colonialism - the MPLA in Angola and Frelimo in Mozambique. Both regimes have been shaped by their economic integration into a region dominated by South African capitalism.

Frelimo's victory grew out of a peasant war in northern Mozambique, where its guerillas succeeded in freeing large portions of the countryside from Portuguese rule. Southern Mozambique, much more urbanised and integrated into the South African economy, had not been liberated at the time of the Lisbon coup. The ports of Beira and Lourenco Marques (now Maputo) fell into Frelimo's hands, not as a result of struggle, but through agreement with the disintegrating colonial power.

This is not to say that urban workers were not mobilised. When, on 7 September 1974, white settlers attempted a *putsch* in Lourenco Marques, it was blocked by an African rising. Then the Portuguese and Frelimo forces intervened, as much in response to the mobilisation by black workers as to the settler rebellion.

From the start the new government drew a distinction between the liberated zones in the north and the 'occupied areas' in the south, where Frelimo collaborated with foreign capital in order to quell the waves of workers' struggles that the fall of the dictatorship unleashed. One example, of a Mozambique firm employing 1,000 workers, will have to do. After the April coup the workers demanded, and won, a 100 per cent wage rise. A workers' commission was formed on Frelimo instructions in response to the white uprising in September 1974. The commission demanded a further increase, and transport to and from work. Productivity and 'labour discipline' deteriorated sharply. Finally two Frelimo political commissars intervened: they lectured the workers on the need to work harder and restored discipline. The relieved employer commented: 'I am convinced that there is a future for us in Mozambique - it's just a matter of adjustment.'[21]

Independence in June 1975 did not mean an end to the economic links between Mozambique and South Africa. Mozambicans continued to work in the gold mines, although their numbers fell from 100,000 to 75,000 in 1976, because of the mining houses' desire to reduce their dependence on Mozambican labour.[22] Part of the mineworkers' wages are still paid in gold as deferred payments in Mozambique, earning the government desperately needed foreign exchange. The Cabora Bassa project, built to provide South African industry with electricity, was not stopped. The electricity supplied to Mozambique by the dam will be routed through the South African electricity grid. The Mozambican economy has been shaped to fit the needs of South African capitalism - as long as Frelimo's struggle remains within narrow national limits, it will not be able to break out of its dependence on the apartheid regime.

In some ways, Mozambique's dependence on South Africa has *increased* since Frelimo came to power. The exodus of Portuguese settlers has created a tremendous shortage of skilled labour. In May 1976 it was reported that Maputo was operating at 60 per cent of capacity and that the South African Railways and Harbours Administration was offering skilled staff and technicians to operate the port.[23]

The South Africans have been careful to keep on good terms with Frelimo. The general manager of SAR&H has put heavy pressure on South African businessmen to use Maputo. [24] (Vorster is taking no chances, though. In September 1975 it was announced that a 400-kilometre fence was being built from the Crocodile river to the Limpopo river in the Kruger National Park, which borders on Mozambique. The government story - that it is an 'elephant deterrent' - is a bit too good to be true.[25])

The flight of the settlers caused a fall in agricultural production (at least half the land had been white-owned.) Although land has been nationalised, a large proportion of output is still cash crops for export. Queues have become a feature of life in the towns. The *aldeamentos* - strategic hamlets built by the Portuguese to control the movement of the rural population - have been turned into resettlement camps for the urban unemployed.

The army, swollen by the needs of war and of maintaining order during the Portuguese withdrawal, has filled the streets with idle soldiers whom the government dares not demobilise because there are no jobs for them to go to. The army and police went unpaid for long periods. As a result, drunkenness, corruption and brutality were rife among the troops. In December 1975, 400 Frelimo soldiers mutinied as they were boarding a troopship bound for Angola, where they were pledged to fight on MPLA's side. The rebellion spread to sections of the Macua and Makonde tribes in the north, and to sections of the police. Although the uprising was put down by loyal troops, unrest continued. Particularly significant was the disaffection of the Makonde, traditionally loyal to Frelimo.

The grim situation the Frelimo regime found itself in was

reflected at the level of the party leadership. Divisions here followed the Sino-Russian split. President Samora Machel led the pro-Chinese faction, which saw salvation in the guerilla war in Zimbabwe, which would rekindle the loyalty of the peasants, many of whom belong to the same ethnic group as the Shona in Rhodesia. The pro-Russian faction, led by Marcelino dos Santos, the vice-president, argued for closer reliance on Russia and Cuba as a counterweight to the South Africans.

In Angola the situation after independence was exacerbated by the need to rebuild an economy battered by the war. Food rotted in the agricultural south while queues lengthened in Luanda because of disruption of the internal transport system. The country was starved of skilled labour, as 300,000 Portuguese settlers fled during the six months of the war. Agricultural production fell. The MPLA mounted a campaign to get in the coffee and sugar harvests in order to earn foreign exchange. No attempt was made to take over the multinationals, although many Portuguese firms and farms were nationalised when their owners fled the country. Gulf Oil resumed production and royalties payments.

The government's difficulties were compounded by the presence of Unita guerillas in the south, which prevented the Benguela railway reopening on schedule. In November 1976 MPLA and Cuban troops launched an offensive in the south of the country aimed at wiping out Unita. Moreover, the South Africans continued their incursions across the border.

The MPLA leadership quarrelled about the direction they should pursue. Neto resisted demands to nationalise foreign interests, stressed the unity of all classes as the basis of the regime, and argued that the private sector would continue to play its part in Angola's development. His aim was clearly to encourage settlers to return and to attract foreign investment. The Russians were reported to fear that Neto might 'do a Sadat' - follow the example of President Sadat of Egypt who, in 1972, expelled 20,000 Russian advisors and drew closer to the West. A more pro-Russian faction was identified with Nito Alves, Minister of the Interior, although he based his appeal on a demagogic quasi-racist attack on the *mesticos* who had filled many of the places left vacant by the Portuguese.

The government clamped down hard on the wave of working-class activity that followed victory over the FNLA and Unita. Strikes were denounced as harmful to the economy and a 'battle for production' was declared. The government refused to permit workers to take over nationalised enterprises.

Another note entered MPLA propaganda - denunciation of 'ultra-left saboteurs and traitors'. A revolutionary opposition to the Neto leadership had developed. Unfortunately, this opposition was confused and divided. Its most important group was the Amilcar Cabral Committee (CAC), with links with the Maoist UDP (Popular Democratic Union) in Portugal, and some support within the MPLA. This group was subjected to repression by the regime. Less significant was Active Revolt, a small group of intellectuals some of whom, like the Andrade brothers, had once been part of the MPLA leadership. (Discredit fell on the revolutionary left as a whole from the activities of the Communist Organisation of Angola [OCA], which is linked to the CIA-backed MRPP [Movement for the Reconstruction of the Proletarian Party] in Portugal. The OCA described the MPLA as 'populist-fascist' and followed the Chinese line of 'neutrality' during the war. Its existence provided the regime with an excuse to clamp down on the revolutionary left as a whole.)[26]

In both Angola and Mozambique the new regimes have been forced to collaborate with imperialism, to put down strikes and to tie the peasantry to the old pattern of cash-crop production for the world market. They have done so not out of their leaders' bad intentions. Given the initial decision to base their strategy upon the fragmentation of the world into distinct national units and to seek the solution of their problems within the confines of these units, everything else followed. For the division of the world into nation states serves to underpin the dominance of the imperialist countries; it provides the multinationals with the political and military force to back up their interests and prevents the mass of workers and peasants from uniting to smash world capitalism. Any attempt to solve the problems of the poor countries along national lines will simply reproduce the international division of labour that accords economic predominance to the advanced capitalist countries. It will also exacerbate the class struggle within the poor countries, as their rulers strive to accumulate capital at the expense of workers and peasants or, as in Zambia, Zaire and Tanzania, are forced to cut jobs and living standards to meet the demands of their Western creditors.

The conclusion of this argument is not that there can be no genuine liberation unless proletarian revolution breaks out simultaneously throughout the world. On the contrary, the victories of the liberation movements in Angola and Mozambique *before* any successful revolution in more advanced countries like South Africa, let alone Britain or West Germany, is a natural product of uneven development. Capitalism does not take the same form throughout the world; the unique combination of backwardness and colonial oppression that it produced in Angola and Mozambique made them the weak links in the Southern Africa complex. But this does not free these countries from the hold of the world economy. Revolutions will take place in some countries before others — say, in South Africa before West Germany; but in order to survive the revolutions must be spread to other countries, above all, the advanced capitalist countries. In the case of Southern Africa, for the revolution to go forward in Angola and Mozambique, it must be spread to South Africa.

The South African Working Class and World Revolution

South Africa is the key to Southern Africa, indeed to the rest of Africa. It is both the most advanced economic power and the most important operational centre for Western capitalism on the continent. We have seen how the expansionist drive of the South African economy leads it to spread throughout the rest of Africa, with the active participation and encouragement of the advanced capitalist countries. The destruction of South African capitalism is the key to the overthrow of capitalism and imperialism throughout the African continent. Victory for the black working class of South Africa would both fatally disrupt the web of Western interests stretching over Africa and be a catalyst to the struggles of the workers and peasants of black-ruled Africa against their own ruling classes.

The struggle against apartheid in South Africa is inseparable from the struggle against capitalism. This statement has been the nub of our argument throughout this book, and there is little need to go over it again. We have shown how apartheid is not something external to capitalism in South Africa, a deformation or excrescence that can be got rid of without changing the system as a whole, but is central to the specific needs of capitalism in that country.

It would be ridiculous to conclude from this that there is no place for the national struggle in South Africa. On the contrary, apartheid requires the national oppression of the African people. The cheap labour system can only operate as long as blacks are denied all political rights. Separate development can only satisfy the political aspirations of the African petty bourgeoisie if they accept the fragmentation of the African nation into tribal rural statelets overshadowed by Pretoria. The African national struggle in South Africa, insofar as it challenges the basis of capitalism in South Africa, has a revolutionary content. To the extent that nationalist organisations like ANC, PAC and BPC fight the apartheid system, they should be supported. What our argument proves, however, is that the national struggle in South Africa can succeed only if it is transformed into the struggle for black workers' power.

The task of smashing the apartheid system falls on the shoulders of the black working class. We stress the *black* working class. We have seen how white workers in South Africa, while remaining workers, nonetheless enjoy huge wage differentials and other advantages, including all the appurtenances of white privilege, like black servants, as a result of the white monopoly of power. They will, as they have in the past, fight to defend these privileges. (They can be compared to the proletariat of ancient Rome which, although propertyless and impoverished, depended upon the exploitation of slave labour. [27]) Their interests are so tied to the survival of the apartheid system that black liberation will be fought for against them.

While the capitalist class in South Africa cannot dispense with the apartheid system because the economy could not operate along capitalist lines without the existing structure of exploitation, the system reproduces many of the features of an advanced capitalist country. These features force South African capitalism to depend on the urban black working class.

1976 saw a series of massive political general strikes. As and when the economy recovers from the present recession, and while starvation wages and inflation continue to impoverish the mass of black workers, we can expect to see massive struggles developing on the wages front.

Wages struggles inevitably raise the demand for independent black trade unions, independent of the employers, the white unions and the state, and independent also of black leaders like Buthelezi and Lucy Mvubelo who are eager to collaborate with these forces. The struggle for higher wages and for trade-union rights will be the battleground on which the mass of black workers acquire the confidence and organisation to take on, and win, the broader political struggles.

Indeed, the political and economic struggles in South Africa cannot be separated. The fight for higher wages and for trade-union rights raises a host of other issues: the pass laws and the migrant labour system; the denial of all political rights and the Bantustans; the repressive legislation and the police state.

Together these economic and political struggles add up to the struggle for a black workers' republic in South Africa, to the seizure of power by the black working class and the destruction of the white state machine.

It is impossible to predict how this process will come about. Revolutions are the products of complex combinations of factors arising out of developments in the world economy and in the particular society in question. In South Africa the major obstacle to revolutions is the integrity of the predominantly white armed forces of the state. Although it is quite possible that demoralisation in the army will be a factor in the South African revolution - there have already been a number of desertions by white conscripts serving in Namibia and Angola - it is unlikely to be a key factor in the disintegration of the settler state, as it was in Russia in 1917, or Germany in 1918-19 or Portugal in 1975.

However, the uneven development of the liberation struggle in Southern Africa means that the South African forces have to guard a border more and more of which adjoins black states; the armed struggle in Namibia is also a growing military burden. Rural unrest and, of course, continued resistance in the townships, will play their part in overstretching the white military machine.

Although it is impossible to anticipate how the various factors at work in Southern Africa will combine to produce change in South Africa itself, it is certain that liberation will be the product of a long and bitter struggle, and that the central factor in that struggle will be the black working class. Whether a revolution does take place under its leadership cannot be left to the spontaneous working of events. It will require the activity of numerous revolutionary socialists to translate the hatred of apartheid shown during the black youth rebellion of 1976 into the struggle for power within the factories. As yet, none of the existing organisations of the black resistance see that task as central - to build a mass revolutionary workers' party independent of the nationalist organisations.[28]

South Africa is part of the world economy. The workers of South Africa, in isolation, will not be able to resolve the problems of a society shaped by Western capital's needs for gold and investment outlets. The ultimate survival and success of a revolution in South Africa will depend on revolutions in the advanced capitalist countries.

The ties of solidarity and common interest go both ways. British capital in particular has massive interests in South Africa. Victory for the South African revolution would be a heavy blow for the British ruling class. Moreover, it is Britain that would probably receive a large portion of the settlers fleeing from black revolutions in South Africa. We should remember how important the *retornados* - the settlers driven from Angola and Mozambique - were to the Portuguese right. The best way to counter the reactionary tide that would sweep Britain after black liberation in South Africa is to build a massive campaign of solidarity with the black resistance in Southern Africa now. In many ways, South Africa could be Britain's Vietnam or Algeria.

But the best form of aid to the South African revolution is to destroy the enemy on its home ground. The companies that exploit black workers in South Africa are based in the capitalist heartlands of Europe and North America. They can only be broken once and for all by the workers of these countries. British, West German and American workers would be striking a real blow for the South African revolution as well as their own liberation if they overthrew 'their' capitalists.

Bibliography

Books and articles

African National Congress (1969) 'Strategy and Tactics of the South African Revolution', in A. Le Guma (ed.) *Apartheid*, London, Lawrence and Wishart 1972

Ainslie, R. (1973) *Masters and Serfs*, London, International Defence and Aid 1973

Angola Solidarity Committee (1976) *MPLA is the people*, London 1976

Arrighi, G. and Saul J. (1973) *Essays in the Political Economy of Africa*, New York, Monthly Review 1973.

Baldwin, A. (1971) 'Rural Administration and the response of the people of South Africa', MA Thesis University of London 1971

Benson, M. (1963) *The Struggle for a Birthright*, Harmondsworth, Penguin 1966

Bukharin, N. (1917) *Imperialism and World Economy*, London, Merlin 1972

Bundy, C. (1972) 'The Emergence and Decline of a South African Peasantry', *African Affairs*, vol.71 no.285, October 1972

Bunting, B. (1964) *The Rise of the South African Reich* Harmondsworth, Penguin, 1969

Cabral, A. (1969) *Revolution in Guinea*, 2nd ed. London, 1974 Stage 1

Callinicos, A., and Turner, S. (1975) 'The Student Movement Today', *International Socialism 15*

Carter, G.M., and Karis, T. (eds.) (1973) *From Protest to*

Challenge, vol. 2, Stanford 1973

Clarke, D. (1975) 'African Workers and Union Formation in Rhodesia' *South African Labour Bulletin* 1:9 March 1975

Cliff, T. (1961) 'Permanent Revolution' *International Socialism* 9 and 61

(1971) 'The Class Struggle in Britain' in Harris, N. and Palmer, J. (eds), *World Crisis*, London, Hutchinson 1971

(1975a) *Lenin* vol. 1, London, Pluto 1975

(1975b) 'Portugal at the Crossroads', *International Socialism* 80

(1976) *Lenin* vol. 2, London, Pluto 1976

Cohen, B., and El-Khawas, M.A. (1975) *Introduction* to National Security Council (1975)

Davidson, B. (1972) *In the Eye of the Storm*, Harmondsworth, Penguin 1975

Davidson, B., Slovo, J., and Wilkinson, A. (1976) *Southern Africa: the New Politics of Revolution*, Harmondsworth, Penguin 1976

Davies, R. (1973) 'The White Working Class in South Africa' *New Left Review* 82, November-December 1973

(1975) 'Leadership and Unity in Black Trade Unions in Rhodesia', *South African Labour Bulletin* 1:9 March 1975

Davis, D. (1976) 'African Unions at the Crossroads', *African Communist* First Quarter 1976

De Figueiredo, A. (1975) *Portugal*, Harmondsworth, Penguin 1975

De Kiewet, C.W. (1941) *A History of South Africa*, Oxford University Press, London 1942

De Klerk, W. (1975) *The Puritans in Africa*, Harmondsworth, Penguin 1976

First, R., Steele, J., and Gurney, C. (1972) *The South African Connection*, Harmondsworth, Penguin 1973

Frankel, S.H. (1938) *Capital Investment in Africa*, London, Oxford University Press 1938

Gibson, R. (1972) *African Liberation Movements*, London, Oxford University Press 1972

Hall, R. (1965) *Zambia*, London, Pall Mall 1965

(1969) *The High Price of Principle*, Harmondsworth, Penguin 1973

Harman, C. (1976-77), 'Poland: crisis of state capitalism', *International Socialism* 93 and 94

Harris, N. (1974) *India-China: Underdevelopment and Revolution*, Delhi, Vikas Publishing House 1974

(1976) 'Mao Tse-tung and China' *International Socialism* 92

Hepple, A. (1969) *Workers under Apartheid*, International Defence and Aid, London, 1971

Hirson, B. (1976) *The Reorganisation of the African Trade Unions in South Africa 1936-1942*, Institute of Commonwealth Studies Seminars 1976

Hodges, T. (1976) 'How the MPLA Won in Angola' in Africa Contemporary Record, *After Angola*, London, Rex Collings 1976

Horwitz, R. (1967) *The Political Economy of South Africa*, London, Weidenfeld and Nicholson 1967

Houghton, D.H. (1964) *The South African Economy*, Cape Town, Oxford University Press 1973

Hyman, R. (1975) 'The Durban Strikes', *South African Labour Bulletin* 2:2 July 1975

Innes, D. (1975) 'The Role of Foreign Trade and Industrial Development in South Africa' in Suckling, Weiss and Innes (1975)

International Marxist Group (1975) *Zambia*, London 1975

Isaacs, H. (1938) *The Tragedy of the Chinese Revolution*, Stanford, Stanford University Press 1974

Johnstone, F.A. (1976) *Race, Class and Gold*, London, Routledge & Kegan Paul 1976

Kidron, M. (1974) *Capitalism and Theory*, London, Pluto 1974

Kirk, T., (1976) 'Detente in Southern Africa: the View from Pretoria' (unpublished).

Legassick, M. (1973) 'Class and Nationalism in South African Protest', *East African Studies* XV, 1973

(1974) 'South Africa: Capital Accumulation and Violence', *Economy and Society*, 3:3 August 1974

(1975) 'The Record of British Firms in South Africa',

South African Labour Bulletin 2:1 May/June 1975

Legum, C. (1976) 'The Role of the Big Powers' in Africa Contemporary Record, *After Angola* London, Rex Collings 1976

Lenin, V.I. (1917) 'Imperialism', *Collected Works* Vol. 22, London, Lawrence & Wishart 1964

Lerumo, A. (1971) *Fifty Fighting Years*, London, Inkululeko Publications 1971

Loney, M. (1975) *Rhodesia*, Harmondsworth, Penguin 1975

Luxemburg, R. (1906) *The Mass Strike*, Ceylon, Young Socialist Publications 1970

Martin, A. (1972) *Minding Their Own Business*, Harmondsworth, Penguin 1975

Marx, K. (1867) *Capital*, vol. 1, Harmondsworth, Penguin 1976
(1894) *Capital* vol. 3, Moscow, Progress Publishers 1971
(1973) *The Revolutions of 1848*, Harmondsworth, Penguin 1973

Maxey, K. (1975) *The Fight for Zimbabwe* London, Rex Collings 1975

Mhlongo, S. (1974) 'Black Workers' Strikes in South Africa', *New Left Review* 83 January-February 1974

Millin, S.G. (1933) *Rhodes*, London 1933

O'Meara, D. (1973) 'Class and Nationalism in African Resistance', MA Thesis, University of Sussex
(1975) 'The 1946 African Mine Workers' Strike and the Political Economy of South Africa', *Journal of Commonwealth and Comparative Studies*, vol. 13 no.2 July 1975

National Security Council (1975), *The Kissinger Study of Southern Africa*, Nottingham, Spokesman Books 1975

Ranger, T.O. (1967) *Revolt in Southern Rhodesia 1896-7*, London, Heinemann 1967

Rhodesian Catholic Justice and Peace Commission (1975) *The Man in the Middle*, London, CIIR 1975
(1976) *Civil War in Rhodesia*, London, CIIR 1976

Rogers, B. (1976) *Divide and Rule*, London, International Defence and Aid 1976

Roux, E. (1948), *Time Longer than Rope*, Madison, University of Wisconsin Press 1972

Shivji, I. (1970) *The Silent Class Struggle*, Dar-es-Salaam, Tanzania Publishing House 1974
(1976) *Class Struggle in Tanzania*, London, Heinemann 1976

Simons, H.J. and R.E. (1969) *Class and Colour in South Africa 1850-1950*, Harmondsworth, Penguin 1969

Slovo, J. (1976) 'South Africa - No Middle Road', in Davidson, Slovo and Wilkinson (1976)

Socialist League of Africa (1961) 'South Africa: Ten Years of the Stay-at-Home', *International Socialism* 5

South African Communist Party (1962) *The Road to South African Freedom* in SACP (1970)
(1963) *The Revolutionary Way Out* in SACP (1970)
(1968) *The Developing Armed Liberation Struggle in Southern Africa* in SACP (1970)
(1970) *African Communists Speak*, Moscow, Nauka Publishing House 1970
(1976) 'Defeat Vorster and His Collaborators: Engage the Enemy on Every Front!', *African Communist*, No. 64, First Quarter 1976

Sprack, J. (1974) *Rhodesia: South Africa's Sixth Province*, London, International Defence and Aid 1974

Stoneman, C. (1976) 'Economic Development with Unlimited Supplies of Capital: the Case of Southern Rhodesia', *South African Labour Bulletin* 2:7, February 1976

Suckling, J. (1975) 'The Nature and Role of Foreign Investment in South Africa', in Suckling, Weiss and Innes (1975)

Suckling, J., Weiss, R., and Innes, D. (1975) *The Economic Factor*, Uppsala, African Publications Trust 1975

Tabata, I.B. (1950) *The Awakening of a People*, Nottingham, Spokesman Books 1974

Thompson, E.P. (1963) *The Making of the English Working Class*, London, Gollancz 1963

Trotsky, L.D. (1906) *Results and Prospects*, New York, Pathfinder 1970
(1929) *The Third International after Lenin*, New York, Pathfinder 1970

(1976) *On China*, New York, Monad 1976

Troup, F. (1972) *South Africa*, Harmondsworth, Penguin 1975

Turok, B. (1974) 'South Africa: The Search for a Strategy', *Socialist Register 1973*, London, Merlin 1974

van Onselen, C. (1976) *Chibaro*, London, Pluto 1976

Webster, E. (1975) 'Management's counter-offensive', *South African Labour Bulletin* 2:3 August 1975

Weiss, R. (1975a) 'The Role of Para-Statals in South Africa's Politico-Economic System', in Suckling, Weiss and Innes (1975)

(1975b) 'South Africa and its Hinterland', in Suckling, Weiss and Innes (1975)

Wilkinson, A. (1976) 'From Rhodesia to Zimbabwe', in Davidson, Slovo and Wilkinson (1976)

Williams, M. (1975) 'An Analysis of South African Capitalism', *Bulletin of Conference of Socialist Economists*, VI:1, February 1975

Wilson, F. (1971) 'Farming 1866-1966', in Wilson, M., and Thompson, L., *Oxford History of South Africa*, Vol. II, London, Oxford University Press 1971

Wolpe, H. (1972) 'Capitalism and Cheap Labour-Power in South Africa', *Economy and Society*, 1:4, November 1972

(1974) 'The Theory of Internal Colonialism - the South African Case', *Bulletin of Conference of Socialist Economists*, 9 Autumn 1974

(1976) 'The 'White Working Class' in South Africa', *Economy and Society*, 5:2, May 1976

Newspapers and periodicals

London

African Communist

Chimurenga

The Economist

The Economist Intelligence Unit, *Quarterly Economic Report* (EIU QER)

Economy and Society

Financial Times (FT)

The Guardian
Ikwezi
International Socialism (IS)
New Left Review (NLR)
The Observer
Review of African Political Economy
Red Weekly
Sunday Times

Paris
Afrique-Asie
International Herald Tribune
Le Monde

Johannesburg
Financial Mail (FM)
Rand Daily Mail (RDM)
Star International Airmail Weekly
World

Durban
South African Labour Bulletin (SALB)

Documents

Kaunda's Role in Detente 31 March Lusaka 1975
*Memorandum Submitted to 1. The OAU Liberation Committee
    2. The Tanzanian Government 3. The Mozambique
    Government by ANC Fighters at Mgagao Military Camp in
    Tanzania*
The Price of Detente London 1976

References

References given here in abbreviated form are set out in full in the Bibliography on p.214.

Introduction

1. Quoted in Hall (1965) p.193
2. Houghton (1964) p.209
3. Bunting (1964) p.414
4. National Security Council (1975) p.66
5. *Sunday Times*, 27 October 1974
6. Quoted in *Star*, 9 September 1975
7. Quoted in Bunting, *op. cit.* p.98
8. Interview with Bill Coughlin, assistant to US Senator John Tunney, *The Guardian*, 16 February 1976
9. Notes of the Month, *IS* 87, March/April 1976

1: Apartheid and Capitalism

1. *Star*, 11 October 1975
2. See Houghton (1964) and Horwitz (1967)
3. South African Communist Party (SACP) (1962) pp.128-9
4. *ibid.* p.129. This analysis was adopted by the African National Congress (ANC) whose 1969 conference stated of South Africa: 'Whilst at the one level it is an 'independent' national state, at another level it is a country subjugated by a minority race. What makes the structure unique and adds to its complexity is that the exploiting nation is not, as in the classical imperialist relationship, situated in a geographically distinct mother country, but is settled within the borders.' ANC (1969) p.195

The same thesis, although in a more rigorous form, can be found in the work of the independent South African Marxist scholar, Harold Wolpe: 'The uniqueness or specificity of South Africa, in the period of capitalism, lies precisely in this: that it embodies within a single nation-state a relationship characteristic of the external relationship between imperialist states and their colonies (or neo-colonies).' Wolpe (1974) pp.9-10. See also Slovo (1976).

5. SACP, *op. cit.* p.114
6. For a trenchant critique of this type of formalism see Trotsky (1929). See also Trotsky (1906) for a classical analysis of how the world economy moulded precapitalist forms in Tsarist Russia into a new, capitalist society combining 'modern' and 'archaic'.
7. Hepple (1969) p.54
8. *Star*, 7 August 1976
9. Simons (1969) p.40
10. *ibid*, p.42
11. Frankel (1938) p.89
12. *ibid*. p.84
13. Lenin (1917) p.254
14. The analysis of the South African gold-mining industry given in the text owes much to Williams (1975) and Johnstone (1976). See Chapter 3 below for further discussion of the role of gold-mining in the South African economy.
15. For a sociological definition of African society see Wolpe (1972) p.432
16. De Kiewet, (1941) pp.24-25
17. Quoted in De Klerk *op. cit.* p.23
18. De Kiewet, *op. cit.* p.50

19. Quoted in Troup, (1972) p.136
29. De Kiewet, *op. cit.* p.79
21. *ibid.* p.72
22. Quoted in Tabata (1950) p.81
23. Quoted in Millin (1933) p.67
24. Quoted in Johnstone, *op. cit.* p.28
25. This argument can still be heard today. Something of its flavour is conveyed by this report of a Consolidated Gold-fields meeting in November 1899: 'With good government there should be an abundance of labour and with an abundance of labour there will be no difficulty in cutting down wages, because it is preposterous to pay a Kaffir the present wages. He would be quite as well satisfied - in fact he would work longer - if you gave him half the amount. (Laughter) *His wages are altogether disproportionate to his requirements*. (Laughter)' Quoted in Williams, *op. cit.* p.7.
26. Johnstone, *op. cit.* p.33
27. The carpetbaggers' attentions were not confined to blacks. Many impoverished Afrikaner farmers were swallowed up by land speculators after the Boer War. Big landowners like Smuts made fortunes out of their poorer kinsmen's difficulties.
28. Quoted in Williams, *op. cit.* p.31
29. Wolpe, *op. cit.* p.442
30. Houghton, *op. cit.* p.88
31. *Star*, 24 January 1976
32. Rogers (1976) p.29
33. See Bundy (1972)
34. Wilson (1971) p.141
35. Ainslie (1973) pp.20-21, 24
36. Bunting (1964) p.371

37. Johnstone, *op. cit.* p.53
38. Wilson, *op. cit.* p.133
39. Simons, *op. cit.* p.130
40. Johnstone, *op. cit.* p.105
41. *ibid*, p.100
42. The gold standard was the pre-war rate of exchange between the pound sterling and gold. By going off the standard the government financed war-time production by printing money.
43. Quoted in Simons, *op. cit.* p.279
44. *ibid.* p.285
45. *ibid.* p.286
46. Johnstone, *op. cit.* p.132
47. *ibid.* p.136
48. Quoted in Simons, *op. cit.* p.339
49. The same system operates today. The result is that, for example, between October 1967 and February 1968 over 2 million gallons of milk were thrown away on government instructions, while many rural Africans suffer from *kwashiokor* and other diseases caused by malnutrition. (Bunting, *op. cit.* pp.373-4)
50. See Frankel *op. cit.* Chapter 4
51. Quoted in Williams, *op. cit.* p.9
52. De Kiewet, *op. cit.* p.263
53. Weiss (1957a) p.58
54. Houghton, *op. cit.* p.122-23
55. *ibid.* p.43
56. See Legassick (1974) pp.259-64
57. See Bunting, *op. cit.* Chapters 5, 6, 7
58. *ibid.* p.43
59. Quoted in De Klerk, *op. cit.* pp.214-15
60. Bunting, *op. cit.* p.343
61. De Klerk, *op. cit.* pp.284-85
62. Bunting, *op. cit.* p.379
63. Quoted, *ibid.* p.377
64. *ibid.* p.379
65. De Klerk, *op. cit.* p.288
66. Weiss, *op. cit.* p.61
67. Bunting, *op. cit.* p.384
68. *ibid.* p.390
69. *ibid.* p.391
70. *Star*, 29 May 1976

2: Black Resistance and White Oppression

1. The title of this section was chosen because the making of the working class 'is an active process which owes as much to agency as to conditioning. The working class did not rise like the sun at an appointed time. It was present at its own making', Thompson (1963) p.9. This section owes much to two books that are now classics - Roux (1948) and Simons (1969).
2. See Simons, *op. cit.* Chapters 12, 13, 14
3. Legassick (1973) pp.6-7
4. Quoted in Gibson (1972) p.42
5. See Chapter 9 below
6. Simons, *op. cit.* p.406
7. See Trotsky (1929)
8. See Isaacs (1938) and Trotsky (1976)
9. Quoted in Lerumo (1971) p.64
10. Quoted in Legassick, *op. cit.* p.21
11. Quoted in Simons, *op. cit.* p.473
12. See Simons, *op. cit.* Chapters 17 and 26; Legassick, *op. cit*; SACP (1962) and Chapter 11 below
13. O'Meara (1974) p.50
14. Hirson (1976) p.4
15. O'Meara (1974) p.153
16. O'Meara, *loc. cit.* and Roux (1948) p.333
17. Quoted in Benson (1963) p.76
18. Tabata (1950) p.98
19. In 1890 the basic wage per shift for black miners was 2/6d; in 1942 it was 2/-. O'Meara (1974) p.157
20. Quoted in Legassick (1974) p.274
21. Quoted in Troup (1972) p.278
22. See Bunting (1964) Chapter 9
23. Quoted in De Klerk (1975) p.238
24. Quoted in Troup, *op. cit.* p.305
25. See Wolpe (1972) (although with reservations arising from his continued adherence to the 'internal colonialism' theory of South African history) and Legassick, *op. cit.*
26. See Chapter 3 below.
27. Quoted in Carter (1973) p.102
28. Socialist League of Africa (1961) pp.7-8
29. *ibid.* p.8
30. *ibid.* p.11
31. Quoted in Turok (1974) p.353
32. Benson, *op. cit.* p.282
33. The following account is based on Baldwin (1971)
34. *ibid.* p.9
35. *ibid.* p.17
36. See Chapter 11 below
37. Turok, *op. cit.* pp.360-61
38. See Bunting, *op. cit.* Chapter 10.
39. See Slovo (1976)
40. See South African Communist Party (1963)
41. Turok, *op. cit.* p.361
42. See SACP (1962) and ANC (1969)

3: The Contradictions of South African Capitalism

1. Houghton (1973) p.212
2. Suckling, Weiss and Innes (1975) Table 11, p.181
3. *ibid.* Table 17, p.187
4. First, Steele and Gurney (1972)
5. Cohen and El-Khawas (1975) pp.28-29
6. Houghton, *op. cit.* p.43
7. *ibid.* p.37. The high figure for agriculture reflects this sector's backwardness.
8. Suckling (1975) p.18
9. Suckling, Weiss and Innes, *op. cit.* Tables 9 and 10, pp.179-180
10. First, Steele and Gurney, *op. cit.* pp.26-27. See also Suckling, *op. cit.*
11. Weiss (1975a) p.62
12. Senbank survey - *Star*, 24 January 1976
13. See Marx (1867) Chapters 6 and 22; and Kidron (1974) Chapter 5
14. Innes (1975) p.115
15. *ibid.* p.116
16. *ibid.* pp.119-23
17. *ibid.* p.133
18. *The Economist*, 14 August 1976
19. *Star*, 17 July 1976
20. *FM*, 13 August 1976
21. *Star*, 24 July 1976
22. *FM*, 13 August 1976
23. *ibid.* 2 July 1976
24. *Star*, 13 March 1976
25. *ibid.* 6 March 1976
26. *ibid.* 11 November 1975
27. Houghton, *op. cit.* p.125
28. *FT*, 21 September 1976
29. *Star*, 14 August 1976
30. Houghton, *op. cit.* p.134
31. *FM*, 16 July 1976
32. EIU QER 1975 No.2
33. Quoted in Innes, *op. cit.* p.147
34. Weiss (1975b) p.105
35. Innes, *op. cit.* pp.150, 152
36. Bunting (1964) pp.463-4; *Star*, 1 May 1976

37. Quoted in Innes, *op. cit.* p.155
38. *ibid.* p.157; and Weiss, *op. cit.* p.107
39. Quoted in Bunting, *op. cit.* p.426
40. *Star*, 11 October 1975
41. Mhlongo (1974) p.42
42. Rogers (1976) p.26
43. *FM*, 24 October 1975
44. *ibid.* 17 October 1975
45. Mhlongo, *op. cit.* p.43
46. Hepple (1969) p.64
47. *ibid.* p.70
48. *ibid.* p.67
49. Wolpe (1976) Table 9, p.231
50. The status of the white working class in South Africa has provoked some debate on the left in recent years. See, for example, Wolpe, *op. cit.* Davies' thesis (1973) that white workers participate in the distribution of surplus-value extracted from black workers seems to provide the most fruitful line of research, although it needs further elaboration to be convincing.
51. Legassick (1975) p.13
52. Webster (1975) p.29
53. Hyman (1975) p.60
54. Legassick, *op. cit.* p.16
55. Hyman, *op. cit.* p.63
56. *FT*, 25 February 1975
57. *ibid.* and Legassick, *op. cit.* p.21,
58. *RDM*, 31 January 1975
59. Quoted in Legassick, *op. cit.* p.31
60. Quoted in Davis (1976) p.101
61. *FM*, 17 September 1976
62. Davis, *op. cit.* pp.94, 96
63. *ibid.* pp.99-100
64. *ibid.* p.100
65. *Star*, 12 September 1973
66. *FM*, 19 March 1976
67. *ibid.* 17 October 1975
68. *Star*, 28 June 1975
69. *ibid.* 5 June 1976
70. *ibid.* 3 July 1976
71. *ibid* 19 July 1975
72. *ibid.* 6 March 1976
73. EIU QER 1975 No.1

4: Rhodesia: the Crisis of White Power

1. Quoted in Lenin (1917) pp.256-57
2. Quoted in Ranger (1967) p.295
3. See *ibid.* pp.268-310
4. Van Onselen (1976) p.57
5. See *ibid.* for an analysis of the Rhodesian mines during the early years of the colony.
6. Ranger, *op. cit.* p.329
7. Arrighi and Saul (1973) p.195
8. Loney (1975) p.55
9. Quoted, Arrighi and Saul, *op. cit.* p.195
10. Loney, *op. cit.* p.60
11. *ibid.* p.69
12. Stoneman (1976) p.4
13. Loney, *op. cit.* p.60
14. Stoneman, *ibid.* Tables 1 and 2, pp.13, 14
15. *ibid.* p.9
16. *ibid.* p.8
17. *ibid.* Table 3, p.15
18. *ibid.* p.7
19. *ibid.* p.11
20. Suckling (1975) p.150
21. Sprack (1974) p.56
22. *ibid.* pp.56-57
23. Wilkinson (1976) p.222
24. Stoneman, *op. cit.* Table 3, p.15
25. Clarke (1975) p.4
26. Interview in SALB 2:7, February 1976, p.22
27. See Davies (1975)
28. Quoted in Gibson (1972) p.75
29. This account of the armed struggle in Zimbabwe is based on Wilkinson, *op. cit.* and Maxey (1975)
30. Loney, *op. cit.* p.172
31. Quoted in Maxey, *op. cit.* p.163
32. See Rhodesian Catholic Justice and Peace Commission (1975)

5: Zambia: the Failure of State Capitalism

1. Hall (1965) p.92
2. Martin (1972) p.39
3. Hall (1969) p.90
4. Martin, *op. cit.* p.271
5. *Chimurenga*, 30 June 1976
6. IMG (1975) p.8
7. See Shivji (1976) Parts Two and Three
8. *The Economist*, 25 September 1976
9. Quotations in Shivji, *op. cit.* pp.167-68
10. Martin, *op. cit.* pp.195-96
11. See Shivji, *op. cit.* pp.165-78, and Shivji (1970)
12. See Harman (1976/7)
13. *FT*, 24 October 1975
14. IMG, *op. cit.* pp.10-11
15. *Star*, 12 July 1975
16. *FT*, *op. cit.*

17. *ibid.* and *FM*, 24 October 1975
18. *Star*, 22 November 1975
19. IMG, *op. cit.* p.8
20. *Kaunda's Role in Detente*, p.2
21. IMG, *op. cit.* p.9
22. *ibid.* p.12; *FT*, *op. cit*
23. *FM*, 7 May 1976
24. *ibid.*

6: Detente Phase One: the Vorster-Kaunda Alliance

1. Tony Kirk's unpublished paper, *Detente in Southern Africa: the View from Pretoria*, was a great help in writing this chapter.
2. National Security Council (1975) p.67
3. *Star*, 14 December 1974
4. *ibid.* 9 September 1975
5. Wilkinson (1976) pp.335-36
6. *FT*, 22 October 1975
7. *The Price of Detente* p.3
8. *Kaunda's Role in Detente* p.5
9. *ibid.* p.5
10. *Star*, 20 September 1975
11. *ibid.* 4 October 1975
12. *ibid.* 27 March 1976
13. Mhlongo (1974) pp.45-6
14. *FM*, 18 June 1976
15. *Star*, 13 March 1976
16. *FM*, 28 November 1975
17. *Le Monde*, 1 February 1975
18. *Star*, 20 March 1976
19. See Shivji (1976) Part Five
20. Quoted, *ibid.* p.143
21. *Star*, 10 April 1976
22. *FM*, *op. cit.*
23. *ibid.* 17 October 1975
24. *The Guardian*, 19 November 1975
25. *FM* 28 November 1975
26. *Africa*, February 1976
27. *Star*, 24 July 1976
28. *ibid.* 21 August 1976
29. Kirk, *op. cit.* p.21

7: Angola: the Turning-Point

1. De Sousa Ferreira (1971) p.55
2. De Figuieredo (1975) p.216
3. ASC (1976) p.22
4. Hodges (1976) p.57
5. See the extracts from the investigation into the CIA by a committee of the US Senate, *Sunday Times* 23 November 1975
6. *International Herald Tribune*, 19 December 1975
7. Davidson (1972) pp.229-30
8. *The Guardian*, 22 December 1975

9. *Afrique-Asie*, 8 July 1974 (Extracts from this correspondence are reproduced in the *Review of African Political Economy* No.5, January-April 1976)
10. *Le Monde*, 7-8 June 1974
11. *ibid*. 15 September 1974
12. *International Herald Tribune*, 19 December 1975
13. Hodges, *op. cit.* p.50
14. *ibid*. p.48
15. *ibid*. p.55
16. *Star*, 20 December 1975
17. *ibid*. 6 December 1976
18. *FT*, 2 January 1976
19. Hodges, *op. cit.* p.55
20. *Le Monde*, 5 June 1974
21. Legum (1976) pp.21-22
22. See Introduction, p.8 above
23. Legum, *op. cit.* p.13
24. *Star*, 22 November 1975
25. *ibid*. 13 December 1975
26. *The Observer*, 11 January 1976
27. Legum, *op. cit.* pp.19-20
28. Hodges, *op. cit.* p.57
29. Quoted in Legum, *op. cit.* p.22
30. See *ibid*. pp.31, 33-34
31. *Star*, 20 December 1975
32. *ibid*. 20 March 1976
33. *FT*, 6 January 1976
34. *Star*, 6 December 1976
35. *FT*, 3 January 1976
36. *FM*, 30 January 1976
37. Hodges, *op. cit.* p.58

8: Soweto: the Black Townships Explode

1. *Star*, 28 August 1976
2. *FM*, 6 August 1976
3. *Star, op. cit.*
4. *ibid*. 3 April 1976
5. *FM*, 16 July 1976
6. *ibid*. 6 August 1976
7. *Star*, 22 November 1975
8. *FM*, 30 July 1976
9. *ibid*. 23 April 1976
10. *Star*, 6 December 1975
11. *FM, op. cit.*
12. *ibid*. 17 September 1976
13. *ibid*. 7 May 1976
14. *ibid*. 15 October 1975
15. Quoted in Bunting (1964) p.260
16. *Star*, 1 May 1976
17. *The Observer*, 20 June 1976
18. Interview in *Red Weekly*, 14 October 1976
19. *The Guardian*, 26 August 1976
20. *Star*, 28 August 1976
21. *ibid*. 14 August 1976

22. *ibid*. 17 July 1976
23. *ibid*. 24 July 1976
24. *ibid*. 14 August 1976
25. *ibid*. 21 August 1976
26. *FM*, 20 August 1976
27. *ibid*. 2 July 1976
28. *World*, 19 June 1976
29. See, for example, *Star*, 7 August 1976
30. See Callinicos and Turner (1975)
31. *FM*, 17 September 1976
32. SLA (1961) p.13
33. On the place of armed insurrection in mass struggles, see Cliff (1975a) Chapter 9 and (1976) Chapter 19
34. SACP (1963) p.173
35. *ibid*. p.173
36. Luxemburg (1906) pp.45-46
37. *FM*, 6 August 1976

9: Detente Phase Two: the Kissinger Deal

1. *International Herald Tribune*, 22 June 1976
2. *The Observer*, 7 March 1976
3. *Memorandum ... by ANC fighters at Mgagao Military Camp in Tanzania* p.2
4. *ibid*. p.2
5. *ibid*. p.5
6. *Ikwezi*, August 1976 p.15
7. *ibid*.
8. *ibid*. p.16
9. *Star*, 12 June 1976
10. Reproduced in *Chimurenga*, 30 June 1976
11. *Star*, 24 April 1976
12. *ibid*. 19 June 1976
13. *ibid*. 6 March 1976
14. *ibid*. 31 July 1976
15. Rhodesian Catholic Justice and Peace Commission (1976) p.41
16. *ibid*. p.43
17. *Star*, 14 August 1976
18. *ibid*. 31 July 1976
19. *The Guardian*, 9 March 1976
20. *The Observer*, 3 October 1976
21. *FT*, 1 November 1976
22. *FM*, 13 August 1976

10: Results and Prospects

1. SACP (1962) p.138
2. *ibid*. p.135
3. *Ikwezi*, November 1975 p.3
4. SACP (1976) p.31
5. Cabral (1969) p.88
6. *ibid*. p.88

7. See Legassick (1973) and Simons (1969) Chapter 17
8. Cabral, *op. cit.* pp.89-90
9. Slovo (1976) p.126
10. See for example SACP, *op. cit.*
11. Wolpe (1972) p.442
12. Slovo, *op. cit.* p.140
13. Marx (1973) pp.322-23
14. *ibid*. p.330
15. SACP (1962) p.146
16. See Arrighi and Saul (1973) Chapter 5
17. ANC (1969) pp.193-94
18. There are, of course, the exceptions of China and Vietnam, where the peasant wars were victorious. See Harris (1974) and (1976) on China.
19. See Legassick, *op. cit.* pp.53*ff*, and *Ikwezi*, August 1976 p.3. The latter piece also contains the statement: 'Instead of dancing around over ludicrous campaigns not to buy oranges and peaches we should go for something more meaningful like an Arab oil boycott.' Apart from observing that the writers place reliance on feudal Arab regimes to liberate South Africa, it is worth pointing out that imported crude oil only meets about 21 per cent of South Africa's energy requirements and that South Africa's most important supplier of oil is Iran. But then the Iranian tyranny is politically fairly promiscuous as far as friends and allies go: it enjoys excellent relations with People's China. See Callinicos and Turner (1975) for a refutation of the theory of red bases applied to students.
20. See Kidron (1974)
21. *Star*, 5 July 1975
22. *ibid*. 21 August 1976
23. *ibid*. 29 May 1976
24. *ibid*. 13 August 1976
25. *ibid*. 20 September 1975
26. See Cliff (1975b) Part 3 on the Portuguese revolutionary left.
27. Chris Harman suggested this analogy; it can also be found in Tabata (1959) p.2
28. See Cliff (1975a and 1976) on the revolutionary party and the struggle for power.

Index

226 Southern Africa after Soweto